T0093637

THE MYSTERIES OF MONKEY ISLAND

*This book is dedicated to all those who are still,
to this day, enthralled by a bunch of pixels.*

*To Bret Barrett and Martin "Bucky" Cameron.
To Stan, who suffered the collateral damage
of a corrupt system.*

The Mysteries of Monkey Island. Pirates Ahoy!
Or how to become a mighty pirate™ using a giant Q-Tip and a rubber chicken.
by Nicolas Deneschau
published by Third Éditions
10 rue des arts, 31000 Toulouse, France
contact@thirdeditions.com
www.thirdeditions.com

Follow us: @Third_Editions – Facebook.com/ThirdEditions –  Third Editions US

Publishing Directors: Nicolas Courcier and Mehdi El Kanafi
Editorial Assistants: Ken Bruno, Ludovic Castro et Damien Mecheri
Text by: Nicolas Deneschau
Translated from French by: Michael Ross, ITC Traductions
Proofreading: Anne-Sophie Guénéguès and Jérémy Daguisé
Layout: Bruno Provezza
Pictograms and internal illustrations: Steffi Girinon, Frédéric Tomé and Gom
Classic cover: Sylvain Sarrailh
"First Print" cover: Steve Purcell

This book is Third Editions' way of paying homage to, and helping you, the reader, learn more about the
video game series *Monkey Island*. The author presents an overview of the history of the *Monkey Island* video
games in this one-of-a-kind volume that lays out the inspirations, the context, and the content of these titles
through original analysis and discussion.

English edition, copyright 2023, Third Éditions.
All rights reserved.
ISBN 978-2-37784-398-5
Legal submission: October 2023.

Nicolas Deneschau

THE MYSTERIES OF MONKEY ISLAND

03.rd THIRD
éditions

Table of Contents

Foreword by Larry Ahern™ 07
Preface: Adventure™ by LucasArts™ 13
Introduction 21

Part 1

Chapter 1: Lucasfilm Games™ 33
Chapter 2: From interactive fiction to *Point & Click*™ 41
Chapter 3: The SCUMM™ game engine™ 47
Chapter 4: Reinventing the adventure game™ 59

Part 2

Chapter 5: *The Secret of Monkey Island*™ 69
Chapter 6: From Lucasfilm Games™ to LucasArts™ 101
Chapter 7: *Monkey Island 2: LeChuck's Revenge*™ 107
Chapter 8: iMUSE™! Interactive Reggae Music Man!™ 129
Chapter 9: The end of an era™ 137
Chapter 10: *The Curse of Monkey Island*™ 141
Chapter 11: *The Curse of Monkey Island: The Movie*™ 165
Chapter 12: *Escape from Monkey Island*™ 173
Chapter 13: The adventure game is dead!!™ 191

Part 3

Chapter 14: Telltale Games™ 197
Chapter 15: *Tales of Monkey Island*™ 201
Chapter 16: *Monkey Island Special Edition*™ 221
Chapter 17: The life and death of LucasArts™ 229
Chapter 18: The secrets of *Monkey Island*™ 237
Chapter 19: The legacy of *Monkey Island*™ 247
Chapter 20: Ron Gilbert vs. Disney™ 251
Chapter 21: Conclusion: So long...™ 255
Chapter 22: *Return to Monkey Island*™ 257

Appendix 1: Mix-o-insults™ 283
Appendix 2: Mojo-credits™ 287
Appendix 3: LucasArts™ classics 295
Appendix 4: *Plank of Love*™ 309
Author's acknowledgments 311

THE MYSTERIES OF MONKEY ISLAND

Foreword

Monkey Island Meanderings

A little more than 20 years ago I was offered the chance to co-direct the next *Monkey Island* game with Jonathan Ackley. The series felt like the heart of LucasArts, the big personality of the studio, the crazy thing that everyone points to when asked, "What are you guys all about?" When I started at the company, I was still getting used to the idea of getting paid to make art and probably would have been happy painting George Lucas' house. The last computer game I'd played featured ASCII characters as protagonists,[1] so seeing cartoons I could control in *The Secret of Monkey Island* was a revelation. I went on to work as an animator on *Monkey Island 2: LeChuck's Revenge*, then finally got my chance to dream up Guybrush's next adventure in *The Curse of Monkey Island*.

It felt a bit surreal, like your parents handing you the keys to their Mercedes and saying, "Now, be careful with this. It's really valuable, and everyone will be looking at you. But we trust you." We were momentarily intimidated. "What if it's too much for us? On the other hand, it's just been sitting there... Someone should be using it." Of course, after our initial concept pitch, management said, "What were you thinking?! Maybe you aren't ready for something this nice." And we may have been grounded for a while, but eventually we got things all patched up and... now I'm realizing I really should have used a pirate analogy here.

We knew we had inherited this amazing franchise, but the challenge was trying to figure out where to take it next. Creator Ron Gilbert and writer Dave Grossman were no longer with the company, so we couldn't pick their brains. Writer Tim Schafer certainly gave us some fun suggestions and encouragement, but didn't have any big *Monkey Island* secrets to spill. It's possible he never knew Ron's big plan for the series in the first place. Or maybe he just kept it to himself thinking that was Ron's direction and we should find our own.

---

1. The American Standard Code for Information Interchange (ASCII) is a computer encoding standard for characters, first issued in the 1960s. It offers a simple way to encode nearly all the characters appearing on a keyboard. In the early days of computers, the graphics of certain games were made up of ordinary letters, numbers, and symbols (like a smiley).

So, we had to do a little detective work and a bit of winging it. Luckily, we had a good treasure map in the first two games to point the way (there we go, back on track with a pirate analogy!). Those games were rich in characters, locations, puzzles, and humor and told us most of what we needed to know. Sure, there may be details some fans will argue about (I've heard Ron said that Elaine would never marry Guybrush), but then the world of *Monkey Island* can be full of surprises. And part of the surprise is where the monkey muse will take each game's creator.

Everybody thinks they know Guybrush, but he seems to evolve in interesting ways with each outing. He's a loveable universal avatar, the put-upon everyman pirate who's a little too plucky for his own good, always ready with a sarcastic quip when his enthusiastic naivete walks him to the edge of the plank. Plus, he's got really deep pockets. He's a character with a voice all his own (although often provided by actor Dominic Armato), one that takes over when you write and design for him. You just can't help but channel cartoon pirates when you work on the *Monkey Island* franchise.

Those animated scalawags drive the jokes, inspiring sea shanties and insults, wayward musings of priceless jewels. When we were working on the proposal scene in *The Curse of Monkey Island*, I was simultaneously shopping for an engagement ring for my soon-to-be wife. Sometimes I wondered whether it was me or the game at the helm. Thankfully, that ring wasn't cursed. Although, now that I think of it, my wife and I both lost our rings a while back. We're just waiting on some buried treasure, a rediscovered old royalty check, or a high-paying offer to make *The Curse of Monkey Island: Remastered* in order to replace them.

Plus, gamers like being Guybrush. They want to swashbuckle with him (although there was technically never a "swash" verb in the interface of the first two games). They like making him poke the surly pirate, deliver the witty comeback, and try to use strange inventory items together. He's someone they can relate to and express themselves through. It's the same with those of us who've worked on the series. I have no idea what Ron intended for *Monkey Island 3* (although I'd love to see it someday), but I do know that the early pitch for *The Secret of Monkey Island* had a different tone than the final game. And I even heard tell around the office poop deck that Tim Schafer and Dave Grossman just wrote a bunch of silly jokes as placeholders while wiring up the game functionality, but Ron liked it so much he told them to keep at it. That may not actually be what happened, but since it's now in a book, it's part of history. Also, while I'm at it, all the good ideas in *The Curse of Monkey Island* were mine.

The series has actually evolved significantly to reflect the perspectives of all the people who worked on it. The franchise that Ron created and generously shared with others has turned into a vessel of crazy rogues, from the hapless hero, the heroine who's out of his league, and the constantly transforming villain to an ever-expanding cast of supporting characters whose very concept elicits laughs. In what other world could a throwaway line from an undead skull inspire a recurring demonic antagonist that became a fan favorite?

The different designer's and writer's voices have allowed for a treasure trove of ideas, other interpretations of what Monkey Island is, and other attempts to drive that expensive Mercedes (uh-oh, the weird car analogy is back). What did Ron have planned at the end of *LeChuck's Revenge*? Who knows? I certainly don't. What I do know is we've dug up decades of comedy gold in the meantime sailing around the cartoon seas in search of the secret of *Monkey Island*. Whether we ever find it I don't think matters. I say, "Big Whoop."

Larry Ahern, co-director of *The Curse of Monkey Island.*

Note: This foreword was written for the French release of this book, before *Return to Monkey Island* was announced.

THE MYSTERIES OF MONKEY ISLAND

Preface:
Adventure by LucasArts

T HERE ARE DIFFERENT WAYS TO APPROACH GAMES, particularly video games. A child grabs a ball and has fun knocking it around to get it into a goal, defeat an enemy, or create some sort of competition. Others imagine that the ordinary ball is actually a priceless treasure stolen from a bloodthirsty intergalactic mercenary. You have games and you have imagination. Play of any kind becomes part of a child's world; it allows the child to use various connected forms of expression to bring to life their internal universe, with their most personal interpretations blending experience with creativity. As the ultimate synesthetic activity, calling on multiple senses all at once, video games have a power that no other game before them has possessed, being at once creative, directive, and stimulating. Video games enable both competition and storytelling, provided that the creators and the systems they establish are finely tuned. When video games first appeared—emerging as a minor form of popular art, much like film about a century ago—they were criticized for being too literal and for being dumbed down for children. It took a number of brilliant gems to prove, as we now know, that those early issues were just the result of youthful folly and the technical limitations of a new medium and new artform. Being the visionary that he is, George Lucas, the genius creator of the film sagas *Star Wars* and *Indiana Jones*, began to believe in this new form of artistic expression, seeing in video games the potential to stimulate the imagination with at least as much power as he had recently achieved on the silver screen.

In the early 1980s, Lucas gave a handful of young creators a level of freedom that would never again be seen in video game history. He gave them free rein with time and resources to invent a new mode of storytelling. The result was an incredible series of absolute masterpieces: *Maniac Mansion, Zak McKracken and the Alien Mindbenders, Indiana Jones and the Fate of Atlantis, Loom, Day of the Tentacle, Sam and Max Hit the Road, Full Throttle, The Dig, Grim Fandango*, and, of course, the *Monkey Island* series... Ask around: for anyone in the Western world who was a teenager with a computer in the 1990s, at least one of those names will undoubtedly bring back fond memories. From melodies that have become classics to lines with some real zingers, for over a decade, the "adventure games" produced by LucasArts deployed their universes, making their mark on an entire generation of players. That generation invariably continues to cite those games as untouchable classics, unrivaled models, and sources of inspiration. There are probably as many ways to explain the impact

LucasArts' games have had on our collective imagination as there are ways to experience said games, but nonetheless, we'll do our best...

There is a mythical, almost palpable aura around this generation of games, and *The Secret of Monkey Island* in particular. More than just a genre, "point & click" or, more plainly, adventure games have been able to distinguish themselves and stand the test of time, in spite of a certain rigidity and harshness of opinion tending toward snobbishness. Adventure games offer a different way to view the video game medium. An adventure game is all about a special connection with the story, characters, places, ambiance, and message. As the adventure game deviated from its cousins, the platform games and action games, it exposed its gameplay as being its greatest flaw. The point & click player unconsciously develops an unprecedented temporal link with the pixel-based backgrounds appearing before them. On a long summer night, with the windows wide open in hopes of catching a breeze, or on a rainy Saturday afternoon at home, lulled by the creaky hum of the hard drive and the noisy blowing of the PC tower, that player would spend hours searching every nook and cranny of the backgrounds, rummaging, combining, experimenting, chatting, and drawing on every possibility offered by the game. That rhythm— that slowness, that temporal aspect—is particular to the adventure game genre. Each "screen" calls you on an adventure and immerses you in a world. Moreover, the adventure game genre can legitimately claim to have offered the best graphics in its heyday. The backgrounds were teeming with details, bringing the game's world to life and establishing the models defining the limits of gameplay for each player. Environmental storytelling first earned its spurs with the backgrounds of works by Lucasfilm Games. The mouse becomes an extension of the player's body, directly connected to their vision. The cursor hesitantly sweeps over the screen, thoroughly searching through the masses of pixels. The immersion becomes total thanks to the musical ambiance, with themes that have become classics.

The works of Lucasfilm Games, and later LucasArts, are also renowned for their humor. After all this time, we can say that they are the zaniest games ever created, using physical comedy, deliberately stupid anachronisms, ludicrous situations, and off-the-wall characters. Naturally, they appear to be directly inspired by Monty Python[2] and Terry Pratchett,[3] with very specific visual references to what would later be known as pop culture, as well as featuring a very clear cultural, postmodern artistic erudition that tugs at the player's curiosity. For gamers in the '80s and '90s, occasions for a good laugh while playing

---

2. A famous British comedy troupe that was most active in the 1970s, with the television series *Monty Python's Flying Circus* and the films *Monty Python and the Holy Grail* (1975), *Life of Bryan* (1979), and *The Meaning of Life* (1983).
3. British author of the *Discworld* book series.

were few and far between, and games like *Monkey Island*, *Day of the Tentacle*, and *Grim Fandango* offered their young players cynicism without malice, soft immorality, and perhaps even provocation without darkness or venom.

The Secret of Monkey Island stands out from the studio's other productions because, indeed, it gave rise to an entire series. And that series has carried on through the years and bears all of the markings of video game production over the last three decades. From a stylistic revolution invoking simplicity and stripped-down representations, to the artistic profusion of the unfinished original trilogy, to a brilliantly produced gem of an episode that calls you on an adventure and serves as the swan song for 2D, to the cursed children of 3D, to the episodic format, the series provided equal measures of upheaval and hijinks for the creators who toiled over it. It underwent just as many mutations as its nascent cultural industry, falling victim to a fatalistic duality balancing profit with artistic dalliance. The series is a fascinating subject of study that this book will humbly attempt to elucidate.

Finally, what makes the work of Ron Gilbert so important is the impressive finesse of his writing, its intelligence, and the hidden subtlety of its thematic vagaries. Indeed, while the author's main idea is purposefully hidden from the player to become the titular "secret" of *Monkey Island*, the theme that emerges over the course of the first two installments, and which remains maddeningly incomplete, leaves no doubt in anyone's mind today. The series' kaleidoscopic universe and colorful characters exude wistfulness for childhood. Ron Gilbert's *Monkey Island* is quite simply a work of nostalgia, a daydream that connects directly to the imaginary worlds of a child, the child who we once were and who curiously resonates with the player who dives back into the game over 30 years later, filling their eyes and ears with the memories of a distant past. A past era made up of "chip tunes," EGA graphics in 16 colors, floppy disks, midnight snacks, and parents yelling up the stairs for the umpteenth time: "Dinner's ready!!!"

So... why this book?

A bit more than an homage, the author of this book (yours truly) and, especially, its august publisher felt that it was important to go beyond the nostalgic desire to talk about the good old days when a handful of pixels could knock our socks off. This book's composition will invite you to discover the rise and fall of the legendary Lucasfilm Games studio, as well as the juiciest details and secrets of the making of each game in the *Monkey Island* saga. To do just that, we will need to take another look at the rest of LucasArts' productions and immerse ourselves in the day-to-day experiences of the studio's handful of talented swashbucklers. Meticulously but, I sincerely hope, not too academically, the chapters of this book will take the time to describe more specifically why each of the games in the series has such a distinct personality and holds a crucial place in video game history. We will travel from island to island, from one era to the next, to retrace a three-decade chronicle of video games.

As you will see, the pages of this book are studded with quotations and references, but they also offer a few snippets obtained directly from some of the creators, and I would like to personally thank, in particular, Peter Chan, Steve Purcell, Dave Grossman, Mark Ferrari, Tim Schafer, Khris Brown, and Larry Ahern, who graciously sat down with me to recount their old anecdotes from their buccaneering days. I was not surprised to discover that, in addition to being talented artists, they are also great people. Finally, there's a good chance that you may have bought this book in hopes of finally discovering the secret of *Monkey Island*. Well, after much searching, I will save you a lot of trouble: it is my pleasure to reveal to you that, in fact, the notorious secret closely guarded by Ron Gilbert is...

...oh! Look behind you! A three-headed monkey!!!

About the Author: Nicolas Deneschau

An eclectic connoisseur of *Kaiju-Eiga*, sci-fi films in black and white, and pirate novels, Nicolas is still trying to find his rubber chicken with a pulley in the middle. Having done a stint writing about films with *Cinegenre.net*, then taking his writing talents to *Merlanfrit*, today he collaborates with Third Éditions. Notably, he is the co-author of the book *The Saga Uncharted: Chronicles of an Explorer*.

THE MYSTERIES OF

MONKEY ISLAND

Introduction

A long time ago in a galaxy far, far away...

Before we discuss the adventures of Guybrush Threepwood, mighty pirate, or dive into the creation of the games, we should first look at the destiny of a man without whom this series of games that dazzled players in the early days of video game history would never have become reality. Our story begins in 1944 in the small California city of Modesto.

George Walton Lucas, Senior, and his wife, Dorothy Ellinore Bomberger, had four children: three girls—Ann, Kathleen, and Wendy—and a scrawny little boy named George Walton, Junior. Let's set the scene: Modesto was a sleepy little city between Sacramento and San Francisco, and the Lucas family, as devout Lutherans, maintained a strict, religious lifestyle. George Walton, Jr., was a delicate boy. Bullied by his classmates, he spent much of his time devouring the classic adventure stories of Robert Louis Stevenson (*Treasure Island*) and Daniel Defoe (*Robinson Crusoe*), as well as collecting numerous comic books (notably *Flash Gordon*). Illness kept his mother bedridden most of the time, and his father was often absent as he worked to provide for his family. As such, George was more or less left to his own devices and was a mediocre student at best. In the late 1950s, muscle cars became all the rage in California, and young people liked to blast rock 'n' roll music while flying down the highway. George Lucas, fascinated by this aesthetic and world of cars, became a fan of automobile racing and pushed his modest studies to the side in hopes of becoming one of the most talented drivers to grace American speedways. However, his dream was short-lived and came to a definitive end when he crashed his Autobianchi Bianchina into a tree at full speed on June 12, 1962. Miraculously, George was ejected from the vehicle, of which all that remained was a burning wreck. The accident made headlines in the local news. That was very nearly the end of the story and you would have been very unhappy to have spent a few dollars on this book.

While he recovered, lucky to be alive, George Lucas decided to get his act together and rededicate himself to school. He attended Modesto Junior College, where he managed to earn a two-year degree. But he also found a new passion: telling stories with the help of a camera. Encouraged by his longtime friend Haskell Wexler, an already experienced cinematographer, George enrolled at the University of Southern California School of Cinematic Arts in Los Angeles. In his class, he made friends with a man named John Milius,[4] who introduced him to the work of a popular Japanese director, Akira Kurosawa. Lucas was immediately entranced by the virtuosity of the Japanese master. He praised the incredible potency of *Sanjuro* and *Throne of Blood*, and he watched *Seven Samurai* dozens of times to learn every shot. He discovered the power of images and looks, as well as the science of editing in Kurosawa's films. The chaining of action shots went on to have significant influence on young George, who appreciated the very particular sense of rhythm capable of masquerading as popular film to more effectively transmit a deeper message... In any case, this new passion seemed more promising than car racing. Lucas' first films as a student were well received, even acclaimed, like his science-fiction short film *Electronic Labyrinth THX 1138 4EB*, which took first prize in the 1967 National Student Film Festival. That same year, George completed a six-month internship at Warner Bros., where he met another up-and-coming director, Francis Ford Coppola, who would become a friend. Coppola was finishing up filming of a musical starring Fred Astaire and Petula Clark called *Finian's Rainbow*.

The two buddies became inseparable, and Lucas got his start as a full-fledged director by creating a documentary about the filming of Coppola's latest movie, *The Rain People*. Lucas and Coppola were young idealists filled with new ideas, while the society of the late 1960s clamored for fresh blood to ride the New Wave of cinema coming out of France. So, together, they decided to found their own production company, American Zoetrope, in 1969. In doing so, they hoped to be able to get their respective film projects off the ground while maintaining total creative control. Producer John Calley of Warner Bros. then proposed that George Lucas should adapt his successful short into a feature-length film for theatrical release, dubbed *THX 1138*.

Very loosely yet clearly inspired by George Orwell's *1984*, the film used a script, originally written by Matthew Robbins and Walter Murch, set in a dark, uncompromising future in which humanity lives in a sedated state and suffers under the yoke of a totalitarian power. A worker, THX 1138, and his partner, LUH 3147, after having unauthorized sexual relations, are sentenced to prison. THX ends up escaping from that white hellhole, while LUH is executed. Lightyears away from the George Lucas universes much more familiar to us today, *THX 1138* is a dark, pessimistic, anxiety-inducing film. Still, the movie is striking for its original aesthetic approach and its sense of rhythm, which prominently features both long silences and action sequences. The movie was released in American theaters in March 1971, but its performance was decisively bad: it was a critical and commercial flop. However, its visual

---

4. Who, a few years later, went on to write *Apocalypse Now* and direct the equally popular *Conan the Barbarian*.

choices and uncompromising nature earned it a solid reputation in the years that followed, particularly among young directors whose names you may or may not know: Spielberg, Scorsese, Carpenter, Darabont, etc.

In spite of its undeniable artistic and visual strengths, the poor box office performance of *THX 1138* left American Zoetrope and Francis Ford Coppola deep in debt. Coppola decided to take on a project that Paramount Pictures was pressing him to direct, a little film called *The Godfather*, which, in spite of being a choice made out of desperation, proved to be a good one. Lucas, meanwhile, was upset about the lack of support he was receiving from his fellow director in talks with Warner Bros. He also sensed that their personality differences risked causing permanent damage to their friendship. George distanced himself from American Zoetrope and began working on a small-budget film for Universal Pictures called *American Graffiti*. At the same time, he decided to create his own modest production company, Lucasfilm Ltd., which we will get back to before long. With the encouragement of his wife, film editor Marcia Lucas, George decided to set aside his philosophical ambitions and deliver a movie that would be lighter and less visceral, fresher and more sincere. The result was an homage to the carefree attitude of 1960s America, in which a group of teenagers leave their worries behind for an evening as they cruise around in gleaming muscle cars while listening to rock legends like Chuck Berry and Fats Domino. Lucas filmed the movie in 29 days with a modest budget, creating a fresh, cheerful film offering nostalgia and catharsis for a society entangled in both the Vietnam War and an economic crisis. *American Graffiti* was a surprising blockbuster. The movie was released in summer 1973 and was a huge success. On an original budget of $777,000, by the end of its run, the film had brought in $115 million and earned Lucas independence beyond his wildest dreams. What's more, the movie's success launched the careers of a number of young actors you may have heard of, including Ron Howard,[5] Richard Dreyfuss,[6] and Harrison Ford.[7] It also gave birth to an all-time classic TV series, the aptly named *Happy Days*.

Coppola and Lucas finally reunited and buried the hatchet. For Coppola, the massive success of *The Godfather* allowed him to undertake many other projects; for Lucas, the commercial success of *American Graffiti* restored his reputation. Coppola asked Lucas to direct a film that was particularly near and dear to his heart, based on a script by his friend John Milius: *Apocalypse Now*. However, George declined. He secretly dreamed of adapting for the big screen one of his favorite series from his childhood: *Flash Gordon*. However, the owners of the rights to the pulp franchise featuring intergalactic adventures

---

5. Who directed *Apollo 13*, *Willow* and, as it turns out, *Solo: A Star Wars Story*.
6. An actor who appeared in *Jaws* and *Close Encounters of the Third Kind*.
7. An actor who needs no introduction: *Blade Runner*, *Star Wars*, *Indiana Jones*, etc.

weren't willing to hand them over so easily. So, George Lucas would have to create his own universe.

November 1973. The movie studio 20th Century Fox, led by Alan Ladd, Jr., agreed to finance George's next project, a science-fiction film given the grandiloquent title *The Star Wars: From the Adventures of Luke Starkiller.*[8] The project was ambitious and would likely require the development of an unprecedented number of special effects. So, Lucas decided to found the studio Industrial Light & Magic (ILM) within his production company, Lucasfilm Ltd., so that he could retain total creative control over the visual aspects of the film. However, above all, George Lucas aimed to invest in special effects, which he foresaw as being an essential element for big-budget movies to be produced in the years to come. He installed the pioneering John Dykstra at the head of ILM, with support provided by model designer Colin Cantwell and the brilliant conceptual artist Ralph MacQuarrie.

Casting for the film began in August 1975 at the offices of American Zoetrope. Director Brian de Palma[9] assisted George with this task. While famous actor Toshiro Mifune[10] was for a time considered for the role of Obi-Wan Kenobi, he was ultimately replaced by veteran actor Alec Guinness. Harrison Ford, Carrie Fisher, and Mark Hamill were then hired to play the leading roles. Cunning as ever and possessing an unparalleled sense of business, Lucas obtained from Fox the rights to all future merchandizing tied to the saga. This bold move would pay off big time. Filming of *Star Wars* began on March 22, 1976, in Tunisia, then continued in London, finishing on July 23 of the same year.

The first cut of the film was a complete disaster: it was flat, boring, and totally conventional... Everything that Lucas wanted to avoid, as he was mainly targeting the movie at a teenage audience. Even though the rushes were then placed in the capable hands of George's wife, Marcia Lucas, and editor Paul Hirsch, the release had to be pushed back to summer 1977. The extra 10 months this gave them were dedicated exclusively to creating the complex special effects needed for the film's various scenes. In October 1976, Lucas collapsed in the middle of the studio from what he thought was a heart attack. But the doctors diagnosed the cause as acute stress, and they encouraged him to rest. However, the countdown had started, and Lucas only had a few months remaining to finish his film. He put all his energy and money into the project, about which Fox executives were starting to have doubts.

John Dykstra proved to be crucial to the success of the film's technical aspects. He was probably one of the first people to buy into the idea that computers

---

8. An early version of the name Luke Skywalker, after the original name Mace Windy.
9. Who was also doing auditions for his next film, *Carrie.*
10. *Seven Samurai* by Akira Kurosawa.

had a major role to play in helping create shots that were too complex or costly to be filmed using traditional techniques. His vision was likely a key element for the future creation of video games. Dykstra proceeded to invent the Dykstraflex system by mounting a large camera on a rig whose movements were controlled by a series of computers. Remember that in the 1970s, all of this was very experimental, and a machine with the power of a simple pocket calculator occupied the space of a large antique wardrobe. With the camera controlled by computers, it was able to carry out very precise, rotating shots of fixed objects such as models, creating the illusion of movement.

The final cut incorporating all the post-production effects was finally finished on time after a lot of painstaking work. The soundtrack by John Williams exceeded all of Lucas' expectations and enhanced the entire production, resulting in the film we know and love today. In a few words: a new kind of film that was gripping, epic, well-paced, and visually extraordinary. From the start, Lucas imagined a coherent universe based on the serials[11] of his childhood, and he convinced Fox to produce two additional movies. You can feel this in the construction of the original episode, with the unprecedented depth of its universe.

Star Wars premiered on 37 screens in the United States on May 25, 1977. Audiences fell head over heels for it. While Steven Spielberg's *Jaws*, released the previous year, set a new standard for blockbusters, *Star Wars* became the quintessential example. Everyone wanted to see it; the theaters were packed day after day. Fox's stock price doubled in record time. Lucas, meanwhile, took a well-earned vacation one week after the film's release. On a beach in Hawaii, his friend Steven Spielberg confided in him that he wanted to direct a new *James Bond*. Lucas stopped him there and told him he had a better idea: a movie about an adventurer in the 1940s who goes off in search of mysterious artifacts while fighting the Nazis... The rest is history.

With the success of *Star Wars* under his belt and confident in his universe, George Lucas decided to produce the sequels on his own. Going forward, Fox would simply serve as the distributor of the films in American cinemas. However, Lucas found that he couldn't handle everything singlehandedly, so he decided to entrust the directing of *The Empire Strikes Back* to one of his former university professors, veteran director Irvin Kershner.[12] Filming lasted through all of 1979, for a theatrical release on May 21, 1980. It was another massive success. Americans flooded the theaters; the famous paternal twist[13] stunned the media and fans worldwide.

---

11. Serials were episodic films based on serialized novels that were particularly popular from the 1930s to the 1950s.
12. *Eyes of Laura Mars, RoboCop 2, Never Say Never Again.*
13. "I am your father!"

While work on the *Star Wars* saga was underway, the script for *Indiana Smith*, who would later become *Indiana Jones* per the wise advice of Steven Spielberg, was close to being finished by Lawrence Kasdan. Lucas would be the producer and his friend Spielberg would direct the film. *Raiders of the Lost Ark* was released on June 12, 1981, and was wildly successful with both critics and audiences. George Lucas was officially crowned the independent film king of Hollywood. Additionally, during this same period, Lucas produced one of the greatest Akira Kurosawa films, *Kagemusha*. George had never ceased to be an admirer of the Japanese director.

While the sequel to *The Empire Strikes Back* was being prepared, Spielberg worked on *The Temple of Doom*, the second installment in the *Indiana Jones* series, which was in the writing process.

But Lucas didn't want to stop there. He fully understood the magnitude of the universes he had created and their success with young fans. Movie merchandise took off, more and more films were produced with special effects,[14] Sony launched its CDP-101, the first audio CD player, and the American youth spent much of their time and money at gaming arcades. What's more, Lucasfilm was earning wild levels of profit and was thus threatened with heavy taxes. To minimize that financial hit, there was one solution: invest in new technologies. This convergence of facts gave Lucas the brilliant idea to create a new team within his special effects company ILM, which he did on May 1, 1982. Thus, the Computer Division was born.

14. In 1981, *E.T.*, *Blade Runner*, and *Tron* all became milestones for this category.

THE MYSTERIES OF
MONKEY ISLAND

Part 1

Chapter 1: Lucasfilm Games™

The number-one objective of the Computer Division wasn't to work on video games specifically, but rather to master the production of digital special effects for feature-length films and various other audiovisual productions. The team's first success was integration of the "Genesis effect" into the movie *Star Trek 2: The Wrath of Khan*, directed by Nicholas Meyer (1982), an animation meant to reconstruct landscapes in the form of fractal images. Having secured its budget, the team was able to dive deep into research and development to come up with new possibilities for digital imaging.

Before long, Atari, which at the time was the biggest player in the American video game industry, set its sights on the work accomplished by ILM and proposed a collaboration with Lucas. The CFO of Lucasfilm Ltd. managed to convince Atari to pay the modest sum of $1 million in exchange for a vague "see what you can do!" Ed Catmull was officially the first employee of the Computer Division. Promoted to the rank of director, he was in charge of establishing the scope and goals for his division, as well as selecting the team with which he'd collaborate. He told *Rolling Stone* magazine that George wanted them to make games... and by the end of the year, they had a game designer![15] Lucas said "jump" and Ed Catmull said "how high?" He quickly hired Peter Langston, an ultra-talented Unix developer, who he poached from a Wall Street firm (remember this name, we'll come back to him later on in this book...).

Of course, we have to remember the context: the Computer Division had to invent something; it had to start from scratch and imagine what the future of video game creation might look like. As such, it's no surprise that the team that formed was a motley crew of different talents. Langston was the very first employee of the Lucasfilm Games Group within the Computer Division: "In May of 1982, The Computer Division of Lucasfilm Ltd. hires me to start a new project in electronic and computer games, and I move from New York City to Marin County, California, and I start hiring staff, and we sign a profitable licensing agreement with Atari, and I give a lot of interviews,"[16] he remembers with a laugh. He then established the basis of game design for the team's future productions. David Fox, Rob Poor, and David Levine soon joined him. They all

---

15. *Rolling Stone*, June 10, 1982.
16. *http://www.langston.com/LFGames/*

worked tirelessly to come up with the technology capable of supporting George Lucas' new ambitions. Their only instruction? "Don't touch *Star Wars*!" That was a big disappointment for David Fox: "We were told right up front that we were not allowed to do *Star Wars* titles. I was really upset–I had joined the company because I wanted to be in *Star Wars*!" And Steve Arnold adds: "We were creating a culture that was designed around innovation... We had the brand of *Star Wars*, the credibility of *Star Wars*, and the franchise of *Star Wars*, but we didn't have to play in that universe. We were a group that lived inside a super-creative, technologically astute company and we got to do our own invention... We got to make up our own stories and call them Lucasfilm."[17]

The advantage of such a small team, given total freedom, was that they could weave their way through the tentacular organization that was ILM. The team was able to take advantage of the most powerful graphics machines on the market, used by the Film Division. They were even able to procure the services of the graphics team to work on their preliminary visuals or simply have the studio's specialized teams create sound effects for them. This flexibility allowed them to spend their first several months focusing solely on game design while bearing in mind that they needed to contend with the enormous technical constraints of the machines available on the at-home gaming market at the time.

Rebel Rescue™ & Ballblazer™

In his earliest days at the studio, David Fox spent his time with Loren Carpenter, the graphics developer responsible for the famous "Genesis effect" in *Star Trek*. Carpenter, who loves a good challenge, kept a curious and watchful eye on the Games Group. With Fox's encouragement, he decided to lend them a hand. As Fox tells it: "We lent him an Atari 800 and he took it home. Within a matter of days, he learned the basics of the assembly language for the 6502 processor and understood how the Atari handled its display of graphics. Within a week he came back to the office with a functioning demo. He had created a real-time generator of fractal images within the limits of the Atari's 48 KB of memory and primitive resolution. It was incredible! It was running at about eight to ten frames per second and was probably one of the coolest things we had ever seen on a microcomputer."[18] Upon seeing the result, being the good *Star Wars* fan that he was, David Fox imagined how he could employ such an engine within a game. Thus, the *Rebel Rescue* project was

17. *https://www.usgamer.net/articles/i-actually-was-hunting-ewoks-lucasfilm-games-the-early-years*
18. *https://www.electriceggplant.com/media/RG44_RescueOnFractalus.pdf*

born. "*Star Wars* was an eye-opening experience for me. I wanted the game to take place in that universe. We didn't have permission to use the saga's characters, but we were able to take very heavy inspiration from the style of the ships and places in the movies. Any resemblance between the game and the scenes on planet Hoth in *The Empire Strikes Back* is, of course, pure coincidence..." David Fox remembers humorously. *Rebel Rescue* became a flight simulator in which the player controls a sort of vessel inspired by the X-Wing from *Star Wars*, with the goal being to save rebel pilots lost on the surface of a planet generated with fractal images. "We didn't have a deadline, so we had plenty of time to screw things up!" jokes the game designer. "After a few months of work, you could fly and control the ship with a joystick, and it was a pretty fun game. But there was still something missing and we had to show it to other people to figure out what worked." Charlie Kneller joined the Games Group and improved the ship's flight dynamics. He also began optimizing the fractal engine. Meanwhile, Peter Langston continued expanding the team's influence. He designed the music and sound for *Rebel Rescue* (renamed *Rescue on Fractalus*) and kicked off production of another game, with David Levine serving as the director. When development seemed to be reaching the finish line, the High Admiral, George Lucas, paid a single visit to the Games Group... He found *Rescue on Fractalus* to be pretty fun, but he was surprised by the lack of shooting on the ship. He recommended to Fox that the game should allow the player to shoot at enemies and also include bad guys pretending to be rebels needing to be saved in order to add excitement to the game. When the leader speaks, you do as you're told, even if that means significant production delays for the game. "We secured permission from Atari—who would be publishing the game—to not mention the aliens in the manual or in any of the PR. In fact, the disguised aliens[19] don't appear though the first four or five levels of the game, so that just as you get into the habit of landing, turning off the engine, seeing a guy in a space suit, and unlocking the door for him, you might not notice that the figure approaching has a green head. If the door was open, you'd be boarded and have to fly like mad into space and hopefully expel him from the airlock. Despite Rebel's rudimentary graphics, I recall numerous people regaling [me] with tales of falling from their chairs in fright and getting a huge adrenaline rush from the shock value," recalls David Fox.

Meanwhile, David Levine reused Loren Carpenter's engine to try out another design idea, a project initially named *Ballblaster*, then *Ballblazer*. Instead of aliens and space ships, the game invited two players to face off in matches of a sport similar to soccer, in which machines called "rotofoils" must get the "plasmorb" into the opposing goal. The first-person view enabled 360-degree

---

19. The enemy aliens in *Rescue on Fractalus* are called Jaggis.

movement over a field generated in real time. While the controls seemed quite finicky, the game nonetheless distinguished itself for being well crafted. *Ballblazer* even improved Loren Carpenter's engine by integrating anti-aliasing, a revolutionary process at the time, which smoothed out the enormous pixels of the 8-bit Atari. Notably, even the game's introductory music was randomly generated, following a tempo and rhythms to accompany the match, an idea that later gained traction, as we will see...

The two games were delivered to Atari in return for the million-dollar "see what you can do!" Steve Arnold, who was a newcomer to the Lucasfilm Games Group team at the time, remembers: "The problem was that Atari basically gave away copies of the game. The games were sent under extreme cone-of-silence, non-disclosure, eyes-only, burn-after-reading security... but still appeared shortly thereafter on the underground networks... and the pirated versions even won some awards..."[20] Users of the Atari 800 at the time could take advantage of the earliest network connection modems to exchange files, and pirated copies of *Rescue on Fractalus* and *Ballblazer* were popular targets. What's more, Tim Schafer, the master architect of *Monkey Island* who joined the team a few years later, shares a funny anecdote. When interviewing for the position, "I called David Fox right away [...] I told him how much I wanted to work at Lucasfilm, not because of *Star Wars*, but because I loved '*Ball Blaster*.' '*Ball Blaster*, eh?' he said. 'Yeah! I love *Ball Blaster*!' I said. It was true. I had broken a joystick playing that game on my Atari 800. 'Well, the name of the game is *Ballblazer*,' Mr. Fox said, curtly. 'It was only called *Ball Blaster* in the pirated version.' Gulp... Totally busted. It was true: I had played the pirated version. There, I said it."[21]

At the time, most video games stuck to a very classic structure based on difficulty, a number of lives available, and very well-established arcade routines. The Computer Division had a different approach, and David Fox offers this explanation of their philosophy: "I would say when we're designing a game, the aim is to create some sort of an experience. [...] We really want to get someone feeling like they're in a new universe, and to create an experience of exploring a new universe. It's the sort of thing that happens in a George Lucas film. It's like you've been transported to somewhere else. Most of us like that feeling and we want to be able to transport the person to another universe too, through a game that's really different."[22]

It's worth noting, from today's point of view, in this era of digital media, the packaging for the games looks completely ludicrous. The boxes of both games

20. *Rogue Leaders, The Story of LucasArts* (Rob Smith).
21. *https://www.apl2bits.net/2016/02/29/tim-schafer-lucasfilm-ball-blazer/*
22. *https://www.usgamer.net/articles/i-actually-was-hunting-ewoks-lucasfilm-games-the-early-years*

and their contents were produced as if for a high-class feature-length film. Gary Winnick created the concept art with David Fox and David Levine for their respective titles, then life-sized models of a rotofoil and a spaceship were built by ILM to appear on the jackets and advertising materials. Finally, a photo shoot with David Fox, completely made over to look like a spacecraft pilot, provided illustrations for the game's guide. It was Lucas-style extravagance...

Presented at CES in Las Vegas in 1984, the two games caught the attention of the trade show's technophile audience. Some journalists doubted that such an engine could be real and looked for a hidden VCR that might be playing pre-recorded images on the screens. But they were indeed real-time demos of games on an Atari 800. The commercial success was relatively modest, but nevertheless, Lucasfilm now had an experienced team ready to make use of their cutting-edge technology for future games...

Koronis Rift™ & Eidolon™

Noah Falstein was the newbie on the team. Peter Langston hesitated for quite some time before hiring him: "Peter wasn't very enthusiastic about bringing me on board because I had previously worked at Williams Electronics on the arcade game *Sinistar*, and nobody in the group had previous video game development experience. He was worried that I wouldn't be able to bring in new concepts given that I was already a veteran creator, at the ripe old age of 26... However, after lending a hand on *Rescue on Fractalus*, I got the idea for a game with a new design called *"Tanks A Lot"*[23] and I immediately got the green light, even before the budget and schedule had been set."[24] The new concept, which eventually took the name *Koronis Rift*,[25] once again based on the fractal engine, put the player in control of a vehicle belonging to a futuristic treasure hunter. The goal was to discover artifacts and long-lost technologies abandoned by the ancient inhabitants of a faraway planet. It blended action with strategy and added a bit of complexity to the rudimentary concepts of *Rescue on Fractalus*. However, even though at the time of its release the media recognized it as being a beautifully made game, its searing difficulty leaves me unwilling to recommend it to my readers...

Also in 1985, a newcomer, Charlie Kenner, was working on another game, *The Eidolon*, based on the studio's historic engine. The game propelled players

---

23. A great pun indeed!
24. *Rogue Leaders, The Story of LucasArts* (Rob Smith).
25. *Koronis Rift* gets its name from Noah Falstein's college thesis entitled: *Koronis Strike: A Computer Simulation Game of Mining and Combat in the Asteroid Belt.*

into a heroic fantasy world where they had to make their way through caverns and battle creatures like trolls and gnomes to escape. As it was, the title was a likely precursor to the famous (and incredible) *Dungeon Master*, made by FTL Games, and perhaps even more so to *Ultima Underworld* by Blue Sky Prod. It was an ancestor to first-person dungeon crawlers,[26] but with real-time scrolling, faithful to the Games Group's other productions. The game is fluid, difficult, and handles well... The game design remained basic, but the concept was there and would only be improved upon in the years that followed.

Abandoning Atari, which changed hands several times during that period, Peter Langston took the opportunity to switch the studio to a new distributor, Epyx, which boosted their sales. While the two games weren't the best produced in-house at the time, they offered the opportunity to experiment and to develop solid experience among the young developers.

Lucasfilm Games™

The year 1985 was one of change for Lucasfilm, and for the Games Group in particular. While Peter Langston continued to direct the creative side of the studio, he delegated the sales and finance aspects to Steve Arnold, who came over from Atari. George Lucas was a businessman, and Lucasfilm, even though it served as an experimental laboratory, needed to be profitable. According to Arnold, when he first joined the Games Group: "It was a bunch of hippies in *Star Wars* T-shirts. They started their day around 10 in the morning, but finished very late, and you could immediately feel that the environment was particularly conducive to creativity and humor." One of Steve Arnold's initiatives was to encourage the technical teams to come up with anti-piracy systems to prevent the distribution of illegal copies and to try to generate profit from game production. Then came the second big change for the game developer: it received a recognizable name and label. Thus, the Games Group officially became "Lucasfilm Games." From then on, games would be produced, published, and distributed in-house under the new brand.

Alongside Lucasfilm Games, a second branch of the original Computer Division, led by Ed Catmull, was spun off. Renamed Pixar,[27] its big players included Alvy Ray Smith and one John Lasseter[28]... Within weeks, Pixar was sold to Steve Jobs, the co-founder of Apple, and went on to become a massive,

26. The "dungeon crawler" genre is characterized by first-person exploration of labyrinthine dungeons according to the formula "door-monster-treasure."
27. From the nickname the employees had given to their Silicon Graphics work stations, which were digital compositing computers.
28. He went on to become the head of Pixar Animation Studios and the creator of *Toy Story*, *Cars*, etc.

successful studio, reigning as the undeniable and uncontested world champion of CGI animation. They did OK for themselves, I guess.

For Lucasfilm Games, George Lucas' instructions were clear: "Stay small, be the best, and don't lose money!" However, Lucas rarely castigated or imposed restrictions on the video game teams. According to the director of the game *Indiana Jones and the Fate of Atlantis*, Hal Barwood, Lucas was like "that rich uncle who gives you Christmas gifts each year, but who you almost never see."[29] Peter Langston adds: "I think from the start, he needed us to prove that we understood the business, which is why he was as involved as he was at the beginning. He had seen what the Computer Division had done with the technology in the area that he knows about: film. And he said, 'This is great, I want to do this more elsewhere.' Doing it in this area that he didn't know much about... He was proud of us, and respectful. I think maybe he even had the sense that he wouldn't want us to come in and say, 'this movie should have this change,' so he wasn't going to do that to us either."[30] According to another developer, Chip Morningstar, Lucas viewed Lucasfilm Games as the *Lost Patrol:*[31] nobody really knew who they were or where they were, but they had to be somewhere...

In spite of impressive creativity, with the releases of *PHM Pegasus*, a military simulation; *Labyrinth*, an early graphic adventure game; the *Mirage Project*, a life-sized X-Wing flight simulator; and *Habitat*, the first true graphic-based MMORPG, Lucasfilm Games still hadn't found its path, its trademark, its identity. Certain game publishers began to specialize—in arcade games, in shooters, in role-playing games. But at Lucasfilm Games, in keeping with the philosophy of George Lucas, the main focus was on telling stories. And while, at the time, storytelling in video games remained shaky, there was already a genre building a solid reputation in this area. A genre capable of combining the desire for a real story with unbridled creativity. A genre that was ready to explode...

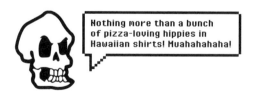

Nothing more than a bunch of pizza-loving hippies in Hawaiian shirts! Muahahahaha!

29. *Rogue Leaders, The Story of LucasArts* (Rob Smith).
30. *https://www.usgamer.net/articles/i-actually-was-hunting-ewoks-lucasfilm-games-the-early-years*
31. A reference to *The Lost Patrol*, an American film by John Ford (1934).

Chapter 2: From interactive fiction to Point & Click™

Given that today's adventure games have marginal popularity and are nowhere near as successful as the big blockbusters, it's hard to imagine that they were once the hottest genre of video game, with each title eagerly awaited like the Messiah. From the early 1980s and for almost two decades, adventure games regularly appeared on the covers of video game magazines and provided the most celebrated sagas of the microcomputer era. Then, from the mid-1990s, the genre began to decline, to the point of becoming a retro, nostalgic pleasure, though current experiments to revive it are showing undeniable inventiveness. The adventure game offered each studio the opportunity to show off its talents, both technical—as most of the games were showpieces for graphics and audio in their day—and narrative, since the genre was one of the only ones to offer players an elaborate, well-developed scenario, whereas action games limited those aspects to a bare minimum. Before we dive into the history and creation of the *Monkey Island* series, we first need to go back in time and return to the origins of the genre, as well as review how it has evolved and its impact on video game history, in order to better understand what Ron Gilbert's series represents in the hearts of so many of those who explored its tropical islands in the early 1990s.

Wander and Colossal Cave Adventure™

Colossal Cave Adventure is often cited as the very first adventure game ever. However, a very serious contender for that title was long forgotten before re-emerging from digital obscurity in 2015. The game in question was created by one Peter Langston (as you'll remember, he was employee number one of the Lucasfilm Games Group: everything is connected), a young computer nerd who had already created *Empire*, the first-ever strategy game, in 1972. In 1974, he created *Wander*. At the time, the term "video game" didn't really exist yet, and Langston himself referred to his software as a "tool for writing non-deterministic fantasy stories." Langston recalls, "I came up with the idea for *Wander* and wrote an early version in HP Basic while I was still teaching at the Evergreen State College in Olympia, Washington. That system limited names to six letters, so: *WANDER, EMPIRE, CONVOY, GALAXY*, etc. Then, I rewrote *Wander* in C on Harvard's Unix V5 system shortly after our band moved to Boston in 1974. I got around to putting a copyright notice on it in 1978."[32] However, *Wander* wouldn't receive historic recognition until decades later. French journalist Raphaël Lucas explains: "The first amateur game developers were university professors and students; they never made the effort to preserve their video games. Moreover, on PLATO (the first networked computer system, created in the late 1960s), the servers were regularly wiped of these freeloading programs that slowed down access to the main programs, which were used to teach classes."[33] *Wander* largely pioneered game elements that would constitute the earliest text-based adventure games. In a question-answer format, the game calls on the player to find the right responses to continue progressing through a branching story, much like in "choose your own adventure" books. The interface was rudimentary and the options were few, but the foundations were there and would be fully established a year later.

In 1975, a broken heart led William Crowther to seclude himself for a few long months in front of his PDP-10 work computer, on which he developed *Colossal Cave Adventure*.[34] The young computer programmer, who by day worked on creating ARPANET,[35] was going through a divorce from his wife, Pat Crowther, and found himself separated from his two daughters. When they came to visit him, he would amuse himself by creating for them little computer challenges that were accessible in spite of the austerity of the interface. In an interview given in 1993, he recounts: "I had been involved in a non-computer role-playing game called *Dungeons & Dragons* at the time, and also I had been actively exploring in caves—Mammoth Cave in Kentucky in particular. Suddenly, I got involved in a divorce, and that left me a bit pulled apart in various ways. In particular, I was missing my kids. Also, the caving had stopped, because that had become awkward, so I decided I would fool around and write a program that was a re-creation in fantasy of my caving, and also would be a game for the kids, and perhaps some aspects of the *Dungeons & Dragons* that I had been playing. My idea was that it would be a computer game that would not be intimidating to non-computer people, and that was one of the reasons why I made it so that the player directs the game with natural language input,

---

32. *https://archive.org/details/wander_201504*
33. *https://www.lemonde.fr/pixels/article/2015/04/28/on-a-decouvert-wander-le-lointain-ancetre-de-minecraft-et-il-date-de-1974_4624439_4408996.html*
34. Or just simply *Adventure*.
35. The precursor to the Internet.

instead of more standardized commands. My kids thought it was a lot of fun."[36] In *Colossal Cave Adventure*, the player reads little paragraphs that describe the geographic location of their avatar, as well as the choices they have before them, just like in "choose your own adventure" novels. The player can then interact by using a combination of two words that seem logical to them, like "go south" or "take sword." In 1975, William Crowther published his game on ARPANET. In 1976, with permission from the original creator, programmer Don Woods made improvements to the game, ported it to different systems, and embellished its universe with names and places directly inspired by J.R.R. Tolkien's *The Lord of the Rings*. Woods continued to improve upon his new version for over 20 years. Up into the early 1980s, *Colossal Cave Adventure* was a major influence on budding creators, to the point of spawning its own genre known as "interactive fiction."

Sierra On-Line™

In 1978, Ken Williams, a young, 25-year-old computer scientist living in Los Angeles with his wife, Roberta, was working on programming accounting software for a client. In order to complete development on time, he brought home a Teletype Model 33 terminal so that he could continue work outside the office. Williams was hoping to soon jump into the software market for the Apple II, but he needed an unexploited niche that would allow him to stand out from the crowd. While perusing the catalogue of downloadable programs for his machine, by chance, he came across *Colossal Cave Adventure*. After buying it, he suggested to his wife that they play it together. Roberta was fascinated with the universe and the endless possibilities offered by such an interface. Discovering that there wasn't much competition in the gaming market, she decided to write the hook for a new story she called *Mystery House*, very loosely inspired by the Agatha Christie novel *And Then There Were None*. Roberta convinced her husband to spend the next two months developing the game on an Apple II lent to them by Ken's brother. She quickly realized that the text alone might seem too austere for the mass market and that the graphics capabilities offered by the Apple computer could greatly enrich her story. So, the couple invested in a VersaWriter, a machine capable of converting line-based drawings into digital images. Coding of the game was completed on May 5, 1980, featuring over 70 illustrations. After packaging the game by hand and creating their own company, On-Line Systems, Ken and Roberta bought ad space in *Micro* magazine and launched sales. Very quickly, and to the great

36. *https://en.wikipedia.org/wiki/William_Crowther_(programmer)*

surprise of Mr. and Mrs. Williams, *Mystery House* became a hit. They sold over 10,000 copies in a matter of weeks, sending off each one "manually" through the U.S. Postal Service. With this success under their belts, the couple kept the momentum going by developing many more games, the most notable of which, *Wizard and the Princess*,[37] was a prelude to the future *King's Quest* saga, another great creation of Roberta Williams, and featured color illustrations for the first time. Meager though they were, the drawings displayed on cathode-ray tube monitors demonstrated enough evocative power to enchant the hundreds of thousands of players who encountered them. Ken and Roberta Williams again met with success and decided to open a true game development and publishing studio, named Sierra On-Line, in 1982. Thus, the graphic adventure game made its debut on the shelves of retailers, though the interface remained rudimentary, given that it was largely based on a text parser and required that the developers anticipate every reaction. These games proved to be particularly frustrating when the player couldn't find the right word or expression to make the system understand.

In 1983, IBM approached Sierra On-Line and asked Mr. and Mrs. Williams to develop a game to promote the company's new EGA color screens (sporting 16 colors!). In response, Roberta created the universe for *King's Quest: Quest for the Crown*. It was a true work of art, given the memory limitations of the machines at the time. *King's Quest* expanded on interactive fiction by having a main character appear on screen. The character was animated and the player could watch him carry out actions ordered by the player through the text interface. The adventures of Sir Graham on his quest for the crown of Daventry were ported to virtually all existing systems at the time, including the PC and Apple II, and later the Amiga, Atari ST, and even the SEGA Master System console.

Point & Click™

January 1984: Apple released its revolutionary Macintosh. With its "high-resolution" screen, its intuitive graphic interface, and… its mouse! Thus began a new era for home computers. The company Silicon Beach Software sensed the opportunity created by the new machine and soon published *Enchanted Scepters*, the very first "point & click" video game in history. In the game— which was objectively unremarkable—the player could use the mouse to select an item from the system's drop-down menus. Innovative but not very intuitive, the new style meant that players no longer had to waste time figuring out if,

---

37. Also known by the name *Adventure in Serenia*.

for example, for an item like an ordinary boulder, the game expected the player to use the word "stone" or "rock." Or some other term!

The next year, ICOM Simulations published the game *Déjà Vu*, which in turn achieved another major milestone for the genre. It marked the birth of the point & click interface as we know it today. It had everything: an inventory you could select with the mouse, a list of actions (examine, open, close, speak, operate, go, hit, consume), and the ability to control just about everything with the "magic appendage" of the Macintosh. But in addition to its innovations, *Déjà Vu* became an instant classic thanks to its high-quality writing and its ubiquitous humor (which was uncommon at the time in the many action and first-person games available to players). The game is centered on the work of a private investigator, set in Chicago in December 1941. Retired boxer Theodore Harding must investigate and exonerate himself from a murder that took place in his office. The game really distinguished itself more for its verve and intelligence than for the actual discoveries in its gameplay. *Déjà Vu* was a great success and launched a series that was ported for the most prominent systems at the time.[38] However, excellent though they were, ICOM Simulations' other games, like *Shadowgate* and *Uninvited*, failed to achieve the phenomenal success of new publications from Sierra On-Line and Roberta Williams.

The new series from Sierra On-Line, *Space Quest*, was a masterpiece and an instant classic of the genre, selling over 100,000 copies within weeks after its release. Taking place in a humorous science-fiction universe, the adventures of intergalactic janitor Roger Wilco as he tries to save the world combine classic imagery of sci-fi universes with extraordinary situations, in which our unlucky hero, in spite of himself, must confront his foolishness and a whole host of alien creatures. The guilty pleasure of the *Space Quest* games, which we all have to admit indulging in, came from finding the dumbest ways to get the main character killed. *Space Quest: The Sarien Encounter* became the first in a great series of six episodes, the fifth and sixth[39] of which come highly recommended by yours truly. Alongside the intergalactic saga, Sierra On-Line produced two other series that would have a big impact on the adventure game genre: on the one hand, the very literal *Police Quest: In Pursuit of the Death Angel*, presenting the adventures of Sonny Bonds, a police officer in California in the early 1980s, as he fights dangerous drug traffickers; on the other hand, the original and more famous *Leisure Suit Larry in the Land of the Lounge Lizards*, released in 1987, which followed the pathetic adventures of a 40-something man, a former IT guy, who's determined to lose his virginity to the easy young women of the city of "Lost Wages" and, secondarily, to find the love of his life. Originally, the

---

38. And even for the PS4 and Xbox One as part of the collection *8-Bit Adventure Anthology*.
39. *Space Quest V: Roger Wilco – The Next Mutation* and *Space Quest VI: Roger Wilco in the Spinal Frontier*.

Leisure Suit Larry series was a reinterpretation of an interactive fiction game called *Softporn Adventure*, which programmer Al Lowe reworked for Sierra based on recommendations from Ken Williams. The result was a marvel of dark humor, in which Larry's unsuccessful attempts to fornicate with anything that moves offered countless occasions to laugh, as well as to test the limits of the developer's imagination. It was yet another game where you could have a lot of fun trying to get the main character killed, showing that Al Lowe has a remarkable talent for abusing his anti-heroes. It's also amusing to note that before players could torture poor Larry, they first needed to complete a test at the beginning of the game to make sure that they were at least 18 years old; only then would they have permission to start the adventure. Players had to prove their age by answering a series of questions on general knowledge and politics. Yours truly was barely 10 years old when I first played the game, and you can imagine the look on my parents' faces when I asked my mother questions like: What were the results of Watergate? Is Perrier a non-alcoholic drink? Is abstinence the most effective form of birth control?

Thanks to word of mouth, *Leisure Suit Larry in the Land of the Lounge Lizards* became one of the best-selling PC games of 1988. Al Lowe even said in an interview given to *Retrogamer* that, one day, a Russian computer scientist told him that Larry was so popular in his country that many people thought that the game's software was just part of the MS-DOS operating system. From that point on, adventure games were all the rage and the aging, frustrating interface of Sierra's game engine didn't hinder the company's sales. It did, however, pose a challenge for developers. It was time for a change.

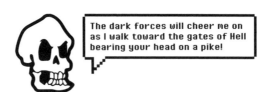

Chapter 3: The SCUMM™ game engine™ [40]

Ron Gilbert™

"When I was a kid, I was not a particularly creative child. I didn't spend my school days drawing pictures of superheroes in my notebooks. I didn't write stories, I rarely read books, and if it was possible for a 10-year-old to be lost, that really felt like me."[41] That's how Ron Gilbert describes himself. In 1978, the Atari 2600 hit the shelves of American stores and young people rushed to buy what's considered to be one of the first cartridge consoles dedicated solely to video games. "Then when I was 12, it's like two things happened that changed my life; changed it absolutely and completely. Now, my father was a physicist at the local university, and one day, he brought home a programmable calculator. This was a TI-59 programmable calculator, and I was fascinated with it. This was long before the home computer would make its appearance, and this little device completely obsessed me. Now, this calculator came with a couple of games, and they were just simple games where you guessed numbers or played a primitive version of *Battleship*. And this calculator could do more than just add numbers. It could make decisions, and it could think, and all this was magical to me. It's like I needed to understand how it did this. So, my father taught me to program it, and from that moment forward, I was completely transfixed by programming. It's like my 12-year-old life finally had meaning. Now, the other thing that happened to me was a little movie called *Star Wars*. Now, when *Star Wars* first came out, it's like it's impossible to describe what it meant to us. It's hard to describe what that movie meant and how different it was. It's like today, all movies are like *Star Wars*. But back

---

40. With regard to the name "SCUMM," there is a heated debate among specialists. Technically, the engine is, in fact, named "SPUTM." SCUMM is actually the interpretation language. It's a very nitpicky point of contention, but in any case, it's now commonly accepted to use the terms "SCUMM engine" or "SCUMM systems." Nevertheless, now you can dazzle your friends by showing off your superior knowledge.

41. *https://www.youtube.com/watch?v=Q6IYgWh-qnY*

then, there had been nothing like it, ever. [...] *Star Wars* was a movie where you went into the theater one person and you came out as another. Now, being 12 years old and seeing *Star Wars* at that time, at that age, is one of those odd things that I'm very thankful for. It changed me, and it changed every one of my friends."[42] Alas! Ron Gilbert, Sr., preferred that his son practice on a more "serious" machine. Thus, Ron, Jr., got his programming start on a North Star Horizon.[43] "With my imagination going crazy from *Star Wars* and being obsessed with programming, there was only really one thing I could do and that was make *Star Wars* games. Now, we finally got a home computer. It was called the North Star and it ran on an operating system called CPM. And it had no graphics, it was just a text terminal, but that didn't stop me from making little RPGs or text-based *Star Wars* and *Star Trek* games. [...] Then, one Christmas, I got a graphics card for the home computer. Now, you hooked it up to a TV and it did a whopping 128 by 128 pixels in 16 colors. That's right: the entire screen was 128 pixels across. People today text emoticons bigger than that to their friends. Now, this graphics card gave me the ability to head down to the local arcades, armed not with a handful of quarters, but with a pencil and a pad of graph paper, and I would copy every graphic on the screens. I'd take notes on alien attack waves and timing, and then I would head home and I would try to reproduce these games on my computer. After a while, I would start to experiment, changing things here and there, add some new alien ships that behaved differently, adding some story, maybe some new ships... And without knowing it, I'd become a game designer."[44]

In high school, Ron had an encounter that would change his life; it was something he'd never felt before, love at first sight: the Commodore 64 (a.k.a. C64). For that time, the machine's power and flexibility felt limitless. Neglecting his storytelling ambitions somewhat to totally invest his efforts in development, Ron expanded on the C64's BASIC programming language with his own routines and libraries,[45] and he created many programs to make the most of the computer's sound and graphics capabilities. "When I got into university several years later, I majored in computer science. It was either that or philosophy. Now, I told my advisor that I wanted to make computer games, and he thought I was completely nuts. You have to remember, this is like 1982, and the Commodore VIC-20 and the Apple II had just started to make

---

42. *https://www.youtube.com/watch?v=Q6IYgWh-qnY*
43. A short-lived 8-bit computer with an outrageous price, released in 1977 and offering a simple version of the BASIC programming language.
44. *https://www.youtube.com/watch?v=Q6IYgWh-qnY*
45. BASIC, like any programming language, comes with a number of "libraries" that can execute functions like "display a character on the screen" or "interpret movements of the mouse." So, Ron Gilbert created and integrated his own libraries that would help him facilitate and optimize the repetitive tasks that he considered to be essential for creating video games.

their appearance, and people still treated them with an odd sense of mystery and confusion and witchcraft. So, when I was in high school, I typed up this English paper on my home computer. The only printer we had was a dot-matrix printer. I printed out my book report, and I was thoroughly impressed with myself for using a word processor. I turned my paper in, and I got an F.[46] I'd completely failed. It was a big red F scrawled across the page. There were no reasons or notes. It was just this F. So, after class, I went up to my teacher, and I asked her why I'd gotten an F. She told me in that stern way that only teachers can: 'I wanted *you* to write your paper, not your computer.' I just stood there. She actually thought the computer had written my book report. I guess she imagined me down in the basement, speaking to my computer: 'Computer, I need an English paper. Three pages long, double-spaced, one-inch margins; three spelling mistakes, just to make it look real.' I tried to explain to her that the computer was just a typewriter: you typed stuff and it showed up on the screen, and then you hit control-P, and you printed it out, but I had done all of the work. She stared at me for what seemed like several minutes. Then, she gave an angry sigh and she took my paper, she crossed off the F, and she wrote a C. Now, if that paper had been turned in riddled with satanic symbols and splatters of chicken blood, and my book report had been written by Satan himself, I might have gotten a B. [...] So, I got to university and my advisor thought I was crazy for wanting to make computer games, and he spent two years desperately trying to talk me out of this plan. Had I considered a degree in witchcraft? Or maybe demonic studies? That would have been OK, but making games? That's crazy talk."[47]

In spite of the medium's scandalous and juvenile reputation, Ron Gilbert persisted. When offered a job making Commodore 64 games at a California-based company called Human Engineered Software, Ron was two years into his university degree, "and taking that job would have meant quitting college. My father, the PhD in astrophysics, was now the president of the university. Now I had to tell my father, the president of the university, that I was quitting his fine institution of higher learning and knowledge, a tradition that goes back 2,500 years to Plato and the ancient Greeks; I had to tell him that I was quitting all of this to go make computer games. He sat silently as I told him what I wanted to do. And then he asked me one simple question: he said, 'How much are they paying you?'"[48]

However, that experience didn't last long. Human Engineered Software closed its doors just six months after Ron Gilbert's arrival. He had to return home to Oregon with his tail between his legs. "I had just been laid off from

---

46. Which is not very good...
47. *https://www.youtube.com/watch?v=Q6IYgWh-qnY*
48. *https://www.youtube.com/watch?v=Q6IYgWh-qnY*

a company called Human Engineered Software (my first job) and had moved back to Oregon and was about ready to start college again when the phone rang. It was someone (I don't remember who) from Lucasfilm Games and they were looking for a Commodore 64 programmer and wanted to know if I was interested in coming in for an interview. 'Holy crap!' I said/thought/shouted to myself. I didn't even know Lucasfilm made games. Lucasfilm was *Star Wars* and the foundation of my childhood. I idolized George Lucas and ILM. I said I could come in for an interview that week and immediately packed my car and moved back to California. I just moved back. There was no way I wasn't going to get that job. I vividly remember interviewing in an office with Noah [Falstein] and Aric Wilmunder, explaining the way you wrote pixels to the C64 screen using their screwed up memory mapping. They seemed impressed. Or confused. Either way, as long as I got the job. My first week at Lucasfilm Games was mind-blowing. I had never met a smarter group of people in my life. From Noah to Aric to Gary Winnick to David Fox to Chip Morningstar to Doug Crockford. I had so much to learn."[49] And young Ron discovered with amazement a world that was conducive to creation, in the ideal setting of Skywalker Ranch: "The first time I met George Lucas was kind of a disappointment. It was the 10-year anniversary of *Star Wars*, and he and Steven Spielberg had shaved their beards to sneak into a showing. I wanted to meet the iconic George Lucas with a beard." Very humbly, Ron continues: "When that person from Lucasfilm first called, I almost didn't answer the phone. I was on my way out to meet a friend for lunch and had just locked the front door and was halfway to my car. I don't know what caused me to go back inside and answer the phone. If I hadn't, I would have had a very, very, very different life." Truth be told, Steve Arnold liked Ron Gilbert first and foremost because he seemed talented and was a total bargain. Noah Falstein liked him because Ron was incredibly funny and proved to be a remarkable programmer.

After a trial run over the summer, Ron Gilbert abandoned his studies for good and made California his home. He proved his talent with such confidence that, before long, his bosses believed him to be capable of leading a new project for the studio, which was constantly looking for new ideas. "We were actually unable to do games based on *Star Wars* and *Indiana Jones* for the first several years of our existence because of pre-existing licensing agreements with other companies. And that was really a godsend because it forced us to be independent, creative and to find our own way, which I think helped quite a bit to establish the company."[50]

49. *https://grumpygamer.com/goodbye_lucasfilm_games*
50. *https://www.mcvuk.com/development-news/not-making-star-wars-games-was-a-godsend-the-early-days-of-lucasarts-part-one/*

A massacre of Ewoks™

In the office of Steve Arnold, the head of the Games Group, there was a very special file cabinet. It contained all of the team's project proposals. Each one more outrageous than the next, and most of them consisting of a single page outlining the game's overall design. Arnold kept them safely filed away because at Lucasfilm, nothing went to waste! That cabinet was home to countless "games" that would never be made. It included quirky titles like *Adventure in the Party Zone, Agent of the Empire, Camper, Murder Cycle, The Star Cage, AlterNet Realities, Cruiser, Booger Hunt,* and even *Ewok Hunt!*[51] There are actually a few stories behind that last one. Chip Morningstar explains, "I always remember, there used to be a thing on the whiteboard behind someone's desk, whenever we'd have journalists in to visit. It said: 'Ewok Hunt Design Meeting 3 PM.'" It was a running gag they had that lasted for a few months. Peter Langston adds, "We pretty much did have an Ewok Hunt during the time when they were filming the Christmas special. They were filling the parking lot with Ewoks. You couldn't park anywhere."[52] However, the wildest anecdote is that, in spite of some light ribbing from his colleagues, Ron Gilbert, being a die-hard *Star Wars* fan, couldn't resist the opportunity to discreetly ask a production team for a small role in the made-for-TV movie *Ewoks: The Battle for Endor.*[53] Thus, Gilbert appeared on screen for a few fleeting seconds dressed as... an Ewok hunter. "It was this really hot summer, and we were up in these dry hills in Marin [County, California], dressed in these rubber costumes. It was just sweltering hot. The glamour of the movie industry!" Thus, Ron Gilbert is officially part of the expanded universe of *Star Wars*. The Hollywood dream. It was a point of pride for him, but it would take him years to embrace the moniker of "furball hunter."

Revolution of a genre™

"There was never a mandate from the company to do adventure games, or go, 'Hey, the adventure game market is big, we should be in that market.' We did adventure games because I was interested in it, David [Fox] was interested in it, so we just pushed forward. A lot of things in those early days at Lucasfilm,

51. The "furball" creatures who help the heroes of *Star Wars: Episode VI – The Return of the Jedi* during a crucial battle. The Ewoks were hated by certain fans (usually older ones) of the series who saw them as a childish distraction.
52. *https://www.usgamer.net/articles/i-actually-was-hunting-ewoks-lucasfilm-games-the-early-years*
53. *Ewoks: The Battle for Endor* is a made-for-TV movie directed by Ken and Jim Wheat, released in 1985. Part of the extended *Star Wars* universe, its story takes place between episodes V and VI. Between you and me, the movie is virtually unwatchable...

there was no company mandate. It was whatever we were personally interested in."[54] So, after joining the team at Skywalker Ranch, Ron Gilbert was finally able to pursue his two passions: development and storytelling.

As we saw in the previous chapter, in 1987, the majority of adventure games, even those considered to be "point & click," mainly based their gameplay on a mostly text-based interface in which the player had to enter—sometimes after guessing—the word or combination of words needed to interact with the environment. With this interface, the player had to imagine what the developer must have been thinking in this or that location in order to solve the riddles. This did not make things easy, and it significantly limited the genre's popularity. That's not to mention the fact that text-based interfaces mostly prevent the exportation of the games outside of English-speaking countries, given that translation is virtually impossible. As an admirer of Japanese action games of the era, which had particularly well-developed interfaces (chief among them *Super Mario Bros.*), Ron Gilbert decided to focus on the interface and gameplay of adventure games. He wanted players to be able to access an array of tools in the form of concise action verbs, leaving no doubt as to the options for interaction available to the player. The player would know that they could use actions like "open," "pull," "pick up," or "use." That way, they could just focus on using these actions within the universe appearing before them. Anything that prevents the player from concentrating on the plot is necessarily a potential source of interference for the player. By displaying these verbs conspicuously at the bottom of the screen, the player would merely have to scan the screen with their cursor in order to discover the "hotspots," i.e., the clickable areas, and then choose among the possible interactions between their inventory and the hotspot. This drastically simplified interface enabled better immersion in the creators' universe and story, and proved to be a nice solution to avoid the terse "I don't understand" that most adventure game text parsers[55] at the time would churn out when an error occurred. This idea single-handedly revolutionized the adventure game.

I Was A Teenage Lobot™

To put this idea into practice, Chip Morningstar, a developer specializing in script languages, offered to help Ron Gilbert. To convince the other members and management of the studio that this new concept was a winner, they needed

---

54. *https://www.usgamer.net/articles/i-actually-was-hunting-ewoks-lucasfilm-games-the-early-years*
55. A game's text parser is a bit of programming dedicated to trying to understand the commands entered by the player via the keyboard. If the player types the word "rock," the parser compares that to its own lexicon to figure out if the input is referring to the musical genre or to a stone.

a game, or at least a rough draft of a game. Ron came up with a scenario based on the movie *Heavy Metal*,[56], which he named *I Was A Teenage Lobot™*. As he tells it: "This was the first design document I worked on while at Lucasfilm Games. It was just after *Koronis Rift* [for the Commodore 64] finished and I was really hoping I wouldn't get laid off. When I first joined Lucasfilm, I was a contractor, not an employee. I don't remember why that was, but I wanted to get hired on full time. I guess I figured I'd show how indispensable I was by helping to churn out game design gold like this. [The *I Was A Teenage Lobot™* proposal] is probably one of the first appearances of 'Chuck,' who would go on to 'Chuck the Plant' fame. You'll also notice the abundance of TMs[57] all over the doc. That joke never gets old, right?"[58] Very modestly and simply entitled *I WAS A TEENAGE LOBOT: A Science-Fiction Role Playing Strategy Adventure Game*, the original design document is dated November 26, 1985. The story, in Gilbert's pure comic and sarcastic style, presents the adventures of a robot made by the company Anybots™, into which they placed the brain of a murderer on death row. In the game's futuristic society, scientists discover that it's easier to just take human brains and put them inside robots than it is to program the robots to think. From there, the "lobotomized" brain and the robot containing it must find the brain's original body to restore the character to his original form. The gameplay is described as a blend of action game with a top-down view and riddles, based on objects and their interactions with the backgrounds. The player moves the robot with the joystick and the actions are carried out using the first letter of each keyword. David Fox and Noah Falstein were impressed with Gilbert's creativity, and they found that he was really onto something with the interface, even if it needed some improvements. What's more, the script-based engine developed by Chip Morningstar gave him invaluable independence in his game development efforts. Having come up with the basics of the graphic interface he dreamed of creating, Ron Gilbert began conceptualizing the engine, and thus the technical tools, for his future games.

56. Film by Gerald Potterton (1981) based on the legendary magazine of the same name.
57. The trademark symbol is a running gag in Ron Gilbert's games, from *Maniac Mansion™* to *Thimbleweed Park™* to *Monkey Island™*. Originally, it was Gilbert's way of joking about how George Lucas liked to trademark everything. Incidentally, any similar usage of the symbol in this book is pure coincidence…
58. *https://grumpygamer.com/teenage_lobot*

Maniac Mansion™

Just a few weeks later, Ron Gilbert and Gary Winnick[59] (one of the studio's longtime artists who had worked there since *Rescue on Fractalus)* shared the desire to finally develop their first *true* game that would be all their own within the studio. It would be an adventure game inspired by B movies of the horror genre.

Winnick showed Ron a drawing of an old manor, in front of which was a sign reading "Trespassers will be horribly mutilated." Ron thought that it would be funny to turn the classic codes of slasher[60] films on their heads by placing in the mansion a bunch of boneheaded kids who are forced to split up in order to escape. Winnick began working on a prototype for the game on paper. It was good. The mysteries unfolded fluidly, and the dialogue was well-crafted and full of dark humor. Steve Arnold, the head of the Games Group, gave it the green light and development of *Maniac Mansion* commenced.

The collection of tools that was developed in the weeks that followed had but one goal: to allow the creatives to completely free themselves from the technical side of development and assemble the game like a jigsaw puzzle. It took Chip and Ron several weeks of hard work to complete their foundational programming. Thus, SCUMM, standing for "Script Creation Utility for Maniac Mansion," came into being. It was followed by a heap of tools given bizarre names based on bodily fluids, like MMUCUS to handle the compression of images, FLEM to place "hotspots" on an image, SPU (for "SCUMM Presentation Utility") to make everything run, BYLE to convert SUN workstation files to a PC format, and SPIT to handle the fonts. All of these modules reflected the team's sophisticated taste for all sorts of foul secretions.

With their legendary flair for storytelling, the sales decision-makers at distributor Electronic Arts were dubious about the project. An adventure game with a never-before-seen interface, presenting a group of dumb kids in a comedy-horror mansion? While Roberta Williams was selling *King's Quest* by the pallet with handsome princes and ponies? Are you kidding?! With all due respect to EA, Steve Arnold believed in Ron Gilbert's idea and thought it could work. So, he made the unilateral decision to fund the game's development and publishing in house, under the auspices of Lucasfilm Games. Meanwhile, Gilbert continued perfecting his interface and proposed that everything would be managed using the mouse and by placing the action options at the bottom

59. Gary Winnick worked as an artist on most of the studio's biggest games, from *Ballblazer* to *Days of the Tentacle*. He reunited with Gilbert 30 years later to launch a crowdfunding campaign on Kickstarter to fund the creation of *Thimbleweed Park*.
60. A sub-genre of horror film popularized by John Carpenter's *Halloween* and which was a major trend in the 1980s.

of the screen. This was the genesis of "point & click" *à la Lucasfilm*. No more need for the keyboard. Between certain screens, narrative scenes without player interaction would provide updates on what was happening with other characters in the story. For the purposes of the SCUMM engine, the name given to these scenes was "cutscenes." Without even realizing it, Ron Gilbert invented a term that would become a global standard. Moreover, here is how he formalized the term years later in the design document for *Monkey Island*: "Throughout the game, the story will be told to the player through selected 'cut-scenes', which are non-interactive animated scenes. Cut-scenes, like scene cuts in movies, cut to somewhere else to show action relevant to the story. As the player's actions change the storyline he will see different 'cut-scenes' to reflect these changes, and to give him information about important events and actions relevant to the story he is creating."

To ensure proper development of the *Maniac Mansion* project, David Fox came to the rescue by writing the dialogue. Originally, this was only supposed to take a few weeks, but it turned into several months. Fox proposed some of the game's wildest and most iconic ideas, like putting a hamster in a microwave to defrost it and bring it back to life... Ron Gilbert confides that they spent and wasted a lot of time developing, screwing up, and starting again. They were all over the place, without really having precise specifications. He remembers thinking to himself at one point that they really needed an adult to help them out. And at Lucasfilm, the only "real" adult was David Fox, who met the qualifications of having a real family life and wearing clean T-shirts. He provided the "kids" with his support so that they could finally complete their project."[61]

Multiple playable characters means multiple plot lines and complicated puzzles. Lucasfilm only had one in-house tester, and in spite of the fact that members of Gilbert's family helped debug *Maniac Mansion*, there remained a handful of flaws in the final version, preventing the player from finishing the adventure in some cases.

First presented at the CES trade show in Chicago in 1987, after several months of hard work, *Maniac Mansion* was finally released in October 1987 for the Commodore 64 and Apple II, and was later ported for the PC in 1988, then for the Amiga, Atari ST, and Nintendo NES console in 1990. While the game was a critical success, its sales were underwhelming, to say the least, compared to the competition. However, over the years, it gained a cult following and would later be labeled a "long-time seller."[62]

---

61. Interview given to the author for the purposes of this book.
62. An expression used to describe games that keep selling in the long term.

Zak McKracken and the Alien Mindbenders™

Having completed his work on *Maniac Mansion*, David Fox decided to reuse the SCUMM engine to launch Lucasfilm Games' next project. Development of *Zak McKracken and the Alien Mindbenders* began in parallel to the final months of work on Ron Gilbert's game, for a release in October 1988. The title presents the paranormal adventures of Zak, a tabloid journalist, who discovers that the stories and clichés he's always served up in his publication's outrageous articles all turn out to be true: Elvis really is alive, extraterrestrials really do walk among us, and those aliens are using San Francisco's telephone system to broadcast waves to throttle humans' intelligence. With help from Annie, Melissa, and Leslie, Zak must travel around the world to prevent the alien invasion and ultimate subjugation of humanity. David Fox got the basic idea for his scenario after an intense conversation with American "New Age" mystical author David Spangler.[63] The New Age movement offered fertile ground for comedy through fantastic and improbable situations. David had no trouble at all harvesting ideas. In the first draft of the scenario, the story's hero was named Jason and he worked for a very serious national newspaper. However, Ron Gilbert pushed Fox to lighten up the atmosphere of his game, suggesting that David come up with more non-conformist characters and that he have Zak work for a sensationalist magazine. The programming side of the operation demanded superhuman efforts from the developers in order to complete the game on time and within budget. While Fox and Matthew Alan Kane worked on designing sound and graphics to fit the adventure, Ron Gilbert improved the SCUMM engine to make it more flexible. With that done, using SCUMM, the team was able to create a framework for the game using nothing more than a page from a word processor filled with common words and key tags. The compiler then analyzed the syntax of the information and translated it into a series of scripts. Basically, it was a game designer's dream. When the game hit store shelves at the end of the year, *Zak McKracken and the Alien Mindbenders* was once again an unequivocal critical success. The media praised the game's humor and ingenuity, as well as the richness of its scenario. They also recognized that Lucasfilm Games' interface left the competition in the dust, particularly Sierra, which was resting on its laurels (or rather, dollars) and barely bothering to update its franchises. But yet again, originality did not automatically equal success, and Lucasfilm Games still didn't have a hit.

While the company kept producing new adventure-game gold, the influence of *Maniac Mansion* continued to grow, and in 1989, The Family Channel launched a series of the same name on American and Canadian television.

---

63. David Spangler created a community in Scotland called Findhorn, where he preached the foundational ideas of the New Age spiritual movement, an improbable melting pot of different religions, anti-consumerism, literal marginalization, and nebulous conspiracy theories.

Although quite different from the game, *Maniac Mansion: The TV Show* was a fairly respectable and funny sitcom with sci-fi overtones. However, it was never a big hit and has been all but forgotten.

Indiana Jones and the Last Crusade™

On their side, George Lucas and Steven Spielberg were preparing to put the final touches on the third episode in the *Indiana Jones* saga before it hit the big screen. The order for a video game to accompany the film release came in very late, while the studio was working around the clock to finish *Zak McKracken and the Alien Mindbenders*. The game *Indiana Jones and the Last Crusade: The Graphic Adventure* was developed in just eight months under the supervision of Noah Falstein. David Fox had no time to catch his breath before coming to the rescue, and Gilbert, who was preparing a new, totally *secret* game (if you know what I mean...), put everything on hold to lend the *Indiana Jones* team a hand. The studio's entire team was mobilized for what might turn out to be the first truly popular game from Lucasfilm Games. In November 1988, the project was still at an early stage and the game absolutely had to be ready by July 1989, by order from the High Commander... It was a new challenge for Falstein and his team because Indiana Jones is a man of action: he resolves most of his conflicts with his fists; therefore, the official adaptation's game design couldn't revolve around solving puzzles. While Steven Spielberg viewed the adaptation as just a merchandizing opportunity—though not in a condescending way—he happily agreed to allow Indy to be killed in the course of the game. However, this went against Ron Gilbert's personal conception of adventure games. Ron preferred to offer the player comfort and flexibility so as to allow them to concentrate on the story and puzzles. Also, the game as a whole had to offer something of interest for someone who'd already seen the film. That meant changing how the puzzles would be solved compared to the puzzles in the movie, while also offering several potential endings (ultimately, three).

One of the main advantages of working directly at Skywalker Ranch was the ability for Noah Falstein to have access to the film's scenario and all its visual production elements. Thanks to that fact, the game includes scenes that ended up being cut from the version of the movie released in theaters. Ron Gilbert recalls: "We went to a couple of advanced screenings early on in the process, mostly for artistic reasons to make sure the look was okay. But we had quite a bit of autonomy, which was always the case in the Games Division"[64] In terms

---

64. *Rogue Leaders, The Story of LucasArts* (Rob Smith).

of innovations, *Indiana Jones and the Last Crusade: The Graphic Adventure* was the first game in the adventure genre to offer a range of responses in conversations with other characters. It was a simple concept producing remarkable immersion in the story, and the approach was then replicated by many other games. The game also included action scenes: Indy was able to resolve certain tricky situations by fighting, or even by inexpertly piloting a biplane. The sound was also particularly well-developed, whereas it had been unanimously criticized in the studio's previous two productions. The game was released right on time in July 1989, and it was a triumph. Critics recognized the outstanding quality of the adaptation and also noted that it did right by its cinematic big brother. With 250,000 copies sold in its first month, *Indiana Jones and the Last Crusade: The Graphic Adventure* was a success and finally earned the handful of young creators the recognition they so badly wanted. They finally did it: Lucasfilm Games had a hit!

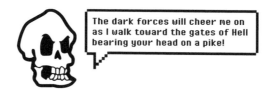

Chapter 4: Reinventing the adventure game™

"Constraints and limitations are a really powerful creative motivator. Sometimes if you remove constraints and limitations, you end up wrecking what you're trying to create. Just because you have too much money or too much technology. I felt, with those early games, especially *Maniac Mansion*, we were so constrained that we had to make really smart choices on stuff. I think that's a benefit."[65]

Ron Gilbert

Why Adventure Games Suck™

Indiana Jones and the Last Crusade: The Graphic Adventure was released and met with success. Lucasfilm Games earned itself a strong reputation and Steve Arnold was a happy man. SCUMM allowed the studio to produce games quickly and, more importantly, to focus on storytelling and creating well-crafted puzzles. All of these factors meant that Ron Gilbert could return to his ambitious personal project, which he had previously put on hold.

In the third volume of the bimonthly *Journal of Computer Game Design*, in the issue dated December 1989, Gilbert published an article succinctly titled "Why Adventure Games Suck." The opinion piece offers a retrospective analysis of 10 years of evolution of the narrative adventure game, with candor and humor. Above all, Ron honed his text by aiming his criticism squarely at himself. In terms of substance, the article summarizes the main issues encountered by players, as well as aberrations in game design to which narrative adventure games invariably succumb. As such, in response, Gilbert proposed a series of simple, common-sense rules based on a keen synthesis of the art of creating good games. These rules went on to become standards, particularly at studios like Naughty Dog (*Uncharted*, *The Last of Us*), Telltale Games (*The Walking Dead*, *The Wolf Among Us*), Quantic Dream (*Heavy Rain*,

---

65. *https://www.usgamer.net/articles/i-actually-was-hunting-ewoks-lucasfilm-games-the-early-years*

Detroit), and Dontnod (*Life is Strange*). Particularly, the rules also informed future productions of Lucasfilm Games.

As Ron Gilbert tells it: "I enjoy games in which the pace is slow and the reward is for thinking and figuring, rather than quick reflexes. The element that brings adventure games to life for me is the stories around which they are woven. [...] One of my pet peeves is the recent trend to call story games 'Interactive Movies.' They are interactive, but they are not movies. The fact that people want to call them movies just points out how lost we are. What we need to do is to establish a genre for our works that we can call our own. Movies came from stage plays, but the references are long lost and movies have come into their own. The same thing needs to happen to story games. [...] The single biggest difference is interaction. You can't interact with a movie. You just sit in the theater and watch it. In a story game, the player is given the freedom to explore the story. But the player doesn't always do what the designer intended, and this causes problems. It is hard to create a cohesive plot when you have no idea what part of the story the player will trip over next. This problem calls for a special kind of storytelling, and we have just begun to scratch the surface of this art form.[66] [...] The same [willing suspension of disbelief] is true of story games (as well as almost all other kinds of games). As the story builds, we are pulled into the game and leave the real world behind. As designers, our job is to keep people in this state for as long as possible. Every time the player has to restore a saved game, or pound his head on the desk in frustration, the suspension of disbelief is gone. At this time he is most likely to shut off the computer and go watch TV, at which point we all have lost. I have created a set of rules of thumb that will minimize the loss of suspension of disbelief. As with any set of rules, there are always exceptions. In my designs, I hope that if these rules cannot be followed, it is for artistic reasons and not because I am too lazy to do it right. In *Maniac Mansion*, in one place or another, I violated all but one of these rules. Some of them were violated by design, others by sloppiness. If I could redesign *Maniac Mansion*, all the violations would be removed and I'd have a much better game."[67]

Below is the full list of Ron Gilbert's commandments. In retrospect, the article is an extraordinary historical document for video games and it's a source of invaluable information for understanding the mindset in which the first game in the *Monkey Island* series was created, and the same for the rest of Lucasfilm's productions. Above all, though, it's one of the few milestones—that can be historically identified beyond any doubt—of reflection and theorization about game design. An important moment in video game history.

---

66. The art of telling stories.
67. *https://grumpygamer.com/why_adventure_games_suck*

THE FIRST COMMANDMENT: END OBJECTIVE NEEDS TO BE CLEAR

From the beginning of the game, the player must understand what ultimate goal must be reached to complete the story and watch the end credits. The player must clearly understand what they are supposed to do with their character if they want to see the final scene. Thus, they enter a phase of pure investigation, in which their senses and intellect are fully dedicated to moving the plot forward. While the objective may change mid-game, the player must still always be able to clearly identify it. It's also a good idea to reiterate the objective because if for some random reason in the storytelling the player loses sight of the objective, they will stumble blindly through the game, which will become nothing more than a series of puzzles stripped of all meaning. The game will completely lose its main purpose, which is to tell a story.

THE SECOND COMMANDMENT: SUB-GOALS NEED TO BE OBVIOUS

Of course, to fulfill their destiny, the character must resolve a slew of different sub-plots. In doing that, it's important for the player to have a clear list of stages to complete. The plan for achieving their goals must be clear. No need to make it complicated: the puzzles will add enough complexity on their own. As with the First Commandment, this is a prerequisite for understanding the plot over the long term.

THE THIRD COMMANDMENT: LIVE AND LEARN

According to Ron Gilbert, it's essential for the player to be able to play right through the game without having to kill their character. For Gilbert, the fact of the main character dying is incompatible with telling a credible story. It causes a break in the narrative and risks shattering the willing suspension of disbelief. Problem-solving through failure emerges as a flaw in the design of adventure games. Danger is, of course, inherent in the story, but the player must be able to avoid it through wisdom and ingenuity. That's the whole point of the adventure genre compared to action games.

THE FOURTH COMMANDMENT: BACKWARDS PUZZLES

There is a very specific order in which a puzzle produces immediate pleasure for the player. First, the player must understand what the objective is, then identify the pieces one by one, and finally be able to guess how to combine the pieces to solve the puzzle. In an ideal progression, to borrow the example given by Ron Gilbert in his article, the player should encounter a crevice before the rope that will allow them to climb down into it. So, the player should see the crevice first; then, as soon as they find the rope, a light will go on in their head and the pieces of the puzzle will suddenly come together. When this progressive design is perfectly orchestrated, there's no greater satisfaction.

THE FIFTH COMMANDMENT: I FORGOT TO PICK IT UP

It can be needlessly frustrating for a player to pass right by an object, then realize much later in the game that it would have been a good idea to take it. If that might happen, the game designers should at least arrange for the player to be able to find the object quickly and easily. Hiding an object at the wrong time is a problem in game design; it's an unnecessary difficulty.

THE SIXTH COMMANDMENT: PUZZLES SHOULD ADVANCE THE STORY

Ron Gilbert recommends that in a story-driven game, designers should shun gratuitous puzzles that have no impact on the story. He suggests stripping down the gameplay to a strict minimum, keeping only interactions that are necessary for moving the story forward (this connects to his original desire when creating the point & click game system and interface that would become a standard after *Maniac Mansion*). You have to free the player from all technical and gameplay interference. Ideally, puzzles should contribute to the story. They should add concrete ideas, like helping humanize an antagonist or giving clues about the context of an event.

THE SEVENTH COMMANDMENT: REAL TIME IS BAD DRAMA

It is crucial for the game designer to master timing, especially in a story-driven game, which uses scene-setting and images to tell the story. To borrow Gilbert's example: "When Indiana Jones rolled under the closing stone door and grabbed his hat just in time, it sent a chill and a cheer through everyone in the audience. If that scene had been done in a standard adventure game, the player would have been killed the first four times he tried to make it under the door. The next six times the player would have been too late to grab the hat. Is this good drama? Not likely. The key is to use Hollywood time, not real time. Give the player some slack when doing time-based puzzles. Try to watch for intent. If the player is working towards the solution and almost ready to complete it, wait. Wait until the hat is grabbed, then slam the door down. The player thinks they 'just made it' and consequently a much greater number of players get the rush and excitement."

THE EIGHTH COMMANDMENT: INCREMENTAL REWARD

The guilty pleasure of the story-driven adventure game lies in discovering new environments and characters, with these aspects perhaps even taking priority over the act of actually moving the story forward. A conscientious game designer will always know how to deliver these rewards frugally yet constantly in order to maintain the player's interest and appease their basic instincts.

THE NINTH COMMANDMENT: ARBITRARY PUZZLES

Just as the First Commandment requires that the designer use deliberate clarity in the game's objectives, the designer must also provide puzzles that can be solved without the need for long text explanations or tutorials. For example, if the player needs six objects to open a door, it absolutely must be obvious to them that they need six, and not five or seven. Otherwise, a player left to their own devices will give up on the adventure before long.

THE TENTH COMMANDMENT: GIVE THE PLAYER OPTIONS

Many games "cage" the player, requiring them to solve puzzles one after another, in the worst kind of linearity imaginable. A more pleasant design, one that's better at maintaining the will and attention of the fickle player, is to allow them to start one puzzle, then switch to another if they get stuck and come back to the first later. That way, the player will feel like they're constantly progressing, and the game will have better pacing.

With these "commandments," Ron Gilbert highlighted the main elements that should make up a story-driven adventure game and enumerated the pitfalls that the informed game designer must avoid. It's interesting to note that this manifesto written over 30 years ago is still instructive for a wide variety of works that we can consider modern adventure games. For example, studios like Quantic Dream[68] and Telltale Games[69] cite Ron Gilbert's polemical article and Ten Commandments as a quintessential model for their game design.

The game engine was ready, the rules were set; all that was left was to come up with an original idea to follow the release of *Indiana Jones and the Last Crusade* and perhaps help comfortably solidify Lucasfilm Games' reputation.

---

68. Quantic Dream and its creative director David Cage produced the games *The Nomad Soul*, *Fahrenheit*, *Heavy Rain*, and *Detroit: Become Human*.
69. The developer, among others, of the *Walking Dead* games.

As Gilbert began thinking about his next project, a new hire, Brian Moriarty (who had previously created text-based games like *Trinity*, *ANALOG: Adventure in the 5th Dimension*, and *Crash Dive!*), was also using the SCUMM engine on the *Loom* project, released in 1990. While Moriarty's game distinguished itself from Lucasfilm's typical production with its more serious tone, it also started a tradition for the studio of featuring heroes with ridiculous names (e.g., Bobbin Threadbare). Moriarty carefully followed Gilbert's precepts in creating his game: he completely reworked the early versions of his scenario to keep only the essence of the story and the main plot line, prioritizing storytelling efficiency over various situations existing purely for fun. He made it a point of honor to build puzzles that fit into the logic of the story, and he pushed this systemic simplicity to the point that the game's text-based interface disappeared completely: no more action words or inventory. All it took was a double-click to interact with an object or character.

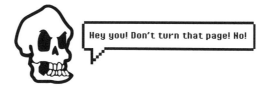

Hey you! Don't turn that page! No!

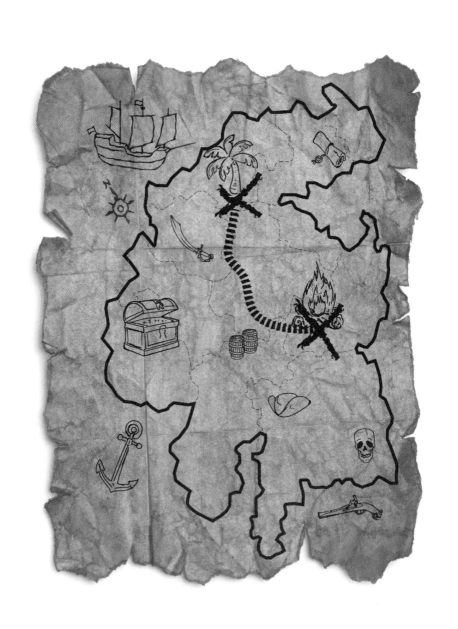

THE MYSTERIES OF
MONKEY ISLAND

Part 2

Chapter 5: *The Secret of Monkey Island*™

"Relentless jabs, and cryptic in-jokes only smart people will understand."[70]

Tim Schafer™ & Dave Grossman™

August 1989. A young, 22-year-old Californian by the name of Timothy Schafer, a recent computer science graduate of the University of California, Berkeley, was desperate to find his first job. "My job hunt was getting kind of depressing. I was building up a pile of rejection letters, most of them from jobs I didn't even want. I got rejected by a company that made library cataloging software. Stuck-up jerks! I bought a tie for that interview! I ironed my PANTS. But then, one bright summer day, I walked into the campus career center and saw this: 'LUCASFILM, LTD. This is to announce an opening for a fulltime Assistant Designer/Programmer in the Games Division [...]. Responsibilities include: 1. Implement designs for graphic adventure games using an in-house game development system. 2. Contribute to game designs. 3. Assist in debugging and testing the game."[71] After a surreal phone interview[72] with David Fox, Schafer figured that he needed to do something big and original to impress the company. He meticulously prepared a cover letter in the form of an illustrated design document. Revealed 20 years later and infused with a twisted sense of humor, the document asks the reader to choose between three different jobs: improving the destructive potential of arms manufacturer Yoyodine Defense Technologies, becoming an office drone at HAL Computers,[73] or working to produce games at the fantastic Lucasfilm studio. The cover letter was as

---

70. A description appearing on the box of *The Secret of Monkey Island*.
71. *http://www.doublefine.com/news/comments/twenty_years_only_a_few_tears/*
72. See chapter 1.
73. A reference to HAL 9000 from the film *2001: A Space Odyssey* (Stanley Kubrick, 1968), which in turn was a reference to the company IBM (each letter in the name HAL comes just before the letters in the name IBM).

unconventional as it gets, and it easily convinced Fox and Gilbert of the young creator's comedic potential. On September 11, 1989, Schafer received a letter signed by Steve Arnold offering him a position on the team as a "scummlet," i.e., a trainee specializing in using the in-house game engine (the bottom of the social hierarchy for developers, according to those who have held the position). Tim Schafer would be assisting Ron Gilbert on his new project.

The second historic "scummlet" to join the team alongside Schafer was another young novice named Dave Grossman. "My mom was a computer programmer in the late seventies. She used to bring home this tremendous dial-up terminal—it was like a fifty-pound electric typewriter, with a really long roll of paper and rubber cups in the back where you stuck the handset of your phone. I thought it was the coolest thing. And you could call up the mainframe and play games. There was a text adventure on there, and I used up an awful lot of that paper. I guess from that point onward I wanted to do something with computers, but if you'd told me then that I'd be writing games, I would have been surprised. It didn't seem like the kind of thing people do for a living. It still doesn't. Fast forward ten years or so, I'm out of grad school about six months, looking around for some sort of job that doesn't involve building missile guidance systems, and as it happens, the Games Division at Lucasfilm is looking to hire a few people to program stuff and be sort of apprentice designers."[74] In another interview, Dave says: "Somehow, I managed to get in, and then, bafflingly, they hired me. I don't know why. Looking back, I wouldn't have hired me. But I don't think the pool was very large. Game designer would not become a Dream Job until years later when we'd managed to spread enough lies about what game designers actually do all day to sucker more people into it."[75]

On September 22, 1989, filled with wonder, Tim set foot on Skywalker Ranch for the first time. He arrived about 15 minutes early, officially making him the very first "scummlet," a few minutes ahead of his comrade Dave. For the first few weeks, Tim and Dave spent their days studying at "SCUMM University," learning the SCUMM engine's programming language, even before they actually knew for sure what they'd be working on. "It was probably the best job ever. No one in history has ever had a better time than being a Scummlet at Skywalker Ranch in 1989. We were very proud of the name 'Scummlet' and didn't even think of trying to lose it," Tim Schafer confides some years later. "SCUMM was a slightly leaky but astonishingly useful tool for making graphics adventure. We were the guinea pigs and had fun playing the software limits."[76] At the very end of 1989, Ron Gilbert showed up in their office and presented to them the

74. *https://scummbar.com/resources/articles/index.php?newssniffer=readarticle&article=1005*
75. *http://www.arcadeattack.co.uk/dave-grossman/*
76. *Rogue Leaders, The Story of LucasArts* (Rob Smith).

foundations of the game he'd been working on for two years; the script was entitled *Mutiny on Monkey Island.*

"I hated fantasy" (Ron Gilbert)™

"I started thinking about my next game [after *Maniac Mansion*]. I knew it was going to be an adventure game. [...] When I'm trying to come up with a new idea for a game, I'll write a lot of one-page design documents, and I'll write them as fast as I can just in one sitting. [...] I had an adventure game concept called *Space Party Aliens.* This was about these two aliens named Pesto and Basil that flew around the galaxy looking for parties, and their ship was powered by the tears of these cute aliens they kept locked up down below. I didn't say these were good ideas... The point is just to design stuff. Write down your ideas, no matter how crazy and stupid they are. Now, the other idea I had was a game called *Commit the Perfect Murder.* It was an adventure game that took place in an enclosed environment, like a cruise ship or some secluded mountain resort, and it followed in the tradition of the Agatha Christie novels or *Murder, She Wrote.* A group of people thrown together, unable to communicate with the outside world, and a murder is committed. Now, the twist on the idea was that you were not the smart detective that was trying to solve the murder; you *were* the murderer. The game was divided into two acts. In act one, you planned and you plotted the murder. [...] You would then commit the murder. [...] Just by chance, there happens to be a famous detective among your group and he or she is now going to solve the crime that you just committed. [...] Everybody loved the *Commit the Perfect Murder* idea and I presented it to my boss. His reaction was: 'Great idea! I love it! But Lucasfilm cannot make a game about committing a murder.'"[77]

A few weeks later, Gilbert had another project in mind and a few, very specific ideas about the universe he wanted to develop. Here was the issue: "I really hated fantasy. [...] But it's what sold, and I needed to find something that embodied what people loved about fantasy, but it wasn't fantasy. And the first thing that jumped into my mind... were pirates!" And the fantasy genre was everywhere in 1987. Countless titles were released, with varying levels of inspiration taken from *Dungeons & Dragons* or *The Lord of the Rings.* "I'd wanted to do a pirate game for a long time. You see, one of my favorite rides in Disneyland is Pirates of the Caribbean. You get on a little boat and it takes you through a pirate adventure, climaxing in a cannon fight between two big pirate ships. Your boat keeps you moving through the adventure, but I've always wished I could get off and wander around, learn

---

77. *https://www.youtube.com/watch?v=Q6IYgWh-qnY*

more about the characters, and find a way onto those pirate ships. So, with *The Secret of Monkey Island™*, I wanted to create a game that had the same flavor, but where you could step off the boat and enter that whole storybook world. The pirates on Monkey Island aren't like real pirates, who were slimy and vicious, the terrorists of the 17th century. These are swashbuckling, fun-loving pirates, like the ones in the adventure stories everyone grows up with."[78] (We'll see later in this book that the relationships between the Disney *Pirates of the Caribbean* universe and the *Monkey Island* saga went through a funny series of mutual influences over a 15-year period.) However, the most likely and important inspiration for the game's universe came from a less-obvious literary source. "I read a lot of novels and reference books, more for the flavor of the period than for accuracy. This isn't a historically accurate game. In fact, you'll see when you play that there are a lot of anachronisms, like the vending machine at Stan's Used Shipyard. They're there to add humor to the game, of course, but they also have a secret, deeper relevance to the story—but I'm keeping that secret for the sequel." Some years later, Ron Gilbert wrote on his blog that the main literary influence for *The Secret of Monkey Island* was a lesser-known adventure novel. "Some people believe the inspiration for *Monkey Island* came from the Pirates of the Caribbean ride—probably because I said it several times during interviews—but that was really just for the ambiance. If you read this book [Tim Powers' *On Stranger Tides*] you can really see where Guybrush and LeChuck were ~~plagiarized~~ derived from, plus the heavy influence of voodoo in the game."[79]

On Stranger Tides™

In summer 1987, Ron Gilbert immersed himself in the novel *On Stranger Tides*. The book by Tim Powers didn't sell all that well; however, the author had previously earned a strong reputation in 1983 when he received the Philip K. Dick Award[80] for the best science-fiction novel, for his novel *The Anubis Gates*. Considered to be one of the founding fathers of the "steampunk" fantasy subgenre, Powers distinguished himself as a writer by blending historical facts with extraordinary supernatural phenomena. He mixes genres; he allows readers to lose themselves in phantasmagorical universes with wacky characters; he twists readers' preconceived notions

---

78. The official magazine *Lucasfilm Adventurer, Vol. 1* (fall 1990).
79. *https://grumpygamer.com/on_stranger_tides*
80. A literary award that has gone to a number of writers whose names the reader will undoubtedly recognize, like William Gibson for the book *Neuromancer* (the origin of cyberpunk!) or Jane Jensen (game designer of *King's Quest VI* and the *Gabriel Knight* series… from Sierra). Like I've said, it's all connected!

and infuses each of his stories with a spirited tempo. The attractive qualities of *On Stranger Tides* are manifest. The novel is wild, with numerous misunderstandings, tone changes, and turnabouts. The universe could easily be described as a cross between the works of Robert Louis Stevenson and the movie *Heavy Metal*, with an added dose of humor. Powers makes heavy use of situation reversals, making his story feel like a mad dash, but one has to admit that it all works together marvelously. *On Stranger Tides* is an excellent adventure novel. Read it.

Here's a brief summary: in 1718, the young John Chandagnac—a cross between Errol Flynn and Tintin—is sailing toward Jamaica, hoping to find his fortune in the New World by claiming an inheritance that was stolen by his uncle. However, his ship, the *Vociferous Carmichael*, is savagely attacked by a band of bloodthirsty pirates commanded by Captain Philip Davies. Following a fierce battle that appears to feature supernatural phenomena, our young hero is taken prisoner, but not before he injures his antagonist in one-on-one combat. The other passengers, including Elizabeth Hurwood, her strange father Benjamin Hurwood, and the father's mystical sidekick Leo Friend, appear to receive special treatment from the pirates. Chandagnac has two choices: die here or become a pirate.

John chooses the latter. He and his new shipmates set sail for New Providence Island, where he will discover the violent and dispiriting world of the "Brethren of the Coast." However, along the way, the pirates cross paths with a Royal Navy ship. After a series of improbable events, at the last second, Chandagnac saves Captain Davies, who, in spite of the crew he associates with, appears to be a man of honor. Renamed "John Shandy," Chandagnac discovers that magic is powerful in the Caribbean, far away from the "technology" of the "Old World." Voodoo controls the fate of people there and is key to the power of the great pirate captains. A few weeks later, Shandy meets the terrible and imposing Blackbeard. Completely ravaged by curses, the terrifying captain hires the novice pirate to go out in search of the Fountain of Youth, a legendary spring hidden somewhere in the swamps of Florida that's supposed to give eternal life.

After a perilous journey through otherworldly and toxic lands, the wretched crew discovers the Fountain; at the same time, Shandy realizes that old Benjamin Hurwood is plotting to cast a cruel spell involving his daughter Elizabeth (who also happens to be our hero's love interest). Indeed, Benjamin wants to use his daughter's body to reincarnate the soul of his late wife. After some incredible misadventures, Leo Friend, the mysterious sorcerer, kidnaps Elizabeth and escapes with her aboard the *Vociferous Carmichael*. John Chandagnac then pursues them with help from an improbable crew. This is followed by a series of battles, pursuits, and adventures in which Shandy must fight Friend's crew of zombies, with Friend having himself become a sorcerous captain. Through the mix-ups and situation reversals, we see no less than four important and dangerous characters pitted against each other: Blackbeard, Benjamin Hurwood, Leo Friend, and John Shandy. Without spoiling the plot for you, I'll say that it's only after incredible ploys, enormous risks, and pure dumb luck that Chandagnac manages to survive, save the damsel in distress, and, importantly, prevent a forced marriage between Elizabeth and the infamous Blackbeard (sound familiar?).

More than just an inspiration, the similarities are immediately evident to anyone who has played the *Monkey Island* series. It's all there. The novel's universe blends different aspects of 18th century piracy in a loving tribute to the novels of Stevenson, Defoe, and Rafael Sabatini, while never hesitating to dive into animistic fantasy, borrowing terms from African folk religions of the 17th century. The concept works beautifully, and it immediately won the heart of Ron Gilbert, who found in the novel an extraordinary alternative to medieval heroic-fantasy universes. What's more, Powers demonstrates a superb talent for bringing his characters to life, especially Blackbeard: even if he didn't manage to achieve eternal life in his universe, he has in ours. The result is a novel with formidable power, that's fast-paced, gripping, and almost cinematic. It's no surprise that some years later, Disney decided to make it the main source of inspiration for the fourth installment in the adventures of the pirate Jack Sparrow, in *Pirates of the Caribbean: On Stranger Tides*. And thus, it all comes full circle. Quite clearly, Gilbert took inspiration from John Chandagnac in creating the character Guybrush Threepwood, the legendary captain LeChuck is a cross between Blackbeard and Benjamin Hurwood, and the visual aspects of the game's universe come from a clever blend of the genre's clichés and the zombie pirates from Powers' novel.

Mutiny on Monkey Island!™

Ron spent several months refining his phantasmagorical universe, writing a multitude of characters, and coming up with a handful of puzzles. However, in late 1988, he had to hit pause on his ambitions in order to help out Noah Falstein on the development of *Indiana Jones and the Last Crusade*. "I started designing *Monkey Island* about two and a half years ago. But I was only about a fourth of the way through the design when *Indiana Jones and the Last Crusade* came up. That had to be done quickly, so we had to put *Monkey Island* on hold for a while. That's why it took so long to complete. The first thing I do when I'm designing a game is sit down and write a short story. I wrote a lot of four- or five-page stories, lots of different plots. Then, I'd read each story and ask myself, Is that interesting? Does that make sense? And I'd say, 'Well, no.' So I'd throw it out and write another. I kept writing these stories and showing them to people around the office, until I hit upon something that was really intriguing. I had put some ghosts into one of the stories, and that seemed to catch everyone's interest. I'm not sure why there's such a close connection between pirates and ghosts, and so many stories about ghost ships and ghost pirates. In all the reading I did, I never found out where all that began. Still, when I put in the ghost pirate LeChuck, that's when everything started to come together for me. Because now I had a good, strong antagonist."[81] Once writing of the hook and most of the main characters was finished, Ron Gilbert developed his story in depth, breaking it up into stages to define specific objectives that the player would have to attain in order to progress through the story. So, the idea was forming in Gilbert's mind, but "I didn't really have a name yet, and that really bugged me. I just called it *The Pirate Game*. Then, one day, I was hanging out with a friend and he told this stupid joke. It's not even a joke; it's really just a quick one-liner, and he said it quickly, and he never said it again. He said, 'Hey, welcome to Monkey Island: grab a chimp and grind your organ.' It's a stupid joke. It's a sophomoric, junior high school joke. [...] But when I heard 'Monkey Island,' I knew that that was the name I was looking for for the game."[82] According to Ron, he never admitted to the Lucasfilm marketing department where the name came from. He was too embarrassed to ever explain it in a meeting.

The preparatory document that he revealed to Steve Arnold in early summer 1989 was around 40 pages long and described most of the adventure's puzzles. "I looked for ways to make the story nonlinear, to give players a choice of which puzzle to solve next. If you have a lot of bottlenecks, you're going to increase the chance that players will become frustrated with your game. Because they're sitting in one room trying to get through one door, and there's nothing else to do in the game until they get through that door. If you can give them other things they can do while they're trying to get through the door, they can put that puzzle aside for a while and do other stuff. Maybe they'll even see something along the way that'll help them figure out the puzzle." The early design document, of which a few precious fragments resurfaced in 2016 thanks to Aric Wilmunder, was entitled *Mutiny on Monkey Island*. It is an exceptional source for us players and video game historians, and we are incredibly fortunate that such a document is now available in the public domain with permission from Lucasfilm/Disney. Below, I have transcribed publicly available portions of the document, and you will notice that the story and game design evolved quite a bit to become the game we know and love. It's also worth noting that the influence of the Powers novel *On Stranger Tides* was still very prominent.

81. *Lucasfilm Adventurer, Vol. 1* (fall 1990).
82. *https://www.youtube.com/watch?v=Q6IYgWh-qnY*

Mutiny on Monkey Island – By Ron Gilbert[83]

Deep in the Caribbean, the small town of Méleê, on the south end of the Island, is alive with activity. From as far away as anyone has heard of, pirates of all types have converged on the small town in search of fame and fortune; and in this case fame ranks slightly higher than fortune. The event that has brought them all here was the discovery of a map leading to the legendary Treasure of Monkey Island.

Where it came from or who buried it is long forgotten, but rumor has it that the treasure is well over a thousand years old, and the wealth brought upon him who finds it will be inconceivable. So far, no one has come even close, but that is about to change.

Governor Fat [a character who will return in a different form in Monkey Island 2] has been the ruler of Méleê for the past 30 years. He came to the Caribbean in his youth, but lacked the courage to travel the seas and fight for his wealth as the pirate life demands. Instead he chose to remain on land and start a small town that catered to those who had what he lacked. He lived the pirate's life vicariously, watching them as they came and went, lived and died, prospered and languished. Due to his ingenious business sense and the ideal location of his Island, he became quite wealthy over the years.

Yet being the powerful and wealthy ruler of one's own Island was not enough for the Governor. He craved something more. Whether more money, more power or more respect was unclear; but his obsession grew ever worse, and the appeal of the jolly ol' town run by the jolly ol' Governor faded steadily. With each passing month, the governor tightened his grip until he held almost nothing. Pirates no

83. *http://wilmunder.com/Arics_World/Games.html* (link active as of the writing of this book, but since rendered inactive).

longer frequented Méleê for business or pleasure. It has been a vicious circle for the Governor. The more then [sic] he wants, the less he gets.

However the news that Governor Fat has fallen privy to the legendary map of Monkey Island has spread quickly, and Méleê is once again a thriving port teeming with scum and villainy. Many doubt the authenticity of the map, but the chance is too great to pass up. During the height of map hysteria, Méleê has been a virtual who's who of Pirates. Everyone who is anyone has shown up to undertake the Governor's challenge: find the treasure and return to wealth and fame. The Governor's deal is simple. He will supply the captain with food, supplies and a ship if needed. In turn, the crew who finds the treasure will return with it to Méleê. Governor Fat will keep one third; the other two thirds will go to the captain and crew to be divided according to the rules of common piracy. Any pirate who finds the treasure and fails to return will have heinously violated the code of piracy thus calling upon himself the revenge of all the others ending in certain death.

Of course, the fate of dishonest pirates is, at present, a moot point. In these three years spent looking for Monkey Island, not one pirate has returned alive. Some of the greatest pirates of the day have met their demise while on the Governor's quest. Each has left with a fully loaded ship and a full crew. What is reported of them afterward is nearly always the same: the questing ship was spotted a few times at sea, it had visited the few islands specified on the map and then vanish [sic] without a trace.

Two theories are popular concerning the fate of these crews. The first blames the bank of endless fog that looms miles out toward Monkey Island. It is said that navigation through this fog is impossible, that there are reefs and small rock islands dotting its interior. Many doubt whether the crew exists of sufficient skill to pass the fog bank and live. The second theory recalls a local superstition. The saying goes that there is a tribe of cannibals living on Monkey Island, and if anyone where [sic] to reach it, they would not survive more than a few hours before becoming dinner. Some even suggest that the Tribe is not really alive, but rather the walking dead which must feed on living flesh to survive. The telling of this last tale is usually followed by a deep silence and then the fevered drinking of rum.

On the evening of September 15th, 1590, a young man comes upon the town of Méleê. The first person to spot this traveler is the night lookout who discovers during a heated conversation that this is the infamous Pirate Captain, Smear West. West is well known for a previous exploit in which he captured one of the largest treasures ever plundered. This feat was followed by continuous bragging and a string of failures which destroyed his reputation, after which he disappeared in disgrace. In short, he is a has-been pirate and the lookout is surprised that he has dared to come at all. As Smear heads down the cliffside toward Méleê, the night lookout laughs. Smear knows that if he is ever going to regain respect, he must succeed in finding Monkey Island and return with the treasure. It is his last chance.

Smear West, intent on undertaking the voyage, spends the next few days searching the island for a crew. He finds few willing to risk a venture with him. The crew he ends up with is a rag-tag bunch to say the least. None has any real pirating experience and most have spent little time at sea.

The Governor reluctantly agrees to supply the fewest funds possible for the purchase and stocking of a ship. His willingness to go along at all is designed more to get rid of Smear than to finance a serious attempt for the treasure. No one expects Smear to survive, let alone succeed.

For those of you interested in the final outcome, rather than the gory details of the ensuing voyage, there is not and never was a Treasure of Monkey Island. The legend is nothing more than a legend. Of course the Governor knows this. The map he has is a fake. He made it himself and conjured up the whole story about how he came upon it. The Governor would have no real interest in the treasure if it existed. Wealth is not his ambition. Power is. A chest full of gold and silver could never bring him the kind of power he truly desires. The only thing that can is, indeed, on Monkey Island, but it cannot be removed. It is not a thing. It is a place. To be specific, it is a small opening in the earth.

Deep in a cave near the center of Monkey Island is a crevice that glows red. Anyone peering in would feel the unmistakable rush of evil billowing upward. It is a heat so intense that it overcomes your mind, drawing you deep into things better left unseen-undone. That crack descends to a place at the center of the earth, the name of which changes from religion to religion, from faith to faith. Most pirates call it Hell.

The crack has a harrowing effect not only on the living, it can bring the dead to life as well. Every Pirate that has taken on the Governor's challenge has felt its heat. A few have felt it while they lived, most have felt it dead. Governor Fat is putting together a crew of the most terrible, bloodthirsty pirates ever to sail the sea, and not one of them is living.

The cannibals on Monkey Island are not as vicious as their reputation suggests; but their image is not an accident. They live there to guard the crevice. It is their sacred purpose to see that no one discovers its secret or location.

West and his crew will make it to Monkey Island, and once there, discover the true nature of the Governor's scheme. Being nice people, they will decide they must stop the Governor and his "Crew from Hell." However, the ship of the dead will prove to be invincible until they follow the [sic] it through the boiling underground rivers of Monkey Island to challenge it in the realm of darkness-a fight not to be missed... (Suggested retail $49.95)

I'm sure that you noticed that the story in the design document really has little to do with the game we know today. Guybrush, Elaine, and LeChuck didn't exist yet. The hero, Smear West, is already a pirate; the junction of two worlds is taken straight from Powers' novel and his Fountain of Youth; and the story as a whole has a much more serious tone that's not as zany as the final version. Gilbert hadn't yet fully processed his influences and inspirations, but the game design was there. He supplemented his design document with a note on the game's flow. Overall, the progression described in the document appears generally similar to the game we're familiar with. The hero must put together a crew (a good third of the game) to set sail on the high seas and take part in Governor Fat's treasure hunt. At this point, Gilbert imagined having a system of ship battles and pillaging, seen from a top-down view, with the ability to build experience (more or less directly inspired by the game *Sid Meier's Pirates!*, published by MicroProse in 1987). Once he lands at Monkey Island, after an eventful journey, West must steal the key from the indigenous population, free his crew, and fight the bad guys. After West liberates a poor native woman, the cannibals offer to help our hero prepare a potion that will allow him to defeat his ultimate antagonist on the ghost ship. West travels across the sea and visits several islands to find each of the ingredients that will allow him to concoct the potion. By following the enemy ship into the bowels of Monkey Island, he will find the last ingredient. West finally returns to Mêlée for the final battle, an explosive conclusion in which he defeats the evil governor. Then, at last, the credits roll: "Everything done by Ron Gilbert with no help from anyone else."

Ahoy there, fancy pants! The New Monkey Island™

While the project seemed solid, the influences hadn't been thoroughly processed, and after reviewing his steadfast principles, Gilbert found the game to be too complex on the whole. There were too many game phases, they were too long and too repetitive, and above all, a crucial, central element was missing: humor. Another significant defect was the deplorable lack of a strong, independent female character, a heroine who Gilbert wanted to have evolve from a simple romantic distraction for the main character into a veritable protagonist in the story. Ron reworked his script and simplified the progression of puzzles in a new preliminary document entitled: *The New Monkey Island*.[84] The story underwent a radical change in tone.

---

84. *https://web.archive.org/web/20180226005830/http://wilmunder.com/Arics_World/Games.html*

In this new version, some of the antagonists were already perfectly fleshed out. We find the ghost pirate LeChuck, of course, and the governor (who was not yet named Elaine at that point), but the hero was still seriously lacking depth. "The original design for *Monkey Island* had the central character suffering from amnesia, so he didn't know his name. I dropped this story element, but then had to come up with a name. Steve Purcell (the guy who invented [the comic book series] *Sam and Max*) was drawing characters for me to look at. He was doing the editing in DPaint, and when you pick up an object, they call it a 'brush.' Since we didn't have a name, we were just calling him 'the guy.' Steve kept saving his brush files as 'guybrush.lbm.' It kind of stuck."[85] Mark Ferrari, one of the artists in the group, remembers a discussion that ensued:

> "**Gary Winnick: So, what are we going to name him?**
> – **Steve Purcell: Fred? Fred the Pirate?**
> – **Ron Gilbert: No. He's an action guy. He needs an action name.**
> – **Steve: Bob then.**
> – **Gary: How about Flynn? You know, like Errol Flynn.**
> – **Ron: No. Something original. And the Flynn estate will probably sue us anyway."**
> **Ron turned to Bucky Cameron and said:**
> **"We're going to need a girl pirate too. Just make a girl version out of the guy brush.**
> – **Steve: That's it! Call him Guy!**
> – **Ron: Yeah! Guy Brush! Why not?"**[86]

As for our hero's last name, it came directly from the novels of Pelham Grenville Wodehouse, a humorous 20th-century British author whose books Dave Grossman devoured. Grossman had used the alias "Threepwood" while playing role-playing games in the early 1980s. The entire team agreed that it was sufficiently ridiculous to become the official surname of Guybrush.

In addition to striving to follow his game design manifesto to a T, Ron Gilbert wanted to introduce a major evolution to the genre. Up to that point, whether it was the games of Sierra or *Maniac Mansion* or *Indiana Jones and the Last Crusade*, conversations between characters were limited to scrolling text at the top or bottom of the screen, without any interaction possible. The visual feedback of dialogue appeared as austere as a public school teacher's pay stub, and conversation with other characters couldn't be paired with any rhythm

85. *Edge* magazine, No. 96.
86. *https://advgamer.blogspot.com/2014/04/game-43-secret-of-monkey-island-herring.html*

or timing. But Gilbert wanted his game to be more than just a "pixel hunt." He wanted the puzzles to be based on searching for objects and managing the inventory, as well as on verbal sparring.

As such, Ron needed to build from scratch an innovative dialogue system, which, once again, would go on to be replicated in numerous other games. Indeed, *The Secret of Monkey Island* can be considered the first in the point & click subgenre to use a complex dialogue-tree system. Additionally, upgrades to the graphics libraries in the SCUMM engine improved the interface appearing on the screen. Dialogue boxes would appear directly above the characters with assigned color coding. What's more, their display duration could be controlled. What may seem trivial today was a mini revolution at the time. Players discovered with wonder the beginnings of control over scenes and pacing. This novelty was particularly crucial given the series' corrosive humor. For any good joke, timing is everything.

Once the project was approved by the supreme leader, Ron Gilbert began work on the most thankless job for a project manager: planning and budgeting. Over the course of five weeks, he went back over his scenario and trimmed the fat. He had to assess on a case by case basis which employee would design which place, for how long, and at what cost. To optimize the creation process, he prioritized all of the necessary production tasks. He found himself forced to abandon swathes of puzzles and characters. Ron Gilbert kept in mind that his project was not the only one in the production phase at the studio, which had a team of about 30 people at the time. Still, he could count on Tim Schafer and Dave Grossman, who were freshly trained, to assist him not only with programming, but also, particularly, with writing dialogue.

16-color EGA and color cycling™

Gilbert entrusted the game's art direction to Steve Purcell, who had previously worked on *Zak McKracken and the Alien Mindbenders* alongside David Fox. Working at a feverish pace, Steve produced preliminary drawings and the visual profiles of the characters. In spite of his youth, Purcell was already viewed as a veteran at the studio. In addition to his work for Lucasfilm, he had created the *Sam and Max* comics (which were later remarkably adapted into games) and collaborated with Marvel Comics.[87]

Mark Ferrari was in charge of virtually all of the game's backgrounds. We likely have him to thank for the colors and ambiance of the backgrounds, which

---

87. *Defenders of Dynatron City* (Marvel Comics, #1 to #6, 1992).

were scoured by hundreds of thousands of players, in spite of the limitations of the EGA screens, which are hard to imagine today, with a resolution of 320 by 200 pixels in 16 colors. He recounts: "I was hired by Lucasfilm Games in 1987, just AFTER the production of *Maniac Mansion*–which was certainly made using a very different tool–HUGE square pixels like cinder blocks, and only FOUR colors if I recall correctly. [...] But the first game I worked on there was '*Zak McKracken And The Alien Mind Benders*,' and we used the EGA version of D-Paint I–16 EGA color palette and standard 8-bit pixels at 320 X 200 resolution–to do the art. So Deluxe Paint I was definitely used before Monkey Island. We all drew using a mouse. If tablets were even a thing yet then, I have no memory of it. And I, at least, never made pencil sketches of my backgrounds ahead of time. The digital medium, with its 16 horrible colors and still jaggedy pixels was almost incapable of translating much of what I would have drawn in pencil, so what was the point? If I was asked for sketches, I just 'sketched' them [...] with a mouse, right on-screen in D-paint." [88]

It's likely that, more or less intentionally, the very simple nature of the backgrounds of the first game in the saga contributed to its effectiveness. That effectiveness would never be surpassed, either by its sequels or its competitors. Furthermore, the EGA version of *Monkey Island* is a masterpiece for lovers of pixel art. The first game in the series was the only one to adhere to that particular visual style. As a reminder to my readers, pixel art basically involves placing each pixel on the screen by indicating X and Y coordinates for where they must appear, then assigning colors to them. The lines of code written to produce pixel art were much simpler and more optimized than the code for the 2D techniques used in subsequent series installments. Indeed, *Monkey Island 2* and *Curse of Monkey Island* abandoned pixel art in favor of scans of actual paintings. But where Mark Ferrari really excelled, in spite of the machine's lack of power and the ridiculous size imposed on him by the floppy disk format, was with discreet animations that he scattered throughout the backgrounds. For example, the pier on Mêlée Island changes color and ambiance according to the light that hits it during the day, at sunset, and at night. Rather than entirely recoding this manually multiple times, he used the old "color cycling" technique. To put it simply, the technique involves changing only the color codes used on a selection of pixels, a basic machine instruction that takes up just a few bytes. The colors then change before our eyes according to a timer. The whole process takes up a lot less space than the animated sprite technique, in which a series of images move across the screen, like you would

---

88. Interview granted to the author for the purposes of this book.

see in any animated production. When done right, the result is phenomenal. Color cycling can also be called "palette shifting" or "palette cycling," and Mark Ferrari became one of the greatest masters of the technique.

Prepare to board!™

Once the planning phase was complete, *The Secret of Monkey Island* officially entered the production phase in November 1989. Ron Gilbert had two top objectives: to follow his own established precepts for good adventure games and to prove to his managers that the new formula would immediately make the game stand out from the competition and from the studio's previous productions. *The Secret of Monkey Island* needed to be a perfectly balanced game designed with the player in mind, in addition to offering an original atmosphere and environment. Thus, the tiny team worked tirelessly for the next four months to produce a perfectly functional prototype that was representative of the final game. The fully playable mock-up was presented to Steve Arnold in March 1990. The animations were rudimentary and many backgrounds were not yet finalized, but everything was there. The puzzles worked and the game's progression was clear. Thanks to that, in the months that followed, at the same time as the release of *Loom*, the team was able to put the finishing touches on development, fine-tune the timing of certain scenes, and dig deep into the humor and reactions of the characters. Gilbert, as we will see in future chapters, won't hesitate to cut out entire segments of the plot to improve the overall flow of a game. Any developer will tell you, having such a healthy period of extra time to perfect your game is a dream. And the team intended to take full advantage of it.

Humor that cuts like a saber™

The osmosis between the three musketeers (Schafer, Grossman, and Gilbert) was at its apex. The usage of humor as a perpetual MacGuffin[89] allowed them to serve up any idea whatsoever to players. "Comedy makes everything easier in adventure games," says Gilbert. "If you really look at adventure games, they are pretty stupid. Nothing really makes sense. Why is it that I need a pencil to solve a puzzle, and the only one in the world is back in New York City, huh? So, if you can make fun of situations like that, it makes your life easier. I really

---

89. A "MacGuffin" is an unexpected object, event, or person that serves as a pretext for advancing the plot of a story. The term is attributed to Alfred Hitchcock, who used this plot device in some of his films.

can't think of any good graphic adventures that were not comedies."[90] Mark Ferrari remembers a few years later: "The thing I remember most clearly about those days was the tremendous and constant humor woven through everything we did. We were all 'funny guys' back then, but the comic ring leaders were definitely Ron Gilbert and Steve Purcell. Their combined senses of humor set the tone and much of the content for *Monkey Island*. Steve was 'monkey-manic' in those days. There were few things he liked better than monkeys and monkey references. I suspect that this helped determine the name of the island in question. I'm pretty sure the soft drinks vending machine in the pirate port was Steve's idea too."[91] *The Secret of Monkey Island* would prove to be a polished and meticulously cut gem, down to the smallest details.

The writing of dialogue was divided between Ron, Dave, and Tim. "There's a myth that goes around about how it wasn't a comedy until Dave and I came along,"[92] Tim Schafer recalls, "but that's not true. [*Monkey Island*] was always going to be a comedy." With a false blend of cheeky amateurism and anarchy, the small team developed their game. "The thing that I think gets misunderstood is that I thought we were writing temporary dialogue for it and so we were just writing really silly, stupid dialogue. Then Ron was like, 'That's the dialogue we're going to use.' I was like, 'What!?' It was great." The writers divided up the characters, and so the three of them handled all of the writing of the dialogue trees. According to Schafer: "Ron wasn't as controlling with the dialogue as I am. I like to write everything for the games. Ron said, 'Let us write our own sections.' So, I wrote certain sections: Stan the used ship salesman, I was writing the puzzle where you try to go and buy a ship from him. I made it way more complicated than it probably had to be. It was the most in-depth dialogue puzzle tree ever written, probably. Then, the shopkeeper. Dave would write his stuff. He would focus on Herman Toothrot and the Men of Low Moral Fiber. We had all of the little set pieces that we would work on. Ron would work mostly on the ghost ship, the puzzles on the ghost ship, and all the LeChuck cut scenes. So we were all working together. We would all check out each other's stuff in mid-afternoon. Some of the first play testing we would do is, 'Let me see your dialogue,' and Ron would play and we would watch to see if he would laugh or not. Then we would go change stuff furiously. Dave got a laugh, so I'd want to get a bigger laugh than that. Then we would encourage each other. There was no internet back then, so we were just trying to use the people in the room with what we wrote. It probably led to a certain style of humor." When a segment with dialogue was complete, it would be subjected to a special ritual specific to the studio: "[Lucasfilm Games] had this thing called the 'Pizza Orgy' where

90. *Edge* magazine, No. 96.
91. *https://mixnmojo.com/features/sitefeatures/LucasArts-Secret-History-The-Secret-of-Monkey-Island/7*
92. *https://www.usgamer.net/articles/Tim_Schafer_Interview/page-2*

they would bring in all of their friends and family and they would stay all night and everyone would just play the game and eat pizza. And not have sex, hopefully. It was an orgy of gameplay and pizza eating. Then they would get everyone together to talk about the game. That's something that we keep going at Double Fine."[93] When asked if he remembers any particular influences on the type of humor and the series' famous sarcastic style, Tim Schafer doesn't hesitate even for a moment: "Right around the time we were starting *Monkey Island*, *The Simpsons* premiered. The very first *Simpsons* came out. We were like, 'this is a phenomenon! This is the funniest thing that has ever existed in the world!' So we were all watching that together and I think that had a very big impact on what we were doing. Before then, my writing influences were Kurt Vonnegut[94] and I think there's a lot of Monty Python in *Monkey Island*."

Pack it up™

September 1990 was a frenzied crunch time[95] for the team. All of Lucasfilm Games' resources were dedicated to finishing the project. While some helped write the manual, others focused on hunting down every single superfluous pixel to save a few bytes (for the PC, the game took up eight 5¼-inch floppy disks for the EGA/CGA version and seven 3½-inch floppy disks for the VGA version[96]). Meanwhile, Steve Purcell developed and designed the title's highly original anti-piracy system. At the time, pirated copies of games were everywhere: floppy disks would be passed around and on the now-defunct Compu-Serve network, you just needed a few hours to download the files for the studio's previous creations. So, Purcell came up with a double wheel made of cardboard dubbed the Dial-A-Pirate. By turning the top wheel to match the drawings on the screen, you would obtain a code allowing you to start the game. To be perfectly honest, though the system was ingenious and amusing, all a pirate (and I mean a real one) would need to do was photocopy the two wheels of the Dial-A-Pirate and spend two minutes putting the pieces together to create a new copy.[97] To finish everything off, Jim Current and Bret Mogilefsky wrote a

---

93. Studio founded by Tim Schafer in July 2000.

94. Kurt Vonnegut (1922-2007) was an American author known for creating the character Kilgore Trout, an unsuccessful science-fiction writer.

95. In the video game industry, "crunch time" is a period of intensive work. Generally, the team works a lot and sleeps very little. They drink a lot of coffee and eat copious amounts of chips and pizza.

96. The superb and incredible Amiga version occupied four floppy disks. As for the Atari ST version, for me, it never existed (though in reality, of course it did...). Now you know: in the rivalry between Amiga and Atari, the author of this book definitely chose a side.

97. Any resemblance to real-life events inspired by the author of this book is, of course, pure coincidence.

guide for the game that's now rare and valuable (in English only), containing a great rewriting of our hero's adventures entitled *The Memoirs of Guybrush Threepwood: The Monkey Island Years.*[98]

The finish line was on the horizon, but the adventure still wasn't finished. The team still had to create the packaging and box everything up. Ron Gilbert recalls: "It was more than just Dave and I, it was also Tim and pretty much the entire company. We needed to get all the boxes assembled and packed to make a ship date to a retailer (I don't remember who) and the warehouse that assembled the boxes couldn't do it in time due to needing to give its workers time off, so we all went down and worked through the night. Tim, Dave and I signed a $1 bill and placed it in one of the boxes. We never heard from that dollar again. I wonder if anyone found it."[99]

The Secret of Monkey Island was finally released worldwide in October 1990 with its 16-color EGA version. However, not long after, in December 1990, Lucasfilm offered a VGA version with its 256 incredible colors and MIDI music. An Amiga (and Atari ST...) version soon followed. It should be noted that the audio processor of Commodore computers offered much better sound quality than the IBM PCs and PC-compatibles of the era (though the screen only displayed 32 colors). An Amiga CDTV[100] version was ultimately canceled.

Two years later, Gilbert's game was also adapted for the SEGA CD console (a.k.a. Mega-CD, offering 32 colors and capable of playing music CDs) and the FM Towns computer, a testament to the title's global success and its indisputable blockbuster status by the standards of point & click adventure games. I'll finish with the most popular and well-known version, released in 1992 on CD-ROM with a remastered soundtrack. No matter what machine you were playing it on, the first few steps into the game were a siren song calling you on an exotic adventure...

Now, in order to better refresh your memory of the events of *The Secret of Monkey Island*, I would like to share with you some extracts from certified archival documents™, written by none other than Guybrush Threepwood himself and brought to us by the files of Ron Gilbert. These documents are both invaluable and enlightening. For highly sensitive readers, hit Ctrl + Shift + W on your book to skip straight to the end.[101]

---

98. A version of this "hintbook" (a guide offering solutions to all of the game's puzzles) is available for free on the website of the Museum of Computer Adventure Game History: *http://www.mocagh.org/lucasfilm/miuk-hintbook.pdf*

99. *https://mixnmojo.com/features/sitefeatures/LucasArts-Secret-History-The-Secret-of-Monkey-Island/7*

100. CDTV: Commodore Dynamic Total Vision, a turbocharged and dead-in-the-water version of the Amiga.

101. Ctrl + Shift + W was a secret code allowing you to finish *The Secret of Monkey Island* instantly. Which is quite a dumb idea when you think about it.

The Memoirs of Guybrush Threepwood, Part 1™

From The Memoirs of Guybrush Threepwood:

For the benefit of those of you who have ever dreamed of becoming a pirate, of mastering sword and sea, of stealing unimaginable wealth, of swilling grog until your head reels and your stomach wrenches, and of questing for that mysterious and powerful elixir, true love, I, Guybrush Threepwood, do here set quill pen to paper in the hopes of discouraging you from trying. Learn by example, if you please...

The story I'm about to tell you started long before I came into it. I entered somewhere around the middle, just when things started to go from strange to downright weird.

It all began a few years ago when a very famous Pirate, by the name LeChuck, fell in love with the beautiful Governor of the Island of Mêlée. The Governor had taken over the Island from her father, a very well-liked ruler, when he died of a sudden illness. Her popularity grew until her command of the island and brilliance as a ruler could be questioned by no one. The Pirates that lived on the Island learned to respect her with a faith equal to, if not greater than, that which they had bestowed on her father. All seemed to be perfect in this remote region of the Caribbean.

The Pirate LeChuck, while out tormenting the Spanish, French, British, or whomever he could find roaming the open seas, came upon Mêlée. He was tired and his ship and crew were in dire need of repair and rest. Mêlée always welcomed visitors and LeChuck's crew found what they needed most.

Being a well-known Pirate, LeChuck was asked to dine at the Governor's Mansion on the first evening. He was quite taken by the Governor and by the end of the evening proposed marriage. The Governor refused the offer as politely as possible, explaining that ruling the Island was her first priority and it required her full attention. The truth was she didn't really like the Pirate LeChuck.

The Pirate LeChuck took the rejection and left the Island. As the next few months turned into years he continued to return to Mêlée in the hopes of changing the beautiful Governor's mind. His feelings turned from admiration to desperation to obsession. The Island lookout was soon told to warn of LeChuck's approaching ship and the guards were not to let him onto the Island. The Pirate LeChuck continued to try and prove his worthiness to the Governor by increasingly daring voyages and foolish deeds. His feelings turned to jealousy and he started to torment ships coming from and bound for Mêlée. In a last-ditch effort, the Pirate LeChuck announced he was going to sail to the legendary Monkey Island and return with its secret. The secret was unknown, but legends value it as priceless. This effort would have also gone unnoticed by the Governor if not for its outcome.

A few weeks after setting sail, a strange storm appeared and engulfed the ship. The vessel was thrown upon a reef and the entire crew, including the Pirate LeChuck, were killed. The Governor mourned only the loss of attention. The truth is she was glad to be rid of him and hoped life on the Pirate Island of Mêlée would return to normal. This was not meant to be.

The Pirate ships of Mêlée continued to be tormented, but this time by a far more sinister force than Pirate LeChuck. Soon after his death, and by coincidence some will swear, a ghost ship started sailing the seas in the dead of night. No ships were immune to being boarded by the ghost ship, but it seemed to prey on the ships of Mêlée more than on others. The sightings continued for some time and appeared to be moving closer to the Governor's Island. The Pirates of Mêlée had feared Pirate LeChuck, but they always had a [sic] even chance at outrunning or beating him in a fair sea-battle. The ghost ship was unbeatable and was merciless towards the captured crew. It was not long before the Pirates of Mêlée refused to set sail and spent day and night on the Island. The Governor sent out many calls for a crew, which would be led by her, to hunt down and destroy the ghost ship, but none were willing.

This is where I came into the story. I was tired of my life in England and had decided to journey to the Caribbean in search of the Pirate's life. I was a young man of twenty and had much to learn. If one was serious about apprenticing to become a pirate, Mêlée was the place to go. The news of the ghost ship had not reached the old world and I set off unaware of what was happening. As we were approaching the island, our ship was hit by a terrible storm and we were shipwrecked just off of the coast.

The evening I arrived on Mêlée, I immediately began my training to become a Pirate. As a rite of initiation, I was given three trials by the Pirate

Council, a less-than-enthusiastic group of drunkards. This treasure hunt involved the discovery of a fantastic T-shirt, a bout of sparring—which, I must humbly admit, I am very good at, my wit being as sharp as my sword—and finally, a theft, which indirectly led me to meet the marvelous Elaine. For that last trial, I had to battle fierce, savage, man-eating beasts, do hand-to-hand combat with the Island's infamous sheriff, and steal an insignificant statuette from the Governor's house. The first time our gazes met, I was lovestruck. She is so beautiful, so strong, so independent. And she loves my ponytail! I had no idea that the late LeChuck was obsessed with her. After completing my final trial, I intended to return to the Pirate Council, have a bit of grog and toast my promotion to Mighty Pirate (plus send in my papers to the Official Pirate Pension Plan™) when I was confronted with a terrifying sight... Out at sea, sailing off into the distance was the ghost ship. I then learned that Captain LeChuck, back from the dead, had kidnapped her to take her to his lair on Monkey Island. The vile villain left warning to all pirates of Mêlée Island that any attempt at rescue would meet with horrifying disaster. I had to find her! But to do that, I needed a solid crew, and I found the best... well, I found the least terrible pirates on the Island to help me on my rescue mission. I also needed a ship, and it was that crook Stan, the "brand-new used ship" salesman, who ended up selling me one, the Sea Monkey™, though I had to make some unfortunate concessions on certain options, like the porthole defogger, the anti-lock anchor, and the heated tiller.

We set sail the next morning..... The voyage to Monkey Island presented only one major obstacle: none of us knew how to get there. As luck would have it, I found a map... well, sort of, in a cabinet in the captain's cabin of the Sea Monkey™. Rumor has it that the ship we had purchased had been owned by a pair of intrepid Pirates who made it to Monkey Island, but were never seen again... The Sea Monkey™ reappeared a few months later, allegedly sailed by a crew of chimps. It took quite a bit of effort to gather the ingredients listed on the recipe for the voodoo spell found in the cabin, and my crew wasn't willing to help me for long, coming up with obscure union rules that I won't repeat here in this journal. I finished the recipe, which had the immediate effect of causing an impressive, supernatural explosion that propelled us to Monkey Island.

When I came to, I found myself gazing upon the beaches of Monkey Island. I again used my new skills as a human cannonball to launch myself onto the Island. It didn't take me long to meet an old hermit living there named Herman Toothrot (Ha! What a ridiculous name). I soon discovered many mysteries on this dangerous island. The cannibals, a Giant Monkey Head, but most interestingly, an ancient voodoo root that would allow me to reduce zombie pirates to dust. After several clever ruses that required me to use my objectively superior intelligence, I managed to negotiate with the natives and received the mummified, and quite friendly (that's right, it talks), head of an old navigator, whose nasty necklace of eyes renders its wearer invisible to ghosts. After entering the Giant Monkey Head, which turned out to be the entrance to a vast underground network, I made my way into the bowels of the earth to discover the secret hiding place of LeChuck's ghost ship. Thanks to the disgusting eye necklace, I made myself invisible and managed to stealthily get my hands on the coveted voodoo root. But there was no trace of Elaine... My dear Elaine. I learned that LeChuck had taken the Governor to Mêlée Island to marry her. I needed to stop that wedding, and fast! I brought the root back to the native cannibals so that they could perform their secret ritual, then I left, armed with a new weapon, and returned to Monkey Island™.

In my mad dash to save Elaine, I managed to get our ship back to Mêlée Island very quickly (don't ask me how, that's another story...). Once in town, I made my way through waves of menacing zombie pirates thanks to my concentrated root juice. In fact, it was really effective, and I have to tell you, I didn't have a lot of confidence in that kind of exotic imported stuff...

When I reached High Street, I saw the lights and I heard a somber melody coming from the Mêlée Island Church. I knew that I needed to make a sensational entrance to make an impression (especially on Elaine... oh Elaine...). I burst into the church just in time to hear the zombie minister say, "If there be any man with reason that these two...er...people should not be united in blissful matrimony, let him speak now or forever hold his peace." I yelled out, "The groom isn't a human!" LeChuck pounced on me, both surprised and furious. I told him to prepare to fight and I was readying my voodoo-root potion when Elaine burst onto the scene (wait, so who was that in the wedding dress then?!): "I'm impressed that you came to rescue me, but it really wasn't necessary. I had everything well in hand" she shouted at me. I was suddenly racked with doubt. But, that meant that Elaine wasn't a prisoner!

It turns out, standing in for the bride, there were two monkeys, who were also armed with a voodoo-root concentrate. They immediately fled. Elaine ran after them and I found myself alone, facing the terrible LeChuck, who was terrified by my charisma. So, I took out my root juice, but the bottle jammed (I knew that kind of imported equipment wasn't reliable). I then entered into fierce hand-to-hand combat with the zombie captain. He just barely had the upper hand, but with my cunning, I was able to control my forced landing on Stan's shop, grab another cursed voodoo root beer, and spray the ghost with it. He immediately vanished in a torrent of tricolored fire. It was quite a show. What an ending!

Likely drawn by my irresistible charm, Elaine drew near me to watch the spectacle before us. I shared with her the deepest thought I had from this incredible adventure: "It's not the size of the ship that counts..."[102]

The End

Game design and anecdotes™

"Deep in the Caribbean, the Island of Mêlée..." It's in this idyllic setting, on a dark night, with a few notes of music playing in the background, that Guybrush's great adventure begins. The music initially evokes the image of someone falling asleep before transitioning to a more upbeat, rhythmic reggae tune. And that's no coincidence (we'll discuss this in greater detail later in this book) because Ron Gilbert wanted his universe to exude a faraway, impalpable, dreamlike quality, as if the player had just fallen asleep and plunged into the world of pirates.

From the game's first scene, Gilbert's vision for adventure games is set into motion. Guybrush meets the lookout (who appears to have poor eyesight... The irony!) and announces his objective–our objective: "My name's Guybrush Threepwood, and I want to be a pirate!" It's clear, direct, and perfectly explanatory.

Likewise, after Guybrush learns the three tasks he will have to accomplish to become a pirate, the player can tackle them in any order of their choosing. Once again, the team put into practice Gilbert's recommendations about giving the player freedom in order to avoid frustration. It's also a great example of

---

102. Unfortunately, here, the discovered manuscript stops abruptly.

how to design combined puzzles and define clear objectives. The team thought of everything.

And so, Guybrush gets to know the small town on Mêlée Island and its residents. He first has to figure out how to steal a precious artifact from the governor's house, then retrieve the legendary treasure of Mêlée Island, and finally duel with the Sword Master.

The first trial, in addition to bringing you face to face with both the sheriff (who is actually LeChuck in disguise) and Elaine, is also an opportunity to enjoy one of the adventure's most hilarious gags. As I mentioned in previous chapters, Gilbert didn't want his character to be able to die, and normally, it's impossible for Guybrush to perish in *The Secret of Monkey Island*. However, there is *one* moment where you can end up with a "game over." Indeed, Guybrush brags that he can hold his breath for 10 minutes, and when he's thrown in the water, weighed down by the very statue he's looking for, all the player has to do is wait 10 minutes and one second to finally see the fatal ending screen (thankfully, you can watch a hysterical conversation between two people on the dock while you wait). Once Guybrush dies, the actions of the game's interface are replaced with others like "Float," "Bloat," and "Order hint book."

Anyway, it's back to the kitchen of SCUMM Bar (indeed, the local tavern bears the same name as the game's development tool!) for the second puzzle. The various tasks you must complete in order to find the legendary treasure of Mêlée Island will take Guybrush into the island's lush jungle. The forest is actually generated randomly from a repetitive pattern in order to optimize the space used up on the original game's floppy disks. If, by chance, Guybrush tries to enter one of the tree stumps in the labyrinth of the jungle, a message appears asking the player to insert disk number 22... Of course, no such disk exists. However, a few days after the game's release, the Lucasfilm Games hotline (called the "Hint Line") was overwhelmed with calls for refunds as some players were furious that they didn't receive all of the floppy disks in their box! Naturally, this joke disappeared in the CD-ROM versions.

What's more, the Hint Line received calls from some notable players. Ron Gilbert: "I met a lot of amazing people working at Lucasfilm Games and I think one of my favorites was Steven Spielberg. [...] Spielberg was a true gamer. It's like he really did love games. He played them a lot, and he could talk about them non-stop. Whenever he was in town visiting George, he would always drop by the Games Group to see what we were working on. Now, he wouldn't just stand there and nod politely as we demoed the game. You could not get two minutes into the demo before he was wrestling the joystick or the mouse out of your hand. I grew up idolizing George Lucas and Steven Spielberg, and here I was, about to get in a fistfight with one of them over a joystick or a mouse. It was just oddly surreal to me. Of course, being Steven Spielberg does have its privileges. When he would get stuck in *Monkey Island*, he would not call the [1-900-740-JEDI–no joke!] Hint Line or log into CompuServe; he would just call me! My phone would ring and I'd hear: 'Hello, this is Diana, I have Steven on the line. He needs some hints for *Monkey Island*. Can I connect you?' The first few times, this was thrilling. After spending 10 minutes on the phone with Steven Spielberg giving him hints on your game, you can just pretty much go home for the day. You could pretty much go home for the whole week. But after a while, I would be poking my head into Noah's office and I'd be saying, 'Spielberg's on the phone: do you want to talk to him?' And he'd say, 'No, I talked to him last time. Let's see if Dave wants to talk to him. I don't think Dave has talked to him in a while.' It became the 'Spielberg hot potato.' How quickly the exciting can become the mundane. There actually is a point to this story... I got a chance to work with Spielberg on a project we did at Lucasfilm called *The Dig*.[103] [...] Noah Falstein and I were the first of many project leads to be assigned to the project before it came out years later. During one of those meetings, Spielberg said something that has stuck with me all of these years. I don't remember exactly what we were talking about, but this concept of believing in what you're creating came up, and Spielberg said: 'You have to believe in your idea enough to dance naked on top of it.' This really stuck with me, and I think it's a critical point in the journey of creativity. If you believe in what you're making, if you believe in it so much that you will dance naked on top of it, then it doesn't matter what anyone else thinks."[104]

The third trial, probably the most famous, requires that the player indulge in the pleasures of verbal sparring, for which the saga has become legendary. The idea originally came from Grossman and Gilbert after the two of them watched a number of swashbuckler films in which the characters spent more time blabbering on than actually crossing swords. It should be noted that the writing of the insults themselves was entrusted to writer Orson Scott Card, who had previously been a scenario writer for David Fox's "Mirage" project for Lucasfilm Games. He recalls: "The writing I did for projects with Lucasfilm Games (as they were then called) began when I was invited to visit 'the ranch' (back when they were still in the carriage house) and look in on some of the games. I loved what they were doing and learned a lot. I'm not sure of the value of my contributions, but I did come up with the insults for *Monkey Island* (with the help of my kids, who drew on their grade-school experience to create the lame starting insults)."[105]

---

103. A LucasArts game released in 1995.
104. *https://www.youtube.com/watch?v=Q6IYgWh-qnY*
105. *https://www.gamefront.com/games/gamingtoday/article/gaming-todays-exclusive-interview-with-author-orson-scott-card*

To remind you, as Guybrush travels across Mêlée Island, he encounters sinister pirates who want to sword fight. As he attacks, our hero lobs an insult, to which his adversary must respond in kind. If the enemy nails our pirate apprentice with his zingers, the antagonist takes the upper hand; otherwise, he will lose ground. The verbal sparring repeats until one of the adversaries surrenders. In practice, this learning system, which seems great on paper, proves to be very repetitive and, in the end, too mechanical. Honing your comebacks as a pirate serves as a humorous counterpoint allowing you, the player, to delight in some spicy dialogue. The very construction of the system for learning insults and fitting comebacks forces the player to remember, guess, or search around for the insult that will give them the advantage over their adversary. Even the slightly more complex variation seen in the duel with Carla the Sword Master calls for just a bit more of the player's intelligence. The player will quickly come up with the keys to the algorithm and will easily win the fight and earn the 100% Cotton T-shirt.

Still, this innovation in game design remains one of the most memorable parts of the game. The insult sword-fighting offers a number of lines that are real gems, and you can find them in the appendix of this book (Mix-o-insults™ p. 283). "Soon you'll be wearing my sword like a shish kebab!"

After completion of the three trials and the kidnapping of Elaine, Guybrush gets a crew together and meets Stan the used ship salesman to buy a vessel. The idea for Stan's character came from Tim Schafer, who was inspired by a "how to be a good salesman" guide. He wrote the fantastic dialogue for the insufferable character in one sitting. The grog vending machine at Stan's dealership unsurprisingly bears a few interesting similarities to a well-known soda brand. Originally, Gilbert wanted to have a Coca-Cola vending machine, but the Lucasfilm legal department immediately put the kibosh on that. This interference from the legal team became a recurring gag in later episodes. Notably, the Lucasfilm legal department's requirements gave rise to the trademark-symbol gag. Also, the troll guarding the bridge and barring access to Stan's dealership is actually... George Lucas himself.

Let's talk about one of the characters that Guybrush meets while putting together a crew: the kindly Meathook. He was originally supposed to be part of a quest with three steps, but Gilbert, just a few weeks before the game's release, decided that the game was quite complex and that the time it took for the player to finally discover Monkey Island was too long. As such, this quest was simply eliminated, even though it had been fully coded and illustrated.

I already explained that Gilbert originally imagined having ship battle sequences while sailing to Monkey Island. As the idea was too complex and didn't really fit into the game's design, this component was abandoned and replaced with the voodoo recipe that we know today. Still, Tim Schafer had developed the algorithms and preliminary visuals for the ship battles, and he still has some pieces of this work in his personal files.

After Guybrush finally reaches Monkey Island, he soon meets Herman Toothrot. It wasn't until the game's testing phase that the team got the idea to add this character. Gilbert wanted to have an element capable of continuously refreshing the humor and rhythm of the game in this section.

There are lots of fun facts tied to Monkey Island. Once there, Guybrush discovers a giant monkey head that serves as the entry to LeChuck's cavern. Originally, Dave Grossman wanted it to be a giant robot; that idea ended up being used years later in *Escape from Monkey Island*, the fourth game. In front of the Giant Monkey Head, there are a number of idols placed on the ground, one of them being an effigy of Sam and Max.[106] To open up the passage, you have to use a key in the form of a giant cotton swab that our hero must steal from the harmless cannibals. They capture Guybrush and move to put him in jail, but first they say to him, "Is that a banana in your pocket or are you just happy to see us?", a riff on the famous quote, "Is that a gun in your pocket, or are you just pleased to see me?" attributed to Mae West in the film *She Done Him Wrong*.[107] The quotation was also used in the 2009 game *Uncharted 2: Among Thieves*, made by Naughty Dog, whose developers proudly profess their unconditional love for *Monkey Island*.[108] It's funny to note that when Guybrush escapes from the cannibals' hut and later returns, the entrance is increasingly reinforced, to the point where it becomes a futuristic fortress requiring an access code.

In the highlands of the island, Guybrush gets the opportunity to indulge in the joys of catapulting, at the risk of sinking his own boat. He can also (almost) die at the edge of a cliff that collapses, resulting in the understated message, "Oh, no! You've really screwed up this time! Guess you'll have to start over! Hope you saved the game!" It was pretty clearly a joke at the expense of adventure games from Lucasfilm's competitor Sierra, in which the player could die here, there, and everywhere.

A bit further along, Guybrush must cause an explosion to unblock the river. In the Amiga version of the game only, a mysterious chest is launched out. When asked about the presence of this mystery chest, Dave Grossman simply responded that it held the secret of Monkey Island...

---

106. Sam and Max are characters created by Steve Purcell, *Monkey Island*'s art director, and went on to star in their own fantastic, eponymous adventure game: *Sam and Max Hit the Road,* released in 1993.
107. A musical by Lowell Sherman released in 1933.
108. I also very strongly recommend that you read the book, published by Third Éditions, entitled *The Saga Uncharted: Chronicles of an Explorer,* co-written by... well, um, on second thought, let's talk about something else.

In the game's hilarious ending, based on an idea from Grossman, Guybrush bursts into the church like Dustin Hoffman in the movie *The Graduate*.[109] Hoffman's character interrupts the wedding of the woman he loves by yelling her name six times, with that name being... Elaine! Thus, the heroine of *Monkey Island* got her name. Soon the credits roll, stating that Ron Gilbert created the game almost entirely on his own, with just a little help from the rest of the team. This was a private joke among the team because after the compilation of the beta version of the game (thus, before it was finalized), Grossman and Schafer purposely omitted Gilbert's name from the end credits.

There are two endings to *The Secret of Monkey Island*. If the player previously sunk the Sea Monkey™ using the catapult on Monkey Island, a screen shows Guybrush's crew in an unpleasant position in the cannibals' village. Otherwise, it just shows poor Herman Toothrot hoping in vain that his new pirate friend didn't abandon him on the island...

A few more fun facts:

☺ Between the 16-color EGA versions and their big sister, the VGA version with its 256 colors, there are, naturally, a few differences. In the EGA versions, the inventory is text based; in the VGA version, icons replace the action words. The habitual action from *Maniac Mansion* and *Indiana Jones and the Last Crusade*, "What is," was left out. This action provided a definition of an object observed by the character, making it possible to handle the item. In *The Secret of Monkey Island*, all the player has to do is place the cursor over an object for its name to automatically appear in the action bar.

☺ The pier next to SCUMM Bar offers a superb view of the starry night sky and the moon. If you look closely at the pixels in the image, you can see a man on the moon.

☺ The dog Spiffy, a discreet pooch you can find in SCUMM Bar, also appears in a close-up on the back of the *Monkey Island* game box. However, that particular image didn't actually appear in the final version because there wasn't enough room on the floppy disks (it did finally appear 20 years later in the game's special edition).

☺ A drunken pirate named Cobb proudly wears a badge that says "Ask me about *Loom*": this was a blatant advertisement for the Lucasfilm game released shortly before.

☺ Elaine's face was based on that of Avril Harrison, who was a Lucasfilm Games employee at the time and worked on the first *Prince of Persia* alongside

109. *The Graduate* is a Mike Nichols film released in 1968, starring Dustin Hoffman as a young university graduate who's seduced by an older woman by the name of Mrs. Robinson.

Jordan Mechner. The face of the famous Sword Master Carla was based on Carla Green, a Lucasfilm Games employee working in product support.

☻ It should be noted that the dialogue between the sheriff and Guybrush in their brilliant off-camera confrontation in the governor's palace (developed by Dave Grossman to replace a more classic puzzle) offers a wealth of references... "It belongs in a museum."[110]

☻ In the SCUMM Bar kitchen, when working on the second trial, Guybrush can look at a portrait of the Pillsbury Doughboy.[111] In the same location, the belligerent seagull comes directly from the game *Loom*.

☻ The character Herman Toothrot gets his name from a pop music group from the 1960s called Herman's Hermits.

☻ Many scenes taking place on the island, in spite of being finished, were deleted from the final game, even though they had been presented to the media on several occasions. Notably, some were included in a televised report on an American cable channel. In the end, Gilbert felt that the adventure was too long.

Reception and reviews™

While today *The Secret of Monkey Island* is unanimously considered a cult classic, it's still interesting to look at how it was received by critics and audiences at the time. Sometimes, an artistic work can be poorly understood, held in low esteem, or simply come out at the wrong time.

In North American media, the game was praised by most for its humor, for being accessible, and for its well-crafted interface and overall production. In issue number 109 of the famous magazine *Computer and Video Games* (December 1990), Paul Glancey wrote: "The Lucasfilm adventures have always been favourites in our office, but this is the first one I've wanted to play right until the end. In the week since I got hold of this game, I've spent every spare moment playing it and enjoying it! *Zak McKracken* had a great sense of humour, and *Indy* had a great plot, but this has both! Usually the entertainment you get from an adventure is derived solely from solving puzzles, but the hilarious characters and situations, and the movie-like presentation (with cut-scenes and various 'camera' viewpoints) make playing this more like taking part in a comedy film so it's much more enjoyable. The puzzles are brilliantly conceived too, and success depends more on looking and listening, which I think is preferable to mind-bending lateral thinking. Lucasfilm's easy-to-use, point-and-click command system rides again in *Monkey Island*, so

---

110. A quote from...? Come on, you know this one! (*Indiana Jones*)
111. For readers outside of North America, he's a character used in advertising for baking products from the company Pillsbury.

even the laser-brains with keyboardphobia have no excuse not to get hold of this utterly enthralling game at once! [...] OVERALL 94%." In the magazine *Amiga User International* dated July 1991, Tony Horgan said: "DECISION 93%. Funny, interesting, good looking, enthralling... but that's enough about me." [...] OVERALL 93 %." Finally, Jeff James of *Amiga World*, in the issue dated October 1991, summarized: "If you can live with *Secret*'s shortcomings, you'll be rewarded by a lengthy and involved four-disk adventure of sailing under the Jolly Roger, trading insults with unwashed ruffians and haggling with used ship salesmen."

Overseas, the French media seemed to be more divided in its opinion. *Génération 4*, in its issue dated November 1990, praised the game: "The game's ambiance is truly fantastic, the characters, the places, and the situations making use of all the clichés found in all the books and films starring these 'heroes.' [...] The dialogue, battles (using insults as weapons), situations, and characters encountered, everything is funny and enjoyable, which in no way takes away from the appeal of the adventure. The PC version, in just 16 colors, is a marvel when it comes to the showcasing and usage of those tones. What's more, the game also offers fluid scrolling between certain adjacent screens, sprites of the main character that get smaller as he moves toward the back of the screen and get bigger as he moves to the foreground, numerous outstanding animated scenes that will have you dying of laughter, and more. This game has impressive graphics. Even the PC sounds and music are on point and become phenomenal when you have a sound card, adding a bit more to the exotic and adventurous atmosphere. A superb adventure game that's more enthralling than *Indy* and which will be a huge hit in France. 95%." *Tilt*, on the other hand, deplored the avalanche of point & click games and the lack of originality and freshness in the game: "*The Secret of Monkey Island* is one of those decent adventure games that come out regularly. There's nothing exceptional about it, but it provides you with long hours of fascinating searches. As such, I recommend it only for die-hard fans of adventure games. For everyone else, I would say you're not missing anything special. The price of this game was not shared with us, but I think a maximum of 200 francs[112] would be acceptable." Finally, the magazine *Joystick* took note of the game's strengths: "No more struggling with wording: even with mediocre English, you can very easily play this game. [...] Additionally, the progression is non-linear, with several ways to solve a puzzle. As such, the game doesn't get repetitive. We'd also like to note the typically 'Lucasian' graphics, the gags (a very funny seagull, an ad for *Loom* given by a pirate), and the reggae music that accompanies many sequences if you have a sound card. Truly

---

112. About $30 today.

splendid, *Monkey Island* is a little masterpiece that will delight all those who once dreamed of Treasure Island."

While the critical reception of the game was mostly positive, sales were not as strong as Lucasfilm Games had hoped. Ron Gilbert says as much on his blog: "*Monkey Island* was never a big hit. It sold well, but not nearly as well as anything Sierra released."[113] Indeed, *Monkey Island* only built up a reputation over the long term, though once it did, it never weakened, in spite of the hazards of a genre that fell out of fashion some 10 years later. The title went unnoticed in the United States and across the Americas due to saturation in the genre. However, it became a real blockbuster in Europe, particularly in Germany, a country that historically loved point & click games (as it has an unfailing "PC culture"). Thanks to its high-quality localizations (in French, German, Italian, Spanish, and even Japanese[114]) and its VGA CD-ROM version, as well as its Amiga and Atari ST conversions, the game's sales doubled in the year after its release (1991).

Over time, generation after generation, players, critics, and the entire video game world discovered–or rediscovered–the adventures of Guybrush Threepwood without ever looking down on him.

I'm the real hero of this series, not that numbskull Treepoop!

113. *https://grumpygamer.com/monkey25*
114. Under the name モンキー・アイランド ユーレイ海賊大騒動！, or in the Latin alphabet *Monkey Island: Yuurei Kaizoku Daisoudou!*

Chapter 6: From Lucasfilm Games™ to LucasArts™

Official recipe for grog™:

- Kerosene
- Artificial sweeteners
- Sulfuric acid
- Acetone
- Red dye (or blue, depending on the season)
- Axle grease
- Battery acid
- Rum [115]

While the team finished up development of *The Secret of Monkey Island* and released it, big changes were underway on the little planet of Skywalker Ranch. The company was undertaking a major reorganization, leading to the creation of LucasArts Entertainment Company (LEC). The new company included the teams from Lucasfilm Games, Industrial Light & Magic (ILM), and Skywalker Sound. The second phase of the reorganization merged the ILM and Skywalker Sound teams to form Lucas Digital Ltd. The video games team was thus orphaned and was given the new name LucasArts.

The decision to reorganize was not a random one. In the late 1980s, the video game industry was undergoing massive changes. Microcomputers, particularly IBM PCs and compatibles, were entering more and more homes, causing sales to skyrocket along with the needs of the mass market. This paradigm shift, from using computers in a business setting to using them in a family setting, also translated to the ever-growing game console market. In 1989, Japanese consoles took the world by storm, particularly thanks to the success of the Nintendo Entertainment System (NES) and the brand-new Game Boy, which went on to achieve phenomenal success, with over 100 million units sold.

---

115. Of course, this is a sweetened version of grog from the Southern Caribbean. Drink responsibly! That is, because of the artificial sweeteners: they can be bad for your health.

The Japanese company SNK launched the Neo Geo, the "living room" version of its MVS arcade system, and NEC launched the future wave of consoles using CD-ROMs with its TurboGrafx-16 (a.k.a. PC Engine, with the CD-ROM extension offered as an add-on for the console).

With all this happening, parallel markets opened up and expanded the potential audiences. The combined release and unprecedented success of Will Wright's *SimCity* and the imminent announcement of the revolutionary Microsoft operating system Windows 3 indicated that the video game world was rapidly democratizing, foiling all of the game publishers' forecasts. The era of experimentation was over. Video game developers had to solidify their positioning, as well as make bets on technologies and strong franchises. The 1990s were sort of a transitional period from the carefree attitude of the early years of the video game industry to the development of a certain maturity in the market, with large-scale production largely imposed by the quality standards of a handful of blockbusters, like Nintendo's productions, as well as recent evolutions in the arcade market.

And George Lucas understood all of this. The war chest that had been built up by the success of the *Star Wars* saga began to empty. The lighthearted days of abundance were over. The success of *Indiana Jones and the Last Crusade* convinced the powers that be at the new LucasArts Entertainment Company that they needed to refocus on strong franchises that defined the company's identity. And what name could be more broadly unifying than *Star Wars*? So, LucasArts once again launched several projects for future games directly tied to Lucas' galaxy far, far away. To forcefully invest in the home console market, the studio tasked a team led by industry veteran Akila Redmer[116] with producing a platform game, a genre that was in vogue at the time, but which was relatively new for the developer.

Star Wars exploitation™

Many games had already been released with the *Star Wars* name, most of them dating from the period when Atari held the license,[117] but the title in development had to embody a renaissance for the franchise in the video game world. It was the start of a plan to lend credibility to adaptations by adding LucasArts' mark of quality assurance. The studio very purposefully selected

116. Redmer had previously worked as a producer on the studio's recent titles (*Maniac Mansion*, *Zak*) and, most notably, was the creator of the highly original *Pipe Mania/Pipe Dream*, a puzzle game published by Lucasfilm and released for the Amiga, Atari ST, and PC in 1989.
117. The famous 1983 *Star Wars* rail shooter was released for just about every machine that existed at the time. And its "sequels" *Star Wars: The Empire Strikes Back* and *Star Wars: Return of the Jedi* (1984).

a platform for its exclusive entry into the living room console market. The recent worldwide success of Nintendo's *Super Mario Bros. 3* made the NES an obvious choice, easily beating SEGA's competing console. As such, the NES, with its large number of machines already in homes, would receive the first official adaptation of the *Star Wars* franchise, produced and developed by LucasArts/Lucasfilm.

The scenario used in the adaptation was more or less faithful to the script of *Star Wars: A New Hope*. The game alternated between classic platform phases and "top-down perspective" phases in which the player drives a landspeeder. A fairly good game, in spite of its infuriating difficulty, the title achieved the success the company had hoped for. While LucasArts would continue producing adventure games, the exploitation of the *Star Wars* license had started and would invariably lead to annual releases of games for the most popular consoles of the day.

Leaving Skywalker Ranch™

Initially, Ron and his comrades worked directly on the premises of the prestigious Skywalker Ranch, near Nicasio, California. The restructuring forced the Games Group to move its offices, its equipment, and all its employees to a new facility in San Rafael, with the move taking place just after the release of *Monkey Island* in November 1990. "I arrived at LucasArts in the late Summer of 1990, when the team had just moved their offices from the Stable House at Skywalker Ranch to 'A' Building at the complex of offices that made up Industrial Light and Magic ["ILM"]," recalls Khris Brown, the head of customer support and voice casting for LucasArts. "The teams had just moved from a very warm, home-like environment, where it felt as if one was going to a friend's house to work every day, to a building that was more corporate-feeling. There was an undercurrent of good-natured rebellion about the move, and a lot of joking and customization of the office space to create a more creative and welcoming environment in what would have otherwise been a fairly sterile office space. People hung Christmas lights, their favorite movie posters, and placed pieces of vintage and eclectic furniture in the building to customize it and make it more convivial. There was a feeling of excitement about Monkey Island, and a very collaborative, all for one, one for all, feeling of underdog unity. There was a younger, recently-graduated core group of friends who often ended up staying in the building very late, playing video games and board games together, ordering pizza, or going out for food before going to one another's houses to watch movies. There was an older, more experienced group of people with young families who were very respected, such as David Fox (my boss), Noah Falstein, Douglas Crockford, and our President, Steve Arnold. Everyone shared their knowledge, and there was a lot of laughter."

The employees enjoyed having a more spacious work environment and the various teams working on different projects were no longer stepping on each other's toes. That meant that LucasArts could simultaneously develop multiple projects, like the flight simulation game *Secret Weapons of the Luftwaffe* from Lawrence Holland (which prepared his teams for the future, much-loved *Star Wars: X-Wing*) and Akila Redmer's *Star Wars* game, without interfering with the "Graphic Adventures" team, which included Ron, Dave, and Tim. However, most employees deplored the loss of the magic that existed at the legendary Skywalker Ranch, with its famous, prestigious library and the proximity to the company's other creative teams, which undoubtedly helped create artistic synergy.

According to legend, the creation of the new logo after the reorganization took weeks of intensive brainstorming in the Lucas communications department. Thus was born the "Golden Guy," the little figure extending his arms to form a symbolic and benevolent eye while standing proudly on the "L" for Lucas.

This same period also saw the creation of the famous magazine written and published by the company, which was distributed for free as a newsletter for the general public through classic distribution channels and stores selling games throughout the U.S. *The Adventurer* published 14 issues from fall 1990 to winter 1996. The purpose of the magazine was, of course, to promote the games published by LucasArts, but also to showcase the developers and the games' universes. Inside, you can find dozens of invaluable interviews, presentations of titles based on the *Star Wars*, *Indiana Jones*, and *Monkey Island* universes, hilarious letters from readers, comics (including some gems from Steve Purcell), and the opportunity to discover many preliminary drawings.

The golden age™

With the success of the studio's most recent games and the undeniable talent of their creators, LucasArts became iconic, a major player in the personal microcomputer market, and each release became a real event for players. Noah Falstein remembers: "When it came time to decorate our new offices here, we had a lot of discussion about whether we should use *Star Wars* posters or something. But we decided just to use our own computer game artwork. We know now that the stuff we're doing has its own merit, apart from the connection with the movie end of the company. I was at a Consumer Electronics Show about three or four years ago, and I had my Lucasfilm Games badge on. I was having lunch and someone noticed my badge and said, 'I really like your stuff and I was wondering how big Lucasfilm is.' I said, 'Well, the games division has about twenty people in it, but the whole company has about four hundred.' His jaw dropped and he said, 'You mean you guys do something besides games?' He didn't know we were connected with George Lucas and *Star Wars* and all that. That was a real turning point for me: it was the first time that I realized that there were people who associated the name 'Lucasfilm' primarily with games and not with movies."[118]

After nearly a decade of research, ingenuity, creativity, and a bit of insanity, this new direction for the studio represented a game changer. It marked a new, more mature era for LucasArts. The developer went on to create its best games, including probably some of the best adventure games of all time.

118. *https://1.bp.blogspot.com/-HWjlTivWhI4/Tmq9kleUL6I/AAAAAAAAAVI/xThWqqBJ6-I/s1600/ adventurer_02_pg05.JPG*

Chapter 7: *Monkey Island 2: LeChuck's Revenge*™

"Warning! Contains graphic depiction of gratuitous expectorations."[119]

On his blog, Ron Gilbert recounts: "I started working on *Monkey Island II* about a month after *Monkey Island I* went to manufacturing with no idea if the first game was going to do well or completely bomb. I think that was part of my strategy: start working on it before anyone could say, 'It's not worth it, let's go make *Star Wars* games.'" In an interview, he adds: "The concept of doing sequels was a creative decision, it wasn't a business decision. Nobody said, 'Hey, *Monkey Island* did really well—it actually didn't—so let's make *Monkey Island 2*.' That was more of a creative thing in me. I wanted to make a sequel to that stuff. So I think they were more creative decisions than business decisions. Now it's all about making sequels because you have this product franchise."[120]

Even though he had just spent four years imagining the universe, adventures, and characters of the first *Monkey Island*, Gilbert had a singular goal: to immediately return to his comical, bloodthirsty pirates and his one-of-a-kind universe. While *The Secret of Monkey Island* had clearly been developed as a stand-alone story, Ron wanted to expand its universe and give it real depth, with a solid background. He wanted to go beyond just repetition of the universal, classic pirate imagery and immediately conceived of the sequel as having an open ending, leaving room for a potential third episode. And the first idea that came to mind for the young developer was the subtitle: *LeChuck's Revenge*.

Funnily enough, "revenge" is nowhere to be found in the game itself, but Gilbert liked the title. He later confided: "The word 'Revenge' came from '*Revenge of the Jedi*,' which was the original name of '*Return of the Jedi*.' I had a rare official '*Revenge of the Jedi*' T-shirt that was made before the name of the movie was changed."[121] As the scenario took shape in the months that followed, Gilbert wanted to push things further than the first game, which in the end, for him, was just a way to test his new reforms of adventure game design. The *Monkey Island* sequel would be bigger, more beautiful, funnier, better written,

---

119. A joke appearing on the box of *Monkey Island 2: LeChuck's Revenge*.
120. *https://www.usgamer.net/articles/i-actually-was-hunting-ewoks-lucasfilm-games-the-early-years*
121. *http://www.worldofmi.com/features/interview/gilbert.php*

and also more visual. Above all, *Monkey Island 2: LeChuck's Revenge* would be centered on a theme and would call for reflection and a deeper level of understanding... The first game could not, in all honesty, claim as much. In the end, that theme became the famed "secret" of Monkey Island.

Technical developments™

Monkey Island 2, unlike its predecessor, was immediately designed to support the 256 colors of VGA screens, which had become commonplace, instead of the original 16 colors of the first game. The graphics were developed to take advantage of the more sophisticated screens. The small team in charge of creating the initial visuals had two returning members: Steve Purcell, of course, but also Sean Turner, who focused on the characters. It also included a young newcomer, Peter Chan. A die-hard fan of markers, the young artist drastically changed the habits of his coworkers. To keep up with the pace imposed on them and continue feeding Ron's imagination, Peter shunned computers and drew everything by hand on large transparent sheets, much like was done in traditional animation in the 1940s and '50s. He then created high-resolution scans of his images. The result? Time saved and peerless quality. What players see on the screen are actual handmade drawings converted by computers to work with the weak resolution of monitors and graphics cards of the era. In concrete terms, technically speaking, there is a gaping chasm between the graphics of the first two *Monkey Island* games, in spite of there being just one year between them. *The Secret of Monkey Island* sported a clean, minimalist style, similar to the *ligne claire* style of drawing,[122] communicating ideas of both simplicity and clarity to go with a simple game design. Conversely, *Monkey Island 2* is dazzling, effervescent, and profusive.

The year 1991 also saw the arrival of the CD-ROM in the world of personal computers. From the beginning of that year, LucasArts' competitor Sierra began re-releasing its flagship titles on CD-ROM. *King's Quest V* and *Space Quest IV* thus took advantage of the opening of this new market. In addition to offering optimal sound quality, provided that the player had a sound card, the new medium offered developers the opportunity to free themselves from the storage constraints of the 3½-inch floppy disk.[123] Cheap to produce, relatively strong, and resolutely modern in its aesthetics, the CD had everyone swooning, and publishers saw it as a marketing opportunity to rejuvenate their franchises at a minimal cost. However, Ron Gilbert, talented though he may

122. A style from the Belgian school of comics, centered on the work of Hergé (*Tintin*).
123. As a reminder, the standard 3½-inch floppy disk offered 1.44 MB of storage. A CD-ROM offered 650 MB. That's equal to 451 floppy disks.

be, lacked perspicacity and was not convinced by the new technology. He saw the CD-ROM as a gimmick that wouldn't last... Thus, *Monkey Island 2* would be released on floppy disks, just like its predecessor! His explanation at the time makes us smile today: "Yes, I was concerned about the size of the game, but not nearly as much as our accountants were! I had to cut out five very large scenes from the game to get it to fit on six disks. I think CD-ROM is coming very soon, but I also believe that it won't last more than a few years. It has so many drawbacks that you can't really do the kinds of things that we want to do. It's also 10 times slower to read from than a hard drive and very slow to seek anywhere. There are other technologies out there that will take over in five to six years."[124] In the end, the game was released on CD-ROM a year later, and the new format's sales exceeded those of the game on floppy disks. Bravo, Ron, for that great prediction!

The technical team dedicated to the sequel grew quite a bit. From seven people for the first episode, the staff grew to 14, with all of them working tirelessly to develop one of the greatest adventure games of all time in less than a year. A small portion of the team led by Michael Z. Land worked in parallel on creating a brand-new system for interactive music management, called iMUSE, which we will discuss in greater detail in the next chapter. The SCUMM engine did not change dramatically, which meant that everyone could focus on the title's creative aspects.

Bigger. Better. Stronger!™

"Well, actually, that's why I'm here on Scabb Island. I'm on a whole new adventure.
— Growing a mustache?
— No. Bigger than that.
— A beard?!?"

The first impression we get from *Monkey Island 2: LeChuck's Revenge* communicates a massive magnitude. We see Guybrush caught in a delicate situation before we flash back to the beginning of the story: when our hero is robbed of everything he has. The action begins in the little village of Woodtick on Scabb Island. While, as in the first game, the objective is clear—find the great treasure known as Big Whoop—it also seems that there is an infinite number of paths to get there. From the start, you can visit several locations on the island, you find a wide variety of people, and you come across numerous

---

124. *Amiga Mania, 1992.*

interactive elements, now carefully hidden under much more detailed graphics. All of this contributes to making the game definitely bigger and more beautiful, but also more difficult. Multiple sub-plots quickly take shape. "There is a lot more dialog in *MI2*. We hit our stride with the dialog puzzles in *MI1* and they really flourished in *MI2*. I wanted to have more locations in *MI2*, hence the multiple islands," says Gilbert.[125] Two islands in the first game increased to four destinations in *Monkey Island 2*.

The second time around, Dave Grossman and Tim Schafer wrote most of the game's dialogue. "Between the two of them, it seemed pretty much equal. They had very different writing styles and it was nice to be able to give certain tasks to them based on the personality of the character they were writing. I was very blessed to have both of them on the project." Meanwhile, Ron Gilbert focused on the scenario, the puzzles, the pacing, and, of course, planning and budgeting. Ultimately, we don't know much about Gilbert's dalliances with the story as the second game matured, other than the fact that he says that the game as we know it is quite similar to the very first version of his script and that the writing of the famous ending was rushed, to say the least: "Now, the thing is, I didn't really have an ending for *Monkey Island 2* for a long time. We were almost done with the game and I still had no ending. I didn't have a bad ending that I hoped to make better, or a mediocre ending. I just had no ending, and I was starting to panic. Now, panic can be an amazing motivator. Panic and fear are often the lubrication of the creative engine. So then, one morning, I was lying in bed and I was just staring at the ceiling, and the ending to *Monkey Island 2* just hit me. [...] It was odd and it was strange, and I knew a lot of people would just hate it. But I also knew a lot of people would love it. [...] So, next morning, I got back to the office and I sat down with Tim, and Dave, and Steve Purcell, and we worked through all the details."[126]

Still, some previews released in video game media at the time provided a different version of the original pitch: the "revenge" in question was supposedly by LeChuck's brother. The idea was that the brother began pursuing Guybrush across the Caribbean to avenge the death of the zombie captain. To this day, the latter version of the story has never been corroborated by any original design document whatsoever, nor was it even confirmed by the developers at the time. In some screen captures from prototypes, we can also see that Guybrush looked younger, was beardless, and was wearing the same white shirt as in the first installment.

125. *https://mixnmojo.com/features/sitefeatures/LucasArts-Secret-History-Monkey-Island-2-Le Chucks-Revenge/6*
126. *https://www.youtube.com/watch?v=Q6IYgWh-qnY*

Ron wanted to put serious pressure on the player via more complex puzzles. He figured that adventure game fans were starting to get accustomed to the mechanics of LucasArts' titles, and so he could afford to set the bar a little higher. However, for novices, he made a radically different decision. Thus, *Monkey Island 2: LeChuck's Revenge* was equipped with an "easy mode," which the developers chose to transparently incorporate into the game design and development of the puzzles. The game box even proudly announced, "Optional easy mode for beginners and magazine reviewers" (Ha!). However, easy mode was only available in the floppy-disk version and was strangely absent from the CD-ROM. According to Ron, the reason for including the easy mode was that, "I wanted there to be a way that someone could play the game and not be stumped by advanced puzzles. The hardcore game players are our bread and butter, but we can't get caught in making games hard to suit these people. In the future, adventure games might be a lot easier and only cost a few dollars (like renting a [VHS video] tape). Until that time we need to release [for] both groups."[127] So, correctly predicting the future of adventure games a few years in advance, and also probably to further distinguish LucasArts from its lifelong rival, Sierra, Gilbert equipped *Monkey Island 2* with a version containing fewer puzzles, characters, and sub-plots. A study conducted at the time showed that most players never finished the adventure games that they purchased. In response to a question about this, Gilbert said of the easy mode, "I don't know if it will change the market, it might change my sales numbers. I agree that most people never finish an adventure game. It's sad because I spent so much time on the game and most people don't see 50% of it. We joke all the time about not doing the last part of the game and no one would notice. I hope with the easy mode that more people will finish and see the whole story." Interestingly, the game was even supposed to have an intermediate difficulty mode, but due to a lack of time, the team only created the easy and difficult modes.

In the end, the game was completed on schedule for a North American release in December 1991, just a little over a year after the first installment in the saga. It was a real feat, a marathon, when you look at the incredible depth, richness, and amplitude of the final product. The PC version (on 11 floppy disks!) included MIDI music and graphics in 256 colors. A year later, the new CD-ROM version was released with reorchestrated music. Initially, the development team had planned to add digitized voices, but that plan was quickly abandoned due to a lack of time. Other platforms received ports of *Monkey Island 2*: the Macintosh, of course, but also an Amiga version in 32 colors with more fluid scrolling and a better soundtrack than the PC version. The Atari ST and Japanese computer FM Towns also got their own versions.

127. *Amiga Mania*, 1992.

Now, I would like to present to you the next chapter in the story of Guybrush Threepwood, an illuminating document written by hand by the pirate himself. The contents are unedited and uncensored. As such, some passages may be offensive to more discerning readers. The author of this book will not be accepting any complaints about this document as he is simply working in the interest of science. Consider yourself forewarned!

The Memoirs of Guybrush Threepwood, Part 2™

In the time following the publication of my first volume of Memoirs, I have found myself much in demand as an author of books, discoverer of lost riches, and highly-regarded after-dinner speaker. Throughout my travels, many have found themselves enlightened, entertained, and overawed by accounts of my adventures—both my epic battle to the death with the Ghost Pirate LeChuck, and the many colorful exploits that marked my career thereafter. Yet none of these tales compares with my greatest adventure to date: my second encounter with the diabolical scoundrel LeChuck, and my discovery of the legendary treasure of Big Whoop. Therefore, at the overwhelming demand of my large and loyal following, I, Guybrush Threepwood, do now take quill in hand once more and recount this tale of daring, cunning, and surprising wit, in the hopes that it will find its way into the hands and hearts of a larger readership. I have set down one version of my latest endeavor: it is the Full and Unexpurgated tale, complete in every detail and most suitable for the bold of heart and stomach. I warrant that the recounting is accurate in every degree. Gentle reader, behold and mark well the tale that follows...[128]

Hi! I'm Guybrush Threepwood. You may remember me from such educational books as "How to Become a Mighty Pirate in Less Than Ten Weeks with Just a Seltzer Bottle and a Rubber Chicken™," or "I, Guybrush T., Formidable Pirate," or my best-selling "How I Vanquished the Zombie Captain LeChuck: A Recipe for Vegan Voodoo Grog™." You may even know me simply because you've followed my adventures closely, like my legions of fans who come from all over the Caribbean to take selfies with me. Or maybe you're one of those many groupies who dream of marrying me,

128. Extract from *The Memoirs of Guybrush Threepwood, Volume II, Monkey Island 2 Hint Book*, Sara Reeder, 1991.

even though they should know that my heart belongs to the goddess Elaine Marley. Oh, Elaine!

Things have been a little rocky with Elaine lately. I'm not sure I understand exactly why we're growing apart, but I get the feeling that she doesn't like my new luscious beard. But I digress... The story I wish to tell you begins on a Caribbean island far, far away... called Scabb Island.

The reason for my presence on that godforsaken island was that, after brilliantly destroying the zombie pirate LeChuck, I needed to pull off a new exploit. And what could be more extraordinary than going out in search of the most famous treasure the world has ever known? A treasure so great that it haunts the nightmares of the most formidable pirates. I speak of the treasure of Big Whoop! But clearly, the treasure was nowhere to be found on Scabb Island, and so I needed to charter a new ship to sail off in search of more promising lands.

With my pockets filled with gold, I headed toward the village of Woodtick. However, on the way, I met a pathetic excuse for a pirate, Largo LaGrande. Let me describe this scoundrel: short, stocky, ugly, and tackily dressed. That crook demanded that I pay him a toll to enter "his territory." And it was only out of pity that I agreed to give him a few coins [Editor's note: In the interest of full disclosure, we must note that, in fact, Mr. Threepwood was robbed of everything he had by Mr. LaGrande]. It became clear to me that the brute ruled the people of Woodtick with an iron fist, and I quickly realized that I would have to take him out of the picture and put an end to his embargo if I wanted to leave Scabb Island.

A chance encounter with my old friend the Voodoo Lady put me on an unexpected quest: I would have to find several items so that she could create for me a voodoo doll in effigy of that squat scallywag. Easy peasy! A bone from Marco LaGrande, his ancestor, taken from the cemetery; a highly toxic slime (his spit, if I'm being honest) from the wretch; something from the rogue's head; and improbably... a brassiere. Once the doll was created, I skillfully got rid of Largo, with the knave fleeing without further ado. Another terrible enemy added to my illustrious record of wins. Finally, I hit it off with Captain Dread, a peaceful mariner on the island who, I'm convinced, was very honored to accompany me on the next leg of my adventure...

We traveled to Phatt Island, where I was sure I would be able to learn something more about the treasure in the famous pirate library. However,

113

my reception on the island was very rough. A big, burly guard led me directly to the island's repugnant governor and I was thrown in prison for absolutely no reason. Apparently, the governor was in cahoots with the late LeChuck. With help from a brave little canine friend, I quickly got myself out of jail. After reaching the library, I was able to get my hands on a precious book: Big Whoop: Unclaimed Bonanza or Myth?™. Here's the most important thing I discovered there: "There were four pirates: Rapp Scallion (the cook), Young Lindy (the cabin boy), Mister Rogers (the first mate), and Captain Marley. They buried their treasure along with plenty of booby traps on a place believed to be called 'Inky' Island. They made a map, which they divided into four pieces, each man taking one. Rapp Scallion later opened the Steamin' Weenie Hut on Scabb Island. It was a huge success, but fell into disrepair when Rapp died in a flash fire. Young Lindy drifted aimlessly, down on his luck, until he mysteriously came into money while panhandling on Booty Island. He used the cash to bankroll an advertising firm, which failed after its gross mishandling of the Gangrene 'n' Honey™ account. Mister Rogers retired off the coast of Phatt Island. He marketed homemade contest grog brewed in a bathtub until his recent disappearance. Captain Marley vanished while sailing in the America's Cup race. His boat was leading at the time."

These invaluable pieces of information put me on the trail of Dinky Island, where the treasure of Big Whoop was hidden. I won't get into the heroic details of how I found the four pieces of the map, but just know that I had to disguise myself in order to once again see the ravishing and audacious Elaine, that I had an unexpected reunion with the skeletons of my parents, who performed a musical number, that I had to briefly bring Rapp Scallion back to life, that I won a prestigious spitting contest fair and square [Editor's note: False!], and that my talents as a freediver worked wonders yet again!

Once I had the four pieces of the map, I had a heck of a time figuring out how to put them together. I'm a man of action, not jigsaw puzzles! So, I paid a visit to my old friend Wally on Scabb Island. Being a cartographer, he asked me to wait a few hours. I used that time to catch up with the Voodoo Lady. Little did I know what was happening while I was away... To my horror, I discovered that poor Wally had been kidnapped by zombie pirates working for an unknown, terrible pirate captain mysteriously called "L." I needed to solve this mystery, free the innocent cartographer, vanquish the bad buy, and, above all, find my precious map! Without a second thought, I slipped into a crate, which, as luck would have it, was to be delivered to the island hideout of the infamous "L."

After a turbulent and tumultuous journey, my crate was dropped in the heart of a macabre fortress. I felt like I'd entered the lion's den, but no matter, I'm far too brave to fear such situations [Editor's note: Ha!] [Author's note: I would appreciate it if my editor would stop his meddling immediately!].

I ventured further and further into the labyrinth of the fortress and before long, I discovered that the lyrics of the song my parents' skeletons sang would actually guide me through the maze! In hindsight, the whole situation was pretty weird and made zero sense. But no matter! The developers had to come up with some way to end this adventure. Finally, I arrived at a vast throne room, where I tried to steal a key shaped like a human skull. However, I was immediately caught in a trap. At that moment, who burst into the room? None other than the infamous, odious, mediocre, mouth-breathing, and apparently-not-as-dead-as-I-thought... Captain LECHUCK!

Incredible. If you're familiar with the previous episode in my adventure, you'll know that I had most definitely vanquished that wretch by spraying him with some voodoo root beer. But there he was, standing in front of me: LeChuck in the (rotting) flesh. Maybe I should've gotten a clue from the title of this episode, LeChuck's Revenge. Along with the zombie pirate, Largo LaGrande arrived too. My two most fearsome enemies united against me. The situation was dire! They took poor Willy and me to the fortress' torture chamber. I was chained up, and LeChuck took his sweet time laying out his diabolical plan for me. He intended to drop me in a vat of boiling acid, then collect my still quivering bones to make himself a chair to sit on. Quite the imagination! I had to get out of my chains and disarm the infernal machine set to plunge me into the acid.

With a few well-aimed loogies, I managed to extinguish the candle that would burn through the rope to fire a pistol, whose bullet was supposed to rebound off a shield, then pop a balloon, which would pump a bellows, which would turn the handle that would plunge us into the acid. After being plunged instead into total darkness and removing our chains, Wally and I made a quick escape. Thankfully, I had on me a small packet of matches. I lit one and we discovered that we had entered the room where LeChuck stored his fireworks, sticks of dynamite, and other homemade bombs.

BOOM!

After a tremendous explosion of unknown origin (the leading theory is that it may have been related to my match coming in contact with the fuse of a bomb), I was literally blown sky-high... and all the way to Dinky Island. Crazy, right?!

I awoke gently on a deserted beach next to an idyllic jungle. Next to me, a chatty parrot named Polly kept repeating the last words of the four pirates who buried Big Whoop on the island. And a bit farther along, I saw the old hermit Herman Toothrot peacefully meditating. I must say, this game recycled a lot of characters.

Herman discovered a new passion for the transcendental philosophy of Taoist Zen Koan. Although I found the subject truly fascinating, I didn't have much time to catch up with my old friend. Thanks to Polly's information, I finally found my way through the jungle to a big X marking the location of the treasure of Big Whoop. I was about to become the greatest pirate of all time! Finally, the treasure was within reach; but just then, the ledge under the chest collapsed, and I found myself stuck, dangling from the end of a rope with the precious Big Whoop in one hand. Three days later, Elaine, who had gone out looking for me, finally reached me and demanded that I tell her the whole story. By that time, I could only hang on for a few more hours. At the end of my tale, the rope finally gave way and I had a dizzying fall into the abyss.

All I can say is, the fall was incredibly rough, even for a strapping lad like myself. I must have hit my head on something because I don't really remember what happened next. All I know is, I had a dream, a strange dream that I will now recount.

I woke up in a strange metal corridor and LeChuck appeared, spitting insults at me. Then, he let out a great laugh and gave me earth-shattering news: "I am your brother!" he said... Those unbelievable words drove me mad. He held up a doll in effigy of me, stabbed it with a pin, and made me suffer agonizing pain. With each pin prick, I was teleported to a different room. Thankfully, I regained my composure and set about quickly making my own voodoo doll, meticulously following the instructions given to me at the beginning of my adventure by the Voodoo Lady. The doll worked like a charm. In fact, it worked so well that I went as far as to rip that miserable zombie's leg off.

With a desperate sob, LeChuck begged me to take off his mask. Upon doing so, I discovered that the terrible pirate was in fact Chuckie! My big brother Chuckie... Then, moments later, we got kicked out of the mysterious tunnel by a custodian, and Chuckie and I met our parents outside. Even as I write this, it all seems insane to me... But in my dream, my parents, who were dressed strangely, had brought my brother and I to what looked like a pirate-themed amusement park called "Big Whoop." What a nightmare... I really must have had quite the bump on the head. Although...

The End

Game design and anecdotes™

In the audio commentary that came with the special edition of *Monkey Island 2: LeChuck's Revenge*, Dave Grossman, Tim Schafer, and Ron Gilbert talk about the game's enigmatic ending:

"**Dave Grossman: I think people might not understand this ending because you have to know a lot about numerology and science, there's a lot of physics.**
— Ron Gilbert: Food processing.
— Tim Schafer: The Fibonacci sequence is incredibly important to this, with all the clues.
— Dave: We went back and forth a lot, or around and around I guess, a lot about the ending. You had it in your head and we were like, 'I don't know, should we really do this?' And we were trying to think of something different that was going to be better. I think I may have actually convinced you to do the ending that we did at dinner one night. [...]
— Ron: I think this ending gets mentioned all the time on, you know, the top 10 best endings of computer games.
— Dave: And it's also mentioned among the top 10 worst endings. It's, like, a very controversial ending. People love it or they hate it.
— Ron: But isn't that perfect, though? I'd almost rather make something that half the people loved and half the people hated, rather than a thing a bunch of people felt mediocre about."

And indeed, the famous ending to *Monkey Island 2* gave rise to a flurry of articles. Was it a dream or reality? Was the eponymous secret of Monkey Island simply the product of a child's imagination? In any case, Ron Gilbert is proud of his choice: "If you want to create something everybody likes, take a picture of a cute puppy and a kitten. Everybody loves puppies. But what have you really told the world? You've told the world that puppies are cute. How have you challenged your audience? What part of their imagination have you fired up? What part of their soul have you stirred and engaged? Now, for me, such a thing is the ending to *Monkey Island 2*. That ending really polarized people. Half the people loved that ending and half the people just hated that ending. And really, nothing can make me happier. [...] Now, to this day, not a week goes by that I do not get one or two hate- and profanity-filled emails from people over that ending. I also get emails from people who tell me how much they loved that ending. That ending really polarized people and that means the ending meant something. I could have done an ending where Guybrush and Elaine live happily ever after, but no one would be talking about that ending 20 years later. No one would be sending me ranty emails about how much they loved how happy Guybrush and Elaine were. Ranty emails really start my day. In a lot of ways, they are my morning coffee."[129]

But let's get back to the start of the game. *Monkey Island 2* opens with a pre-credits scene that was fairly original in that, from there, almost all of the game is a flashback. Guybrush tells Elaine the story of everything that's happened. This is an elegant narrative device that is representative of Ron Gilbert's desire to transcend the classic codes of storytelling in adventure games by introducing the trappings of literary scene-setting and by establishing a particular timeframe.

As with the first game, and in accordance with Gilbert's mantra, the game clearly defines the objectives from its very first bit of dialogue. The ultimate goal is to discover the treasure of Big Whoop, and the first step will be to find a way to sail off and escape from Scabb Island. Guybrush starts the adventure with a short-lived fortune he has earned by working for the circus, probably Fettuccini's circus from the first game. However, more than just a gag, the loss of that money when Guybrush is shaken down by Largo LaGrande (whose name comes from the town where Gilbert grew up, La Grande, Oregon) represents a very peculiar relationship with money in the world of *Monkey Island*. Over the course of his adventures, Guybrush is sometimes rich and sometimes poor, to the point that money seems to have no value at all. After all, the true value in an adventure game is found in objects. An adventure game character only has a future if they have the right objects in their inventory. Nothing,

---

129. *https://www.youtube.com/watch?v=Q6IYgWh-qnY*

or almost nothing, can be purchased in the traditional fashion. Basically, it's the opposite of our reality. Additionally, there's a clever nod to the player's kleptomania, a classic trope of the point & click subgenre, in one of the books in the library. Thus, Gilbert, by putting his puppet Guybrush into the worst possible situations, totally erases the value of the game's gold coins and places value instead in physical objects that are actually useful in life. In this sense, you can think of *Monkey Island* as a sort of communist manifesto. But that's a story for another day.

The game design of *Monkey Island 2*, although very similar, is like a denser version of that of the first game. After the introduction, the player follows a linear progression (the adventure opens up later on) in which the search for items to make a voodoo doll of Largo and then the search for pieces of the map serve as both related objectives and as a way of approaching the game through puzzles and the playing of various roles. However, as we saw in the previous paragraph, Gilbert had a specific idea in mind for his sequel. He was laying the groundwork for a spectacular turn of events, with the goal of giving an identity and solidity to his universe, which diverged from the traditional and corrupted imagery of fantasy pirates. Indeed, a number of visual elements make direct reference to the Disney theme parks. The treehouse in the forest on Booty Island is an exact replica of the Swiss Family Robinson treehouse at Disney World. The tunnels through which the player must navigate at the end and the many references to modern technology are all evidence of the artificial nature of the world of *Monkey Island*. The very nature of the treasure of Big Whoop, which turns out to be an ordinary "E ticket" to an amusement park,[130] the many anachronisms, the inability for the player to die, the many references to contemporary pop culture (*Indiana Jones*, *Star Wars*, *Terminator 2*) are all elements which take on new meaning in light of the adventure's ending.

From the beginning, Guybrush Threepwood lives in an artificial fantasy world, as if the player had gotten out of their little boat in the Pirates of the Caribbean ride at Disneyland to stroll through the scenery, with no danger, but with limits that can't be crossed. Really, all of that fits perfectly with Ron Gilbert's original intentions when he first got the idea for the *Monkey Island* universe. We previously discussed this in chapter five. "Your boat [in the Pirates of the Caribbean ride] keeps you moving through the adventure, but I've always wished I could get off and wander around, learn more about the characters, and find a way onto those pirate ships." French scholar Charlotte Courtois gives the perfect example of the scene in which Guybrush Threepwood has to capture Stan in his used coffin store. When the player enters the room,

---

130. The Disney E Ticket is a special ticket that allows you to access all of the amusement park's attractions.

they are automatically put on a fixed track, like when you're on a Disney ride, and during a few seconds of dialogue, the cursor reappears so that the player has the opportunity to "get off the tracks," if you will. "Through this puzzle, the game invites the player to live out the fantasy of breaking the ride's car free from its tracks, to move around freely through the scenery. Still, while the player's character is freer after trapping Stan, they remain limited by the borders of the walk box.[131] The parallel with the management of space at theme parks is very strong in this sequence. It allows us to understand space (in *Monkey Island*) as a function of both game design and storytelling."[132] Finally, Charlotte Courtois concludes: "Beyond being pirate games, the first few episodes of the *Monkey Island* series are adventure games *about* adventure games. The elimination of the specific management of space in Stan's rooms[133] reflects a greater interest for storytelling than for provoking thought." Gilbert's *Monkey Island* games were experimental hatcheries and clearly a laboratory for the major rules that would govern video game storytelling and the way of presenting stories to players in the years that followed. With regard to that, as we will see, the ambition was enormous and would gradually crumble in the subsequent games.

In order to avoid redundancy and transforming everything into nothing more than a gimmick, the emblematic insult fights of the first game were purposely set aside in the sequel. Still, few adventure games have been carried by the richness of their dialogue like *LeChuck's Revenge*. Funny, clever, sarcastic, but never mean, the lines written by Schafer and Grossman showcase the unparalleled comedic and writing talents of the two authors. Like in the hilarious scene in which Guybrush, lost in the jungle on Dinky Island, can call the LucasArts hint line to ask for help from the unfriendly Chester and to ask him the most absurd questions. This Chester character was based on an actual person on the team: it was none other than Khris Brown, who had since become the head of customer support: "I became the manager of the group, and had a fantastic team of collaborators who were passionately committed to ensuring that LucasArts Customer and Product Support stood for the ethos of what we all believed was the heart of the *Star Wars* films: ethics, integrity, service, compassion, and kindness," she recalls. "We answered questions from people ranging in age from 8 to 80, and would sometimes spend an hour

---

131. A technical term tied to point & click games, the "walk box" is the zone within which the player's avatar can move around.

132. Extract from *Jeu d'aventure graphique, parc à thèmes et XIXᵉ siècle dans la construction de l'espace des premiers Monkey Island de LucasArts. Disneyland, le secret de l'île aux singes ?* [Graphic adventure games, theme parks, and the 19th century in the construction of space in LucasArts' first few Monkey Island games. Could Disneyland be the secret of Monkey Island?], Charlotte Courtois (Université Sorbonne Nouvelle Paris).

133. "Rooms" are spaces, or screens, in which the player can move about in the game.

or more helping someone set up their computer so that they could play our games." Larry adds: "We all felt that it was a privilege to work with people in the beginning of their relationship with computer games, and sometimes with computers themselves. Technology and games were second nature to us, but could be very scary for older people or for parents who had an upset child who couldn't easily get past a certain puzzle." It was Tim Schafer who came up with the famous Chester gag.

The name was a twist on the word "tester." "Tim Schafer gave me the nickname "Chester" because it rhymed with "Tester." In addition to spending time helping customers, I would test the games to ensure they would make sense for the players, and I would send my comments to the teams if I thought there would be any stumbling points. Working with the players so directly meant that I had a different perspective than the official testers, who were seeking programming bugs. [...] Player experience is the basis of everything I do. I wish I could thank every frustrated veteran upset about Secret Weapons of the Luftwaffe's[134] imperfections and every child who didn't understand [LeChuck's] sense of humor for teaching me what is important!"

There was some disagreement within the studio, and Brown explains, "I was personally opposed to the charging of a fee for the hint line, and charging for it wasn't something that was considered necessary by the overall Lucasfilm organization, which is very generous with its fans. A business case was made that convinced some managers who were above me to capitalize on the trend of charging for hints in order to recoup operating costs. This is why the voice that originally appears in the first voiced version of the Monkey Island II games sounds displeased."

When asked the age-old question "What is the secret of Monkey Island?" Brown confided that the agents on the other end of the Hint Line didn't have any insight into answer themselves, so when people were really insistent about it, the terse reply was simply that Hint Line agents weren't authorized to divulge such confidential information. If they were talking to really unhappy children, they would send them a free T-shirt, and that would usually fix everything.

A few more fun facts:

☉ The character Kate Capsize was inspired by Kate Capshaw, the wife of Steven Spielberg at the time, who is known in particular for playing the role of Willie in *Indiana Jones and the Temple of Doom*. In fact, there are numerous references to *Indiana Jones*. For example, Guybrush complains, "I hate

---

134. The game *Secret Weapon of the Luftwaffe* was a flight simulator set during World War II, developed by Lucasfilm Games and released in 1991.

snakes,"[135] and uses a rope to swing across the precipice to reach Big Whoop. Similarly, there's a flood of *Star Wars* references, most notably the "I am your brother!" ending twist, which copied the famous dialogue from the end of *Star Wars: Episode V - The Empire Strikes Back* almost word for word.

◎ In the costume shop, there are numerous references to all sorts of characters (including: Bart Simpson, Bullwinkle, Fred Flintstone, and Huckleberry Hound), but with off-the-wall alternative names, probably due to the previously mentioned copyright concerns.

◎ The library on Phatt Island hides little nuggets of humor among the titles of the books, with so many references that it would take too long to list them all here. I'll just give you a handful of examples: *The Time I Blew Up LeChuck*, *When I Blew Up LeChuck*, *Where I Blew Up LeChuck*, and *Why I Blew Up LeChuck*. In the same library, according to the book in the category "Three-Headed Monkey," a recurring gag in the series, the monkey in question is supposedly the son of the Loch Ness monster.

◎ Poor Wally, who disappears after LeChuck's fortress explodes, was supposed to appear in a cutscene in which we would see him on a raft, lost in the middle of the ocean. His monocle was supposed to fall into the water and, in an attempt to recover it, Wally was supposed to disappear beneath the surface. However, in the end, the scene was cut because the team judged it to be too cruel.

◎ *Monkey Island 2* was able to afford the luxury of being self-referential. For example, if you choose the name Herman Toothrot when you sign up for a library card, you can only borrow three books. Indeed, in the first game, the old hermit was notified that he needed to return his overdue library books.

◎ Captain Dread tells Guybrush about his misadventures with the cannibals on Monkey Island: he lost his companion, who, as it turns out, was the head of the navigator who helped Guybrush make his way through LeChuck's secret cavern.

◎ At the very end of the game, if Guybrush takes the elevator and opens the door, he finds himself in a fake background that's a copy of Mêlée Island in *The Secret of Monkey Island*. In the same place, the grog vending machine brings back painful memories for anyone who completed the first game. Indeed, it's the same machine on which Guybrush landed at the end of *The Secret of Monkey Island* during his battle with LeChuck.

◎ The "wanted" poster on Phatt Island showing Guybrush's image lists crimes committed by the player as they're carried out throughout the game.

---

135. A famous line from *Indiana Jones and the Raiders of the Lost Ark*.

Reception and reviews™

Of all the games in the series, *Monkey Island 2: LeChuck's Revenge* is invariably cited as the most emblematic, the most successful, and the most brilliant. Enjoying a cult following today, the series also has the unusual distinction of having been recognized as being exceptional from the moment it was released. As we will see, the game's remarkable qualities were actually praised by testers at the time.

French magazine *Génération 4*, which had previously given a thumbs-up to the first episode, gave *Monkey Island 2* a rating of 96% and had no shortage of compliments: "In addition to its perfect playability, *Monkey Island 2* also shines bright thanks to its comical situations. It is without a doubt the funniest game that I've played. The dialogue is sublime, always putting a smile on your face and sometimes sending you rolling on the floor laughing... That's a rare enough occurrence to make the game noteworthy. The animations of the characters, with their many expressions, add to the situational comedy of numerous scenes. But that's not all... *LeChuck's Revenge* is the first 256-color VGA game from Lucasfilm, with backgrounds scanned from actual drawings. It's even more beautiful than Sierra's games, with a particularly great style for the backgrounds. [...] *LeChuck's Revenge* is perfect from a technical perspective! All in all, it's a fascinating, original, funny, spellbinding adventure game that's accessible to all and is superbly produced. As such, it's not a stretch to say that *Monkey Island 2* is THE BEST ADVENTURE GAME ever made for a microcomputer. The Lucasfilm magic is clearly just as present in the studio's games as it is in its films. I can't wait for *Monkey Island 3* [if only he knew]."[136]

The other leading French video game magazine, *Joystick*, was equally enthusiastic, though more reserved: "I'll remind you, *Monkey Island* [1] was a funny and exciting game. This sequel is at least as much so. [...] It is undeniably very beautiful, technically and artistically speaking: the color palettes chosen are superb. Many nighttime scenes give you the chance to admire the effects of reflections and lights. Likewise, the screens are filled with details. As for the animations, again, there are no problems to be found. [...] It's fast and fluid, and the programmers added numerous details that bring every single scene to life. It goes without saying, the command system is very convenient, since all you have to do is click on an action word or even directly on an object on the screen to interact with the environment. In short, this is a perfect game. 94%."[137] Unlike with the first episode in the series, the magazine *Tilt* was decidedly more enthusiastic: "Did you like *The Secret of Monkey Island*? If so, you will love the second installment in the adventures of Guybrush

---

136. *Génération 4*, No. 40, January 1992, Stéphane Lavoisard.
137. *Joystick*, No. 23, January 1992, Cyrille Baron (Moulinex).

Threepwood, who this time heads out in search of a legendary treasure. All you buccaneers, it's time to set sail: the flagship of Captain Lucasfilm is weighing anchor once again for a memorable voyage, equipped with sumptuous graphics and an ingenious new music system. To your positions, mateys! 18/20."[138]

In English-language media, reviews were just as excellent. The magazine *Computer and Video Games* dedicated three pages to Ron Gilbert's game: "Fab! Ace! Topper! Cushty! Just a small selection of words which describe my view of *Monkey Island 2: LeChuck's Revenge*. The first *Monkey Island* game was great—maybe even better than *Indiana Jones and the Last Crusade*—but this, this soars way over its prequel in terms of quality and quantity. It really is a massive adventure, but at the same time totally absorbing. I managed to finish the first section in what I thought was perhaps an hour, but imagine my surprise when I glanced at my watch to find that three hours had passed and I'd missed my bus and the pubs were shut—and imagine my disbelief when I told myself that I wasn't bothered because I'd enjoyed myself so much! Lucasfilm's new iMUSE music system is incredible and simply has to be witnessed to appreciate just what a difference it makes to the overall package. [...] Everything about *Monkey Island 2* says quality, so buy it! 96%."[139]

In spite of great anticipation and rave reviews, when the game was released, it didn't sell as well as expected. Years later, Tim Schafer provided *Edge* magazine with a bit of information about sales. With just over 25,000 copies distributed, *Monkey Island 2* was a disappointment for LucasArts, which had hoped to quadruple that number within the same period. Schafer recalled that the top brass of LucasArts had told him and the team that the *Monkey Island* series was a failure and that they should focus on something else.[140] Above all, the game's renown came from widespread piracy (very fitting for a game about pirates!). For LucasArts, just as for Ron Gilbert's team, it was time to move on to something else and let Guybrush and his friends rest, at least for a time... In spite of the game's open ending, which was one of the most improbable cliffhangers in video game history, LucasArts had to sail off in search of new horizons!

Legacy and story design™

While *Monkey Island 2: LeChuck's Revenge* received a symphony of praise for its production and humor, at this point, you may be wondering why the game is considered one of the greatest, if not *the* greatest, adventure games

---

138. *Tilt* magazine, No. 99, February 1992, Piotr Korolev.
139. *Computer and Video Games*, No. 123, February 1992, Paul Rand.
140. *Edge*, No. 204, August 2009.

ever created. And why your grandma is always saying that it's the best game she's ever played. And why you invariably find it on lists of the top ten greatest games of all time. The answer is simply because Ron Gilbert's game was an undeniable gem of story design. Allow me to explain.

The Secret of Monkey Island resulted from the direct application of the laws established by Gilbert in his seminal article "Why Adventure Games Suck and What We Can Do About It."[141] As such, the first episode marked a revolution in the point & click subgenre, or even in the adventure game genre writ large. *The Secret of Monkey Island* laid the foundation; it made the creator think deeply about his way of designing his own game. Gilbert tried to highlight the important elements for telling a good story while maintaining the aspects of a video game that make it fun. *Monkey Island 2,* on the other hand, was a revolution in story design with constraints. Budget constraints, time constraints, and scenario constraints.

First, the time constraints: as I'll remind you, *Monkey Island 2* was developed in just one year, though, granted, it was in an era when development times were not nearly as long as they are today. But regardless, for such a long and detail-rich final product, it was a real feat.

Second, the budget constraints: as the studio increasingly set its sights on *Star Wars*, budgets allocated to swashbucklers of the point & click subgenre got much tighter (remember that *Monkey Island 2* was mostly created by three people). And like all good project managers must do, Gilbert had to optimize every resource, every location, and every animation to the max without having negative impacts on the script as originally planned. Easier said than done. In concrete terms, this meant that the team found themselves with, on the one hand, a sheet listing all of the game's puzzles they'd come up with and, on the other hand, a list of locations ("rooms") that the team had created and in which they had to tell their story. They then had to place each puzzle into the rooms while trying to maintain consistency with the game's universe, but also with the scenario, in order to avoid clashes between the gaming aspects and story aspects.[142] They also had to take care to maintain appropriate timing for when the elements for solving the puzzles would be presented to the player. This is where the scenario constraints come in, creating a real headache. Thankfully, Ron Gilbert excels in that kind of situation! This is where the art of story design plays a crucial role.

But let's be absolutely clear: we're talking about an era when none of this had been theorized about. There were no schools teaching video game storytelling.

141. See chapter 4.
142. Dissonance between gameplay and storytelling is felt when there's a difference in how something is handled in gameplay phases and how it's handled in storytelling phases. For example, Nathan Drake (*Uncharted*) is a kind and clever hero, but in gameplay, he'll happily kill hundreds of people at the drop of a hat.

And few academic publications took any interest in the subject. For that reason, the ingenuity of *Monkey Island 2* is absolutely dazzling.

The usage of story design in point & click games, especially in *Monkey Island*, in which anachronisms become an acceptable form of dissonance between gameplay and story, is developed to contextualize the puzzles for the player. Through the game's design, the player must be able to understand what's expected of them, because for any good creator, it's unthinkable to leave the player to wander aimlessly, as had been the case in the most recent Sierra title at the time.[143] For example, a telescope sitting on a table where it has no business being will undoubtedly pique the player's curiosity, and the player will then jump on it and grab it, even if they don't yet know exactly what to do with it. Since the object appears to be out of place, it seems obvious that it must be used for something. Conversely, in real life, a person won't necessarily see a telescope sitting on a table as an opportunity to move up in the world... The story design of an adventure game is very specific to that exact game.

As such, objects must "tell" the player something, and in *Monkey Island 2*, this concept is put to work brilliantly. In the game's universe of eccentric pirates, we know perfectly well that nothing is actually going to go as planned. For example, the Voodoo Lady tells us that we need to create a voodoo doll and that, in order to do so, we need to find four ingredients tied to Largo LaGrande: "something of the Thread, something of the Head, something of the Body, and something of the Dead." We immediately realize that this will not be such an easy task as it may have initially seemed. It's the age-old clash between the art of showing things and the art of telling a story. Of course, it's only by immersing yourself in the game's deliciously comedic universe that you can dream of using a bra, a wig, a loogie, and a bone from Largo's ancestor, freshly dug up from the cemetery, to solve this particular puzzle. That's the trick of story design: maintaining overall coherence that allows you to create complex puzzles while also keeping total consistency within the original universe. All that while also taking the opportunity to tell us things about the character of Largo, without having to actually say anything explicitly. Does Largo wear bras? Does he collect them? Gilbert manages to subtly make use of the same puzzle a second time during the final battle against LeChuck, in which the player must remember that they need four ingredients to create the life-saving voodoo doll.

Contrary to this object-driven design, the adventure game must capitalize on its second major asset to tell its story: the backgrounds. If the player passes through a place like an infirmary, and later needs a syringe, they will undoubtedly remember that perfect place to find it. They will then go to confirm their hypothesis, and the background will be used as an element of

---

143. This is an official troll©.

gameplay. However, the infirmary will still retain its original purpose: to be a background used to convey a subplot to the player. This is known as "environmental storytelling." And I can also mention a third, more meta, way of using this background. An infirmary in the pirate universe of *Monkey Island*? It gives a clue about the reality of the titular "secret."

To cap it all off, Gilbert, because of the abovementioned constraints, optimized each location so that they could be used at different points in the game for completely different quests, like the bar in the village of Woodtick, on Scabb Island, for example.

It's a subtle blend of realistic, linear story design and procedural or random story design specific to the video game, for which a trail was blazed by *Monkey Island 2: LeChuck's Revenge*. Ron Gilbert managed to create the perfect alchemy between the fun of the puzzles, the coherence of his universe, the progression of his story, and indirect storytelling about a character, simply by making you go pick up a bra from a laundry business...

And the game is filled with such clever tricks. You have to understand that in 1991, this was earth-shattering in the world of video game creation and theory! While that richness is transparent for the player, it also influences the depth of the universe. And for all game creators (no matter the genre), because of that, *Monkey Island 2* became an inexhaustible source of inspiration, including to this day, for all sorts of games, from the freest open-world games to the most linear first-person shooters.

I want to feel your soul being ripped slowly from your body! Muahahaha!

Chapter 8: iMUSE™! Interactive Reggae Music Man!™

Monkeys are listening™

If you bring up *Monkey Island* with a bunch of old-time gamers, there's a strong likelihood that one of them will attempt to hum the handful of notes of the main theme, while another will start whistling LeChuck's militant tune. The series has its own place in the pantheon of famous video game themes, alongside the likes of *Super Mario Bros.* and *Zelda*. The famous "pirate reggae" has left a never-ending echo in the minds of all those who have wandered along the shores of Mêlée Island. Undoubtedly thanks to its original style—drastically different from pompous symphonic ballads or rock 'n' roll tunes, more evolved and lyrical than the disgraceful beeps of the Sierra games—the music of *Monkey Island* conveys the game's unusual personality: humor, irony, nostalgia, and a certain epic feeling. We have Michael Z. Land to thank for that. Land is a brilliant theorist of electronic music, as well as a genius computer developer and composer who's well versed in both classical and rock music.

Michael Z. Land™

Young Michael's parents signed him up for piano lessons when he was just five years old. However, the rigidity of classical music didn't sit well with the boy's imagination, and he traded his keyboard for an electric bass and joined an experimental rock group at the age of 13. In 1979, Land began studying music at Harvard University, with a special focus on electronic music. As an enthusiast of music theory and research, as well as a fan of Beethoven, Michael Land proved to be a talented artist with multiple strengths, and he ultimately graduated with honors. Sensing that a revolution was underway, the young man began studying computer programming alongside music. At the time, there was theory on the subject, but the tools were still primitive. Still, Land was sure that he could adapt the specific applied concepts of classical music to digital music. In 1987, he began his career at Lexicon as a technician specializing in audio processors. While there, he developed a complete operating system for using tools in MIDI format. In April 1990, while production of *The Secret of Monkey Island* was in full swing, Michael Z. Land joined Ron Gilbert's team and was given just five months to write all of the game's musical tracks.

Music makes up half a game™

Just like Ron Gilbert, Michael Z. Land wanted to once again stretch the limits of the adventure game genre: "I was the head of music and sound at LucasArts from 1990 to 2000. [...] When I started at LucasArts, there were about 30 people in the company. When I left, there were about 350. Over that period of time, that original core team, especially the project leaders [Ron Gilbert, David Fox, Noah Falstein], had this incredible vision for pushing the envelope of what games could do. And so, the audio and music people—myself being the first, and then everyone else who arrived—were swept up in that vision. And, of course, ultimately, it was the game team's reflection of George Lucas' attitude toward filmmaking. So, it ultimately was working within that overall ethic, and the creative quality that myself and Peter [McConnell] and Clint [Bajakian] sort of established as a foothold when we started out, we really wanted to maintain that level, so that every person we brought in individually, we really wanted them to have something really special to offer as a creative vision. A lot of times it was in the sound design realm. [...] The creative side of the sound design was just as important. So, we basically said, 'let's bring in people who are sonically as creative as we are musically.' And we also wanted to make sure that people had the ability to deal with the vagaries of scheduling and the amorphous nature of game development in the '90s."[144] Starting from Lucasfilm's earliest adventure games, the quality of the studio's music was unanimously praised by the media, whether for adaptations of themes by John Williams (*Indiana Jones*, etc.) or for original creations. "For the first five, six, seven years, for some period of time, I was included in the weekly project leader meeting in which they would discuss whatever their struggles and issues and visions were for whatever the games were they were working on. Let me tell you, those were some of the most fascinating, most amazing discussions I've heard in my life about what games are. To include the composer-sound designer person in that discussion was a great nod from those guys, and that gives you some idea of the culture there [at LucasArts]." That idea may seem

---

144. Interview presented by the Department of Technology and Applied Composition of the San Francisco Conservatory of Music: *https://www.youtube.com/watch?v=-0EqG6RYn9Y*

perfectly ordinary today, but it was a philosophical revolution when the games
were created. Indeed, up until the very late '80s when the first sound cards
became available for PCs, video games only offered simple melodies played
through the computer's "buzzer."[145] The rise of dedicated hardware, then the
CD-ROM, made it possible to bring video games up to the same level as other
audiovisual arts.

iMUSE™

The transition from *The Secret of Monkey Island* to *Monkey Island 2: LeChuck's
Revenge* came with the greatest technical revolution in video game music
since the first beeps in early video games: interactive music. Michael Z. Land
comments: "The motivation for bringing [interactive music] into games really
happened, for me anyway, at a very specific moment working on *Monkey Island 1*
where there was some situation, I think it was the sword fight actually, where
I had some pretty simple ideas for how the music should change during the
sword fight, and there was just no way to do it with the existing audio system,
and it was really solving that problem that was the real impetus behind incorporating all of the flexibility we had for the interactive music." So, Michael Z.
Land came up with the Interactive Music Streaming Engine (iMUSE). "iMUSE
started out as a MIDI-based interactive music system, and it eventually
evolved to include sound and digital audio music. Also, in parallel with that,
there was a migration away from more low-level control up to a much more
high-level graphical interface for the composer. [The idea] came very directly
out of working on *Monkey Island 1: The Secret of Monkey Island*. It was a really
fun game and there was some really cool music use, but at that time, in the
industry, the tradition really was to play a cue for a minute or two, and then
you, the player, would experience a half-hour, hour, two hours of silence, and
then you would get another cue for a minute or two. It just seemed like games
could have a lot more than that. So, we made the fairly radical commitment,
when *Monkey Island 2* came around the next year, to actually 'pave the game
in wall-to-wall music,' and in the process, to make the music conform to the
gameplay experience as closely as we could. Those two commitments were
really the motivation behind iMUSE."[146] His colleague Clint Bajakian, who went
on to compose the fabulous soundtracks for *Outlaws*[147] and *Uncharted: Golden*

---

145. Well before sound cards became available, PCs provided sound via a "buzzer," or PC speaker,
a little speaker directly connected to the motherboard, capable of emitting very simple sounds.
Producing an actual melody through the buzzer was a bit of a miracle.
146. *https://www.youtube.com/watch?v=-0EqG6RYn9Y*
147. A Wild West-themed first-person shooter by LucasArts, released in 1997 for the PC.

Abyss,[148] adds: "I would say that Michael envisioned iMUSE in the beginning and then brought Peter McConnell aboard, who really helped to shape it from both the creative and technical standpoints, and there were more creative and technical contributions over the years by people like Michael McMahon. But I came aboard and kind of functioned as the guinea pig. I was a layman when it came to programming, but I was a composer and a software user, so many of the concepts and things like terminology were run by me for comment, which I appreciated. Working with iMUSE gave an amazingly powerful edge over creating an adaptive score." The team created iMUSE with the same basic goal in mind as they had with SCUMM: to simplify technical aspects in order to allow the creatives to quickly and easily produce games. This technique really paid off in the long run, given the longevity of the system. "I worked on the low-level system stuff [i.e., the in-house machine programming language]; [Peter McConnell] worked on a tool we called Q-Tip."[149] Clint Bajakian adds: "All of us back then had obviously appreciated film and film score, and of course, it's a linear format where the music cue adheres to every frame of the film, and we wanted to see if we could achieve that in a nonlinear domain where you really didn't know what would happen." However, in spite of their great talent, the LucasArts audio team didn't realize the Mt. Everest of work they would have to climb in order to achieve their ambitions.

Hell is Woodtick™

Michael Z. Land recalls: "[*Monkey Island 2*] was probably the least efficient game score that any of us ever worked on in terms of cost per minute and man-hours involved, but it certainly hit a nice bell that we then could try to get back to in more efficient ways over the years. Sort of the most extreme, extravagant place was Woodtick [on Scabb Island], which I think was five, or six, or seven satellite rooms off of a central walking area, and so that was a really good test of the system because we had these things called 'jump hooks,' which means you associate a condition with a number, and then you pepper your music with messages that say, 'when you hit that number in this spot, jump to this place in your MIDI file.' And so, using that technology, it allowed the capability to have a different musical ending written for every couple of measures." In theory, every single part of the game in Woodtick would offer a different overall soundtrack. Imagine how, according to the

---

148. A game released for the PS Vita, from the famous Naughty Dog series, developed by Bend Studios in 2011.
149. Because the previous year, there had been a tool called "Earwax," and so the team thought their new tool could "clean up the sound a little bit."

responses to certain bits of dialogue in the game, the system would have to start an intermediary MIDI track at a certain point so that it could then blend with the MIDI track for the central hub of Woodtick. "That was a ridiculous amount of work. [...] Hundreds of little snippets just for one little section of the game. And that was just, like, OK, we never did that again. That was just too much." Indeed, the little village of Woodtick, built out of shipwrecks, serves as a sort of tutorial for players just entering the universe of *Monkey Island 2*. And that player is likely to move constantly back and forth between locations in the village. From the sweet, inoffensive melody of Wally the Cartographer's office, to the high-pitched organ music of the path through the shipwrecks, to the more rough and martial march of the carpenter's back room, the sound evolves as Guybrush moves around the area. So many different melodies based on similar rhythms, but which must fit perfectly together without any discontinuity or discordant notes. Clint Bajakian remembers that Michael Land had a very complex job of composing all the music for Woodtick while considering how the player might behave. In addition to composing the main tracks and transitions, "there was the logic, there was the guarding against player exploitation. So if a player went in and out of the barbershop, would they cause the music to lurch and ping-pong back and forth in an unattractive way? And the answer is no, there were all kinds of layers of logic that protected against the music doing anything unnatural." Explaining that Land had to create an absurd number of different tracks, Clint Bajakian adds that "The punchline is that after all this hard work and all this benchmark achievement, it was done so well that no one noticed. We got no word back from the industry or from the critics or from anybody that this was going on." According to Michael Land, "For the beginning of the game, I wanted the music to sound like what you'd hear coming out of a radio if you were walking down a street on a Caribbean Island. Scabb Island has a light, happy theme, but as the game progresses—and LeChuck becomes more prominent—the musical themes turn darker, more sinister. Then there are other areas where the music sounds really wacky, more like a 1950s cartoon."[150] When lined up one after another, the musical loops in Woodtick and their variations add up to a total of over 20 hours of music! In the end, the player only hears about a tenth of that. So, if you want to do justice to the monumental work that it took to create the iMUSE system, take ten minutes and go walk all across Woodtick. You'll notice how the music adapts and changes according to your movements, with remarkable fluidity.

---

150. *The Adventurer*, No. 3 (fall 1991), "iMUSE Brings Interactive Sound to Games."

Pirate Reggae™

The work of Michael Z. Land can be described as being very eclectic. And that's precisely what has given *Monkey Island*'s music a personality like none other in the video game world. For each of the games, Land jotted down some notes based on the initial design documents and chose the ambiances of his tracks accordingly. The result was a predominant musical genre that he decided to blend with other influences. In the *Monkey Island* universe, Caribbean music is featured most prominently. Land used a lot of woodwinds and marimbas. Then, he prepared several styles of ambiance, developing relatively complex tracks that could be played in a loop without interfering with the story or breaking the player's concentration. The composer infused his melodies with a heavy influence from traditional sea chanties. He blended European folk music with Central American instruments and an electric guitar using rhythms typical of reggae music. In so doing, Land invented the "pirate reggae" subgenre.

With *The Curse of Monkey Island*, Land made a transition from his previous work to the new technical capabilities offered by the most common machines at the time. No more MIDI music; Land took advantage of advancements in sound compression to offer symphonic pieces, using many simultaneous tracks and faithful playback of the sound of the original instruments. This only further amplified the gentleness, emotion, and finesse of the melodies.

From the very first game and—we must acknowledge—reaching a high point with *The Curse of Monkey Island*, Michael Z. Land and his team produced some absolutely superb tracks. Some rousing (*Monkey Island 1*: "The Scumm Bar Theme," *Monkey Island 3*: "Main Theme"), some deeply nostalgic or powerfully reggae (*Monkey Island 3*: "In the Belly of the Snake"), at times incredibly epic (*Monkey Island 3*: "Rollercoaster of Death") or simply tragicomic ("LeChuck's Theme"). The composers made use of acoustic instruments and sounds rarely heard in video games, like the melodeon or the oboe, and, like Prokofiev for his *Peter and the Wolf*, associated each character with a recurring theme.

Michael Z. Land explains: "I've always had a three-pronged musical background. Rock music: you know, Grateful Dead, Hendrix, all that kind of stuff—reggae, love that; classical: Beethoven, Wagner, and a lot of the early Renaissance stuff; and then electronic stuff, which definitely tied into the programming side. So, really, the wonderful thing about coming to LucasArts was that it tied into all three of those really well. So, the way *Monkey Island* emerged—I mean, such a hilarious game; really cool graphics, beautiful graphics. [...] More broadly speaking, the reggae-pirate intersection, that was really Ron Gilbert's brainchild, and it really works. It works thematically in the game and it just worked musically as well—the English folk song and the reggae groove just went together really well."

A special mention is deserved for the extraordinary combination of verbal sparring and musical number in *The Curse of Monkey Island* entitled "A Pirate I Was Meant to Be," which has to be the greatest and stupidest bit of musical gameplay in all of video game history.

"Haggis: We're a band of vicious pirates!
— Edward: A sailin' out to sea.
— Bill: When you hear our gentle singing...
— Haggis: You'll be sure to turn and flee!
— Guybrush: Oooh... this is just ridiculous.
(...)
— All: A pirate I was meant to be!
— All: Trim the sails and roam the sea!" [151]

I'm not bald! I just like
feeling the warm wind of
Hell on my scalp...

151. *A Pirate I Was Meant to Be*, a popular song of the Barbery Coast Barbershop Quartet (*The Curse of Monkey Island*, 1997).

Chapter 9: The end of an era™

In spite of disappointing sales for *Monkey Island 2: LeChuck's Revenge*, the period that from its release in December 1991 up until the early 2000s is unanimously considered a prosperous decade for LucasArts. It's known for being the period of the studio's great classics. However, it was also a period of big changes for the studio. As I mentioned in chapter six of this book, Lucasfilm became LucasArts, but the company's new orientation toward sales and profits didn't totally kill all of the studio's creativity in the cradle. Between 1992 and 2002, out of a total 55 titles released by LucasArts, a whopping 34 of them were tied to *Star Wars*.[152]

That said, not everyone was on board with the change. Chief among the dissenters was Ron Gilbert, who from the time that production of *Monkey Island 2* ended was thirsty for a new adventure. So, the brilliant game designer jumped ship in early 1992. "It will always be Lucasfilm Games™ to me, never LucasArts. They changed the name a year or so before I left when they rolled a bunch of divisions into this new company called LucasArts and the games group was one of them. [...] It's hard for me not to be sad. I haven't worked there since 1992, but it was still home to me. I grew up there. I learned just about everything I know about designing games there. I became a real programmer there. I made lifelong friends there. Eight of the most memorable and influential years of my life were spent there. I would not be who I am today without Lucasfilm Games."[153]

Ron Gilbert went off to found the studio Humongous Entertainment with producer Shelley Day in Bothell, Washington, on March 2, 1992. There, he continued to create traditional point & click games, almost all targeted at children, including successful series like *Putt-Putt*, *Freddi Fish*, *Pajama Sam*, and *Fatty Bear*. It's funny to note that most of those games were created using the SCUMM engine. In 1996, Gilbert launched an "adult" division of his studio called Cavedog Entertainment, whose teams were mostly made up of former

---

152. Including, but not limited to: *Star Wars: The Empire Strikes Back*, *Star Wars: X-Wing*, *Super Star Wars 2*, *Star Wars Chess*, *Star Wars: Rebel Assault*, *Super Star Wars 3*, *Star Wars: TIE Fighter*, *Star Wars: Dark Forces*, *Star Wars: Rebel Assault II*, *Star Wars: Shadows of the Empire*, *Star Wars: Yoda Stories*, *Star Wars: X-Wing vs. TIE Fighter*, *Star Wars: Jedi Knight*, *Star Wars: Masters of Teräs Käsi*, *Star Wars: Rebellion*, *Star Wars: Rogue Squadron*, *Star Wars: Episode 1*, etc.
153. *http://www.grumpygamer.com*

Squaresoft USA employees. They produced the successful strategy game franchise *Total Annihilation*.[154] For Humongous' more modest productions, Gilbert filled every role: producer, designer, developer, scenario writer, and business manager, in a laudable effort to show honesty and sincerity toward his art. He had the freedom that he'd feared losing at LucasArts and that he had always searched for.

At LucasArts, Ron's departure was synonymous with change. Thankfully, team members were ready to take on new responsibilities. All of the original game designers were given projects, including Dave Grossman, Tim Schafer, Hal Barwood, Steve Purcell, Sean Clark, and Brian Moriarty. And since another *Monkey Island* was officially off the table, the students from the "school" of Ron Gilbert had the opportunity to express their own creativity. Over the course of a decade, they churned out an avalanche of titles, each one more glorious and incredible than the last: *Indiana Jones and the Fate of Atlantis*, *Day of the Tentacle*, *Sam and Max Hit the Road*, *Full Throttle*, and *The Dig*.

The state of the market in 1995™

The bitter realization that came with the release of *The Dig* (lukewarm reviews and a catastrophic development process, see p. 307) couldn't be ignored: the video game market was undergoing a transformation. The golden age of 2D games with dazzling pixels had come to an end. New consoles were coming onto the market, offering new graphics with a flood of polygons, symphonic soundtracks, and games that were fast, frenetic, and ultra-fast-paced. And audiences flocked to the new machines. As such, unsurprisingly, adventure games, with their fixed screens and their slow, literary storytelling, began a very slow but relentless decline in the hearts of players. In 1994, it was essentially *Star Wars: Rebel Assault* and its spectacular success (on CD-ROM and its awful SEGA-CD version) that ultimately saved LucasArts from bankruptcy. In spite of its inept controls and the lack of anything special about the game, *Rebel Assault* was visually stunning for new owners of a CD-ROM drive and provided a technological proof of concept for a market ready to shake off the pixelized and childish image that had long stuck to it. In 1995, the Sony PlayStation took the global market by storm. *Ridge Racer* and *Wipeout* blew their competition out of the water and immediately made all the more traditional 2D productions look old. For PCs, *Doom*, *Duke Nukem 3D*, and *Quake* revolutionized the market. A new genre was born: the first-person shooter (FPS). And that became what audiences wanted, or even craved. As such, a new corner of the

---

154. *Total Annihilation*, (PC, 1997), *Total Annihilation: Kingdoms* (PC, 1999), as well as their respective expansions.

market opened up. LucasArts was well aware of this seismic shift and set the *Star Wars* machine in motion, launching production of *Star Wars: Dark Forces* and *Star Wars: Shadows of the Empire*, both action games.

Still, the studio didn't completely abandon the old ways. In 1995, the adventure game genre continued chugging along, though still on the PC, particularly thanks to the European market. The flood of high-quality titles created a solid base of die-hard fans who were always ready to jump on the latest game from LucasArts, Sierra, or one of the smaller newcomers to the market. While LucasArts had always served as an adventure game innovator, introducing all of the greatest innovations in the genre, it had many talented disciples. I'll just name a few, but the point is that great point & click titles proliferated over a handful of years in the latter half of the '90s. MicroProse, more accustomed to military simulations, released in 1992 the prodigious *Rex Nebular and the Cosmic Gender Bender*, the studio Cyan created a new subgenre with *Myst*, Sierra enjoyed unprecedented success in 1993 with *Gabriel Knight: Sins of the Fathers* and its sequel *The Beast Within: A Gabriel Knight Mystery*. A small newcomer from England released two gems called *Lure of the Temptress* and *Beneath a Steel Sky* that were easily as high-quality as the works of LucasArts. In Japan, one Hideo Kojima broke down the wall between interactive storytelling and adventure game with *Policenauts*. In France, Delphine Software produced the very respectable *Operation Stealth* and *Cruise for a Corpse* (*Croisière pour un cadavre* in the original French). It was a prolific golden age. In 1996, Revolution Software set a precedent for the genre. *Broken Sword: The Shadow of the Templars*,[155] in addition to being head and shoulders above the competition in terms of quality, was a tremendous success and spawned a new franchise. And with good reason: the game is beautiful, funny, perfectly animated, wonderfully written, and pleasant to play. It was a real master class in design and balance for its competitors, and it proved that the adventure game genre, if it used care and finesse, could still connect with audiences. Our favorite band of goofballs at LucasArts surely took notes for their next game.

In the real ending of this game, I was supposed to take over the universe and become the Lord of Darkness!

155. The game was released for the PC and PlayStation and was the brainchild of the talented Charles Cecil.

Chapter 10: *The Curse of Monkey Island*™

"The only pirate adventure that asks the question: what's sharper, your sword or your wit?"[156]

A few weeks out from the release of *The Dig*, at LucasArts, adventure game projects were at a standstill. The long and painful development of the latter had left a bitter taste in the mouths of the studio's leaders. Then, there was also the fact that sales of the last several titles, with the notable exception of *Indiana Jones and the Fate of Atlantis* (released three years previously), had been pretty mediocre. As such, they weren't especially motivated to get the machine up and running again.

That said, let's take a closer look at a little troublemaker who had other ideas in mind. After a few years of studying design, Larry Ahern quietly joined the team at LucasArts. Immediately after earning a bachelor's degree in studio art from the University of California, Davis, he began designing T-shirts and coffee mugs. In 1991, he applied for a job at LucasArts. "[The interviewer] just flipped through my design book. [...] I got lucky in that the technology curve of games coincided with my learning curve of animation." At the time, neither was very mature.

Ahern immediately joined Ron Gilbert's team and provided assistance to Peter Chan and Steve Purcell for animation of the sprites (characters) and of certain graphical elements of *Monkey Island 2: LeChuck's Revenge*. From there, he took on more important work for *Day of the Tentacle* and *Sam and Max Hit the Road* as a graphic artist, before becoming the lead animator on *Full Throttle* (and, indeed, one of the game's greatest strengths is its animations). In a way, he was a man behind the scenes, but still, he was able to prove himself in remarkable fashion. Ahern recalls that when he first joined LucasArts, the company had a laid-back, creative, tight-knit atmosphere. Aside from a handful of console games and preliminary work on the future *Star Wars* games using pre-rendered 3D graphics (e.g., *Rebel Assault*), LucasArts only made adventure games based on original franchises. Then, after a year or so, the policy changed and they started to make shooting games, more elaborate games on CD-ROM,

---

156. Advertising slogan for *The Curse of Monkey Island* (1997).

and then 3D games. From there, the studio started hiring new talent, real "hardcore" gamers who wanted to create era-defining games, and then *Star Wars* became the company's main focus. He found it to be an interesting time to work at LucasArts. *Doom* had just come out. The company's new direction offered the game developers a nice change of pace, but LucasArts had definitively reached the upper echelons of video game studios. In 1994, the company moved to bigger offices and restructured itself to be more like a traditional corporation. Creators were able to maintain a certain independence in their work on LucasArts' many projects, but the company's exponential growth brought about a change in mentalities.

Once production of *Full Throttle* was finished, Larry Ahern was approached by the studio's management: "The main reason it took LucasArts a few years to make a third *Monkey Island* game was simply because Ron [Gilbert] left the company to form Humongous Entertainment, Dave [Grossman] followed soon after, and Tim [Schafer] was focused on coming up with unique games. None of the original designers/writers were going to continue the series for [LucasArts], so they had to look for someone else. Meanwhile, after Jonathan Ackley and I had worked with Tim on *Day of the Tentacle* and *Full Throttle*, management thought we might be ready to lead our own game. And by 'our own game' I mean 'a sequel to an existing franchise,' because that's much safer for first time project leads. It was a perfect storm of commitments, commerce, and creativity."

With his fellow developer Jonathan Ackley, also a big fan of *Monkey Island*, of their own initiative, they decided to develop a script for a sequel to their favorite saga. When asked by PC Zone magazine why a third *Monkey Island* game was made after LucasArts said there would be no more, Ahern responded, "We have no idea. I guess nobody bothered to tell us that we weren't supposed to do one." Jonathan Ackley added, "We wanted to do this game because we're *Monkey Island* fans. Guybrush is [sic] fun character and we just knew that we'd have a great time thinking up scenarios for him."

"The ending of Monkey Island 2 is the real curse of Monkey Island!"™

One of the first difficulties the team had to overcome to start writing a new episode in the cult saga was to deal with the absence of the series' original creator, Ron Gilbert, head on. Jonathan Ackley recalls: "First, I would say that [*MI3*] wasn't made without Ron's influence. Ron influenced not only the style and tenor of the game, but also the very structure of LucasArts at that time. Ron trained Tim and Dave. Tim and Dave trained me. I could insert a classic *Star Wars* reference here about the whole master/apprentice bit, but I'll refrain.

Secondly, we weren't worried because Larry and I had made a large number of these games before and we knew the territory. Mostly we worried fans wouldn't like the game because they wouldn't want to feel disloyal to Ron. So Larry and I knew we had to outdo all our previous efforts just to break even."[157]

The second difficulty was the cursed legacy of *Monkey Island 2: LeChuck's Revenge* and its famous open ending in the Big Whoop amusement park. How could they come up with a plausible continuation of the story after that? How could they perpetuate the universe that had established the series' identity, a world of comical, kindly pirates, without getting bogged down by things like time traveling or an overly conspicuous MacGuffin?[158] Larry offers an answer: "It was definitely something we were kind of all sweating over as we were first working on the designs. It was like, 'OK, we don't want to ignore what happened at the end of *Monkey 2*,' but it was kind of a complicated situation that [the game's developers] left us in. So not to give too much away, what basically happens is that, at the beginning of *Curse* we start with Guybrush not being fully aware of what happened himself. He starts off thinking it was all down to some kind of voodoo curse, and as you play the game it evolves and Guybrush slowly figures out what happened to him. So for people who maybe haven't played *Monkeys 1 and 2* before, or haven't played them in a while, *Curse* kind of retraces some of the steps, and explains lots of little nitty-gritty things that somebody might want to know." Jonathan continues: "We knew that the gamers who played *Monkey Island 2* would hate us if we didn't explain it! We also realize that there are thousands and thousands of people who haven't played *Monkey 2* who will potentially be playing *Curse*, and we want to suck them into the story." Larry adds: "Also, *Monkey Island 2* leaves you at this carnival setting and we didn't want to start *Curse* with, 'Hey, OK, you bought a pirate game, but here we are at a carnival!'" [159]

Bill Tiller, the artist responsible for the game's fantastic backgrounds, talks about the atmosphere in the team: "The *CMI* crew did not like the ending of *Monkey Island 2*—not too many people did. To come up with a logical explanation for it, they brainstormed a lot of interesting ideas. The one they ultimately settled on was the idea that LeChuck had turned Guybrush into a kid at the end, but somehow the spell had worn off and so Guybrush escaped. [...] The cinematics had to be written and storyboarded next. So, four of us locked ourselves in a small office and brainstormed all the ideas for the cutscenes. And that was a lot of fun. I had brought a lot of souvenirs from my vacation to Disney World—all pirate and skeleton themed—and we decorated the office

---

157. *https://scummbar.com/resources/articles/index.php?newssniffer=readarticle&article=1007*
158. You're already familiar with this term (see chapter 5). Look at all the crazy stuff you're learning in this book!
159. *Edge*, No. 44 (April 1997).

with it. One souvenir in particular I think heavily influenced the game, a screaming skull that shrieked at anyone who walked by the office. I placed it in the hall just outside to scare anyone who walked by. We had a great laugh the first few times, but then the guys got annoyed with me because I kept doing it and it went off too often and was interrupting our work. So we had to bring him back into the office much to my great sadness. But I think the screeching skull was the influence for Murray. I still have the skull in my Halloween decorations box."[160]

The Pirate Curse of Monkey Island™

Thus, writing began quietly in May 1995 and lasted three months, resulting in a complete design document entitled *The Pirate Curse of Monkey Island or "Being a Proposal in Which We Make Amends for the Ending of Monkey Island 2."* The document, which resurfaced in 2016 thanks to Aric Wilmunder, is interesting for two main reasons. First, it reveals the initial idea for the scenario of the third episode, which we will examine in detail in just a bit; but more specifically, it reveals that even within the studio, the ending of *Monkey Island 2* was viewed as problematic. According to Jonathan Ackley, "First we wrote an incredibly convoluted story about Elaine being turned into a ship's masthead.[161] You had to change her back before the fiery demon LeChuck burned her down. A lot of great special effects *à la* the *Gone with the Wind* burning of Atlanta scene. We also had a number of puzzles involving Guybrush attempting to return the wedding gifts given to LeChuck for the monster's undead wedding to Elaine. It would've been spectacular, but when we looked at it again, we decided the story was somewhat hollow. We reworked the story until all the puzzles revolved around Guybrush overcoming his own ineptitude and saving the one person who loves him despite his idiocy. The emotional stakes for Guybrush became even higher and the story fell into place."[162]

Below is the full summary of the story from the abovementioned design document:

Governor Elaine Marley finds Guybrush Threepwood dazed and floating in the middle of the ocean in a

---

160. *https://www.adventurecorner.de/pages/532/interview-with-bill-tiller-english*
161. It seems that he means a figurehead, the beautiful sculpture one would find on the bow of an old pirate ship. Can you picture it?
162. *https://scummbar.com/resources/articles/index.php?newssniffer=readarticle&article=1007*

bumper car. Although he can't recall exactly what happened to him (at the end of the last game), he knows LeChuck is to blame. So, they set off with an armada to destroy the zombie-pirate LeChuck once and for all, in an assault on his fortress/summer-home.

Amidst the cannon fire, Guybrush sneaks over to infiltrate the fort, and learns of a treasure hidden in the dungeon. Among the loot is a huge diamond ring, which Guybrush decides to steal and give to Elaine so they can get hitched. He snatches the ring, burns up LeChuck with the evil pirate's own voodoo-flamin' potion in the process, then proposes.

Elaine, however, wants to think about the whole idea, but agrees to take the ring with her. A fire breaks out on Guybrush's boat and he is stranded on LeChuck's island. There he learns that the ring was intended for LeChuck's wedding to Elaine. When the nuptials were canceled, LeChuck couldn't bring himself to return it, so he just horribly cursed it instead.

Guybrush catches up to Elaine in time to see her put the ring on and transform into a wooden figurehead on the bow of her ship. The voodoo lady tells Guybrush that, to lift the curse, he must gather together some strange items, all symbolic of destroying LeChuck's hold on Elaine, and make a voodoo potion.

LeChuck, transformed into a demon-pirate by the mojo-fires, returns and hunts for Guybrush and Elaine. Eventually Guybrush revives Elaine. But, when she's restored to her old self, Guybrush is double-crossed by a crewman and taken to LeChuck's new hideout on Monkey Island. There, they learn about life, love, LeChuck's evil plans, Big Whoop, and the true secret of Monkey Island.

LeChuck tells them he built the amusement park on the site of Big Whoop, situated on Dinky Island, a small atoll off Monkey Island. There, he discovered that Big Whoop was a portal to the demon

> world. The amusement park was a perfect lure for
> sea-weary pirates. LeChuck could send them through
> the portal, and transform them into demons for his
> army-a demon army that he would use to defeat the
> Governor's forces, and to make her marry him.
>
> Once LeChuck had Elaine back, he would transform
> her into a demon also, so they could rule the
> Caribbean together as king and queen of the
> undead. Guybrush and Elaine, instead, thwart this
> plan in a climactic battle on a Matterhorn-style
> roller coaster, which is used to bury LeChuck in
> an avalanche of snow, permanently dousing the
> demon-pirate's hellish fires.
>
> Happy ending.

As I'm sure you'll notice, the original scenario diverges somewhat from the fragment of Guybrush Threepwood's journal reprinted later in this chapter. The project team was able to make a few adjustments in order to overcome management's concerns and get the script approved quite easily.

We haven't gotten into this yet, but the process of getting a project approved was fairly complex at LucasArts. The studio's management was largely made up of businessmen rather than creative types, and for a proposal to be accepted, it first had to go through the head of development, who would then pass it on to the head of marketing, and finally the president of the company. The final step was a meeting with all of the creative directors, who were supposed to give their opinions on the proposal. "These meetings are usually spirited discussions about what is good and not so good about a proposal,"[163] says Steve Dauterman, who was the Director of Development at the time. With such an arduous and slow process, game design documents had to be as striking, funny, precise, and concise as possible. Above all, very few projects were actually approved, only two or three a year. Development of *The Curse of Monkey Island* (which, it's worth noting, was never given the name *Monkey Island 3*) could officially begin.

---

163. *https://www.awn.com/mag/issue2.12/2.12pages/2.12bekinslucas.html*

How do you make a masterpiece?™

From the beginning of the project, Larry and Jonathan took note of the criticisms leveled against the studio's previous games: *The Dig*? Too complicated. *Full Throttle*? Too many cinematics, almost an interactive film (yep, they were even having this sort of debate back then). *Sam and Max*? The puzzles were too convoluted.

Next, the duo analyzed the foundations of the first two *Monkey Island* games in order to select the design elements that interested them the most. According to Jonathan: "We really liked the non-linearity of *Monkey 1*. Particularly the three-trial structure on Mêlée Island. So, in *Curse*, we actually have two complete islands and each one has a three- or five-trial structure. So, if you get stuck in one direction, you can go and explore another, and if you're stuck on that one, there will be another one, so you can always go back and forth and solve puzzles in just about any order."[164] The construction of the puzzles in the third opus also needed to distinguish it from the other games, particularly via their ambiance. Larry continues: "As we started working on puzzles for this game, we knew we wanted to try to get into a few more piratey situations. We were looking at getting the player to actually shoot a cannon at another boat and do some more swashbuckling kinds of things—things we weren't able to include in *Monkey Islands 1* and *2* because of technological limitations. So, that's set us up for a few puzzles."

From late 1995 to early 1996, production chugged along. The team working on the new installment in the adventures of Guybrush Threepwood quickly grew to 18 members, which was enormous for an adventure game at the time. In 1995, expectations in terms of quality and the much-vaunted "production values" of an adventure game began to weigh heavily on titles hoping to achieve blockbuster status, and it felt difficult for the team to maintain the classic trial-and-error production process while keeping costs down. As such, the two directors worked to create perfectly finalized storyboards they could deliver to their artists, whose job it was to enact their vision, without the need to change a single thing. According to Jonathan: "Larry and I spent three months working on the design. That's typical for one of these monster adventure games. We had the complete plot, non-interactive script, puzzle outline, character descriptions, and room connectivity [around 80 screens, each about the same size as those in *Day of the Tentacle*]. While art is in pre-production, the programmers wire up a walkthrough of the game. Background art starts coming in before animation, so before we're bogged down with art we try to make the BG as interactive as possible. We also write the first-draft dialogue." Larry was well

164. *Edge* No. 44 (April 1997).

aware that the recent success of Revolution Software's *Broken Sword: The Shadow of the Templars* had raised the bar for the kind of quality that players expected. The animation, the "acting," the voices, and the overall production all became crucial concerns. More than ever before, the game had to be brilliant and offer perfectly fluid gameplay. As such, *The Curse of Monkey Island* received the shortest pre-production period in the history of LucasArts, but the longest and most intense phase of actual development. The smart alecks at the back of the class (you know, the ones sitting right next to the radiator) will say that it shows in the final product, but we'll come back to that later.

In the meantime, production progressed as scheduled. As Jonathan Ackley narrates, "Then the animation comes in and we have to change the dialogue to match the character the animators have added. Sound effects are added three quarters [of the way] through the project, making a project that you might be tired of fresh again. A little after that, you get the voice recordings. All along the way, [the testing team] has been telling you what's wrong with your game, so you make their changes... 'No, Jonathan. I don't think you understood me. This part SUCKS!' Then comes music, and then you spend months polishing the game until it shines."

A change in visual identity™

Initially, visual development of the characters was entrusted to Steve Purcell. After a series of illustrations of the main protagonists that didn't go over very well, particularly the peculiar, childish design of Guybrush, Larry Ahern wanted to bring in a fresh perspective and decided to hand the task over to a new artist. He chose the young Bill Tiller, who had been hired at LucasArts by Colette Michaud, Steve Purcell's wife, to work on the animations for *The Dig* when the project was still in the hands of Brian Moriarty. The particularly gifted artist was swiftly promoted to create the visual identity of *Full Throttle*, producing the quality that we all know it for. Tiller remembers when he joined the team of *The Curse of Monkey Island*: "My first memory of even talking about a sequel to *Monkey Island* was when I was talking with some of *The Dig* programmers and mentioned how much fun it would be to do a sequel to *Monkey Island 2: LeChuck's Revenge*. I was sort of laughed at by a few of them. They said it would never get made because the last *Monkey Island* game didn't sell well enough to make a sequel, and Ron Gilbert wouldn't do it now that he was no longer working at LucasArts. So that crushed my dream. But after *The Dig* was finished, there was talk of doing a *Monkey* sequel with Jonathan Ackley and Larry Ahern. But Jonathan didn't initially want me to work on it because we had clashed a bit while working on *The Dig*. So, I had to work hard to prove myself. I eventually won him over and got the job as background art director. Before that, I went on vacation to the Bahamas and Disney World. There, I took a lot of reference pictures of the Caribbean and the Pirates of the Caribbean ride at Disney World because *Monkey Island* was a bit of a spoof of that ride."[165]

His unique, slightly crazy, cartoonish and colorful style was probably the best thing that could have happened for *The Curse of Monkey Island*. In an interview given to the website *MixnMojo*, Bill Tiller says: "In the early going, I figured we would do that [make the backgrounds look more like those in *MI2*], but it seemed like a wasted opportunity if we just did the same thing. Plus, we now had high-resolution graphics, and besides, the last Monkey Island game came out five years earlier. We felt the door was open to update the *Monkey Island* look and give *Curse of Monkey Island* its own unique feel and style."[166] And Bill Tiller would regularly offer proposals to the two co-directors to develop the game's famous style until he came up with the right formula. Of the concepts proposed by the artist, Larry and Jonathan chose the most quirky and deformed ones. "But I actually think the backgrounds in *Monkey 2* are very cartoon-like. I mean, you wouldn't mistake them for photographs, would you? Plus, Steve Purcell and Peter Chan did a lot of the *MI2* art and they are both excellent cartoonists. So I think the *MI* art style was already moving in a cartoonlike direction back on *Monkey Island 2*." Tiller and his team just exaggerated that style. "With exaggeration, you get the viewer to clearly see and identify the character's distinctive features easily, and it tends to be more pleasing to the eye." If the visuals had been too realistic, they would have seemed very strange and disjointed. Animation can give each character its own distinct personality, particularly when the animation is very pronounced, even caricatural, as is the case in *The Curse of Monkey Island*.

Bill Tiller, in his speech *How to Draw Monkeys the LucasArts Way: An Analysis of the Funny Pictures in* The Curse of Monkey Island, offers a few tips regarding the traps and pitfalls a graphic artist should avoid when creating the backgrounds for an adventure game: "Because of the unique artistic require-ments of adventure games, and all computer games in general, we actually had to make the game look better than television. Simplistic background art works fine for television, but will create negative effects in a computer game. One negative effect of using simplistic backgrounds is that puzzles become very obvious and are too easy to solve. If, for example, in the Voodoo Lady's hut, there were no objects in the room save for the chewing gum, the paste, and the voodoo doll pin, there would be no challenge in figuring out which items would be useful for later puzzles. The player would have such a limited choice,

165. *https://www.adventurecorner.de/articles/8254/interview–with–bill–tiller–english*
166. *https://web.archive.org/web/20010716110353/http://www.thescummbar.com/features/billtill-er/page2.shtml*

the decision would be overly apparent. The way we designed our backgrounds, and the way I think works best, was to put in all sorts of interesting items and detailed things to look at. This forces the player to search around and examine things more closely. It gives the player a sense that he is exploring the Voodoo Lady's hut and interacting with the environment. This also gives a chance for our programmers to write funny dialogue for each item, even if the player doesn't need the items." But that wasn't the only difference compared to traditional animation: "In traditional animation, the background is only intended to support and compliment the animated characters in it, or for most shots anyway. There are exceptions, like close-ups or long-tracking establishing shots, where the director intentionally has the audience focus on the background. With an animated film, if the background is too interesting, it works against the character, upstaging it and defeating the purpose of the scene. But in a computer game, the backgrounds ARE the game, be they three-dimensional models for the world of *Zelda*, or two-dimensional background sprites for a side scroller. Seeing the backgrounds clearly in a game is usually a matter of life and death for your character. But with adventure games, life and death are usually not the main concern for the character. The important thing in these kinds of games is to keep the player entertained and happy, even if he is stuck in, say, King Andre's treasure cave bargaining for Elaine's diamond. At least the player can look around at all the treasure, shipwreck ruins, and Smuggle Bunnies™ hidden in the room. [...] The composition of the art is probably the most important thing to pay attention to."

From silent to talkie™

The Curse of Monkey Island was also the first episode in the series to be fully dubbed. And its dubbing is incredible! It wasn't LucasArts' first rodeo, given that since *Day of the Tentacle* the studio had been dubbing in voices for each character. Finding the right tone for the most eccentric protagonists had become one of the company's specialties. Voice director Khris Brown, (who some years later would hold a similar position for George Lucas' *Star Wars* prequel trilogy[167]) reveals to us some more of what was happening behind the scenes. "Casting the voices for *Curse of Monkey Island* was done in conjunction with the other Voice Director at LucasArts at the time, Darragh O'Farrell. Most of the focus was on finding the right voice for the feeling of Curse, which was a little more in an animated style than the Ron/Tim/Dave Monkey Island

---

167. The nickname given to Episodes I, II, and III, as opposed to the "original" trilogy of Episodes IV, V, and VI, and the sequel trilogy of Episodes VII, VIII, and IX.

games. Larry and Jonathan worked to ensure that the voices both respected the past feeling of the game while making it align with their vision." As an example of Khris Brown's process, she explains how she proceeded while working on *Sam & Max*: "We solicited auditions from all of the agencies and actors in Los Angeles and San Francisco. I would listen to them all on cassette tapes and then dub the auditions I liked onto a separate cassette tape for each character. [...] My office was full of large plastic tubs of cassette tapes and a two-cassette deck recorder. I listened and dubbed for two weeks–it was like something out of a 1980s movie. We had hundreds of auditions and many callbacks, as we were doing something completely new. We needed actors who would be able to maintain the same level of enthusiasm and authenticity in their performance, even when reading many different dialogue choices." This exercise was totally strange and dispiriting for the actors, who were more accustomed to acting from linear scripts.

"Most animated shows are recorded in an ensemble style, with all the actors in the recording studio together, so that the actors can react to one another in the moment. With video games, every reaction is imagined, and coached by the director, to create a real moment between the characters when they meet in the game. Many video game characters' actors never meet in real life. As a director, I imagine, create, and convey the emotional reality needed to spark the appropriate response in the actor, who is usually alone in the recording booth. Even today, we seek actors who are very comfortable with improvisation and can immediately create any needed emotion with authentic feeling." However, the needs of a series with such off-the-wall humor like *Monkey Island* went even further: "We also needed people who had a deep sense of whimsy and good-natured humor. The games are very zany, but have [a] very innocent and pure heart. If an actor is cynical or sarcastic as a person, it will sometimes carry over into the sound of their performance, and that wouldn't work for these games. [...] Extreme creativity requires extreme trust–there is no room for egos or anything less than 100% risk-taking." And it's worth noting that the voice acting in *The Curse of Monkey Island* is excellent. For Guybrush, Dominic Armato filled his shoes and embodied the character's naïveté and guile-lessness. Khris Brown explains the importance of casting: "An actor's voice can make or break the story. Their ability to inhabit and portray the character's essential truth–whether they are friendly, optimistic, depressed, sinister, or full of hope–will convey more to the player than even the scripted words in the moment." Thus, Larry Ahern and Jonathan Ackley, from the moment they began writing, had to keep in mind that the game would be dubbed. A "silent" game can't offer the same type of dialogue as a "talkie" game. In the former, the humor has to be communicated through the written word; in the latter, the actors are responsible for setting the tone of the scene. Khris Brown continues: "If someone sounds sad in their tone of voice, but they are saying happy words, we, as humans, instinctively know that something is wrong. [...] If the game is text only, with no VO [voiceover], each person playing will naturally imagine the correct tone of voice as they would understand it in their own individual mind. Once those lines are spoken as VO, however, the actor must be able to create a performance that will ring true to every different person playing the game. [...] We don't have the actors 'perform' the role—they live it. It is all imagination, but we often laugh and cry along with the characters in the script when we are recording it." As true fans of the *Monkey Island* series, Dominic Armato and Alexandra Boyd (the voice of Elaine Marley) sometimes influenced the script. "I have had instances of actors saying, 'This doesn't feel right,' and they're usually correct," Khris Brown recalls. "If they're living the role, they'll know what's right. This is an area for great diplomacy for an actor, however. For both the actor and myself, our duty is to bring the writer's vision to life. For an actor to question a line in the studio, something will have to be extremely out of place, and it is always brought up with the deepest respect."

Interestingly, the English version of the game included a scene that was deleted from the international versions. When Guybrush gets together the crew for his ship, *The Sea Cucumber*, they start singing a sea chantey to procrastinate and defy their captain. This results in an incredible musical scene, all in rhyming verse, called *A Pirate I Was Meant to Be*, in which Guybrush must come up with the right arguments to thwart those of the other pirates. As rhymes are a real headache to adapt into a foreign language, the team simply decided to delete the scene. Still, players of translated versions can rewatch the scene from the original version of the game via SCUMMVM.[168] And while we're on the subject, translating the game was a real challenge. In *The Curse of Monkey Island*, the insult battles were typically meant to rhyme. However, as it was impossible to come up with consistent translations that rhymed, in the French version for example, the translators were forced to throw in the towel and either come up with responses that didn't rhyme or ones that did rhyme, but had no connection with the original insult.

Jonathan Ackley and Larry Ahern's game finally hit store shelves on October 31, 1997, in the United States and on February 20 of the following year throughout Europe. The game was only released for the PC (and Mac much later) given that in 1997 the Amiga (and Atari ST) had disappeared from the landscape and game console audiences were not yet very interested in adventure games. It should also be noted that the game has never had a remastered version or a remake, unlike its venerable ancestors. This may suggest two things: either *The Curse of Monkey Island* doesn't have the same legacy as the first two games, and thus is viewed as undeserving of a remake,

168. SCUMMVM is independent software that allows you to run old versions of LucasArts games. Available for the PC, Mac, and various other machines.

or the original version of the game was so timeless that a remaster seems unnecessary. I'll offer some possible answers a bit later on in this book.

Below is the next installment of the disquieting documents found and passed down by the descendants of Guybrush Threepwood. Be careful of who you share this tome with: more sensitive souls may no longer be able to look at you the same way.

The Memoirs of Guybrush Threepwood, Part 3™

Lost at sea for days now. I have no crew or navigational instruments. No provisions except a half-eaten corn dog and, unless I find water soon, I'm surely done for. Only the hope of finding my love, Elaine, keeps me going. My quest for the fabulous treasure called Big Whoop has left me in this sorry state. I thought it would bring me fame and glory. Instead, it delivered me into the clutches of my enemy, the zombie-pirate LeChuck. I had thwarted his evil plot to marry Elaine and he was after revenge. Really, really thirsty now. If only I could have a small drink of fresh water, I might have the strength to sail on. Oh, but I know there's nothing but ocean for miles and miles... If I could reach land, I might find water and some food. Fruit, maybe... Something to fight off the scurvy and help me get my strength back. Mmmmmm... maybe some bananas... Oh, why do I torture myself like this? I might as well wish for some chicken and a big mug of grog for all the good it will do me. Oh, my sweet Elaine... Am I cursed to starve here on this ocean... without seeing your face just one more time? Am I— [Editor's note: certain parts of the manuscript are illegible. The pages have been burned, blackened, and stained with what appears to be organic tomato sauce.]

The vessel drifted aimlessly wherever the winds took it, until... Incredible though it may seem—I'm sure you're getting used to hearing that by now—I found myself caught in the middle of a battle between LeChuck's pirate ship and my darling, the marvelous Elaine. From atop the ramparts of the small fort near Puerto Pollo, she chastised the vile zombie captain. I discreetly approached the hull of my enemy's ship, but he turned his skeleton corsairs on me and they put me in irons. I had escaped starvation and solitude; I was so close to my goal, only to find myself held prisoner in the hold of my greatest enemy! Thankfully, I've been in worse situations before, and I was comforted when I saw a familiar face. Indeed, manning one of the ship's cannons, I recognized good ol' Wally, who I had left in a sticky situation in the course of my previous adventures. Going by the name of "Bloodnose the Pirate," he had ended up taking a Level 2 Mighty Pirate training seminar with a special focus on brutal pillaging. Of course, he was so relieved to see that I was still alive, and so wrapped up in my natural charisma, that within a matter of seconds, he let me take control of his cannon. I turned it against LeChuck's own leaky tub of a ship and fired. The vessel exploded and I found myself in what was left of the treasure hold. I just barely had enough time to do a little plundering of my own and picked up a superb ring set with an enormous diamond before the whole ship sank to the bottom of Puerto Pollo harbor. Once again, LeChuck was done for. But for how long?

Once on the beach, my beloved Elaine was bursting with joy to see me again. And with great emotion, right then and there, I asked her to marry me, trembling as I held out to her the ring I had just picked up. I may see myself as a man of action. A swashbuckler. A rogue. A wanderer! A man who can hold his breath for 10 minutes. I have no ties and no regrets. I sail with the wind and go wherever adventures take me. But still, I'm a big romantic and I was smitten with the most beautiful woman in all of the Caribbean. Naturally, Elaine immediately accepted and I slipped the ring onto her finger. It was such a beautiful moment. But of course, this was not a "happily ever after." If it were any other way, you'd be saying, "I paid a fortune for this game and I finished it in less than 10 minutes! This is what you call an 'interactive film'?"

No, as soon as I put that ring on her finger, my darling Elaine transformed into a solid gold statue! What had I done? Apparently, the ring carried an evil Voodoo curse and I had unwittingly dragged the love of my life into another one of my adventures.

As usual, I headed off to pay a little visit to my old friend the Voodoo Lady. She told me that the ring did indeed carry a terrible curse. It was the ring that LeChuck had himself intended to give Elaine! To break the awful spell, I needed to sail to Blood Island to recover the ring's original diamond. If I did that, my dear Elaine would be restored. Basically, it wouldn't take a genius. And besides, I was the famous, fearsome pirate captain who had twice vanquished LeChuck and discovered the treasure of Big Whoop.

As the full account of my trials and tribulations on Plunder Island is not quite suitable for younger audiences, I'll just say that I gained the trust of my new crew by winning both a banjo duel (fair and square) and a Scottish caber toss competition. Also, that I found the map showing how to get to Blood Island thanks to my own blood, sweat, tears, and some cooking oil. And that I finally acquired a magnificent ship by seizing it from a bunch of ferocious monkey pirates. Along the way, I made the acquaintance of an unbearable and totally devious skull named Murray, as well as a highly conceited rival captain by the name of Rottingham, who stole my precious map.

Our departure from Puerto Pollo was more complicated than usual and my crew quickly got me up to speed. Rottingham ruled the high seas of the Caribbean. If I wanted to sail to Blood Island, I would have to defeat him in single combat. After a few days of sparring, cannonballs, and stinging insults, I finally crossed swords with the terrible bald captain. My words were as keen, quick, and sharp as my sword, and in any case, he fought like a cow. I crushed Rottingham and recovered my map. Blood Island was mine!

The journey there was not an easy one. We suffered through a terrible storm and, after many hours of battling the elements, our ship was carried away by a ground swell. Overcome by the herculean effort I made to maintain the confidence of my crew, I blacked out at the helm and after a few hours of drifting, we somehow reached the shores of Blood Island.

The statue of Elaine had been flung deep into the jungle and my three companions who made up my entire crew informed me that they were ready to give up the pirate life, which was much too dangerous, and return to their previous job of cutting hair. I wished them the best of luck; I no longer needed them anyway. As I made my way through the jungle, I discovered a decrepit old hotel, a relic of a storied past. It was home to the restaurant of the Goodsoup family, a Caribbean culinary institution famed for its delicious tripe with a nacho cheese and goose fat fondue. After sobering up the restaurant's manager, I collected information on the original diamond that was supposed to be set in the cursed ring, and which supposedly came from Blood Island. Griswold Goodsoup was the manager's name, and he recounted to me that sad chapter in his family's history. His great aunt Minnie "Stroni" Goodsoup was a prominent woman in the society of Blood Island. However, she was too romantic for her own good. She had a weakness for pirates. One in particular. She fell head over heels in love with him and within a week, they were engaged. However, on the eve of their wedding, he stole the Goodsoup family diamond from the ring she wore and sold it to smugglers on Skull Island. She continued wearing the diamondless ring and died not long after. She ultimately returned to haunt the Goodsoup family tomb. A very sad story... But if I wanted to free Elaine from the curse, I would have to retrieve the ring from poor Minnie's remains and steal the diamond from the formidable smugglers of Skull Island.

I knew what I had to do. I'll spare you the details, but basically, I had to die twice, cheat good ol' Stan, who had become a pirate life insurance salesman, find a new suitor for the ghost of Minnie, and win an epic game of poker against the dreaded smugglers. Once again, thanks to my natural talent for solving any problem, even if through unconventional means, before long, I was able to acquire the diamond and the ring. I put the two together and slipped the diamond ring onto the finger of the statue of my dear Elaine. She immediately regained her normal appearance and threw her arms around me, covering me in kisses. [Editor's note: To this day, historians debate the truth of these unconvincing claims.] One thing is for sure: things never go as planned, and my eternal rival LeChuck then reappeared! A veritable horde of skeleton pirates armed to the teeth descended on us. In a fierce battle, I killed a good hundred or so of them [Editor's note: right...], but after several hours of combat, they made us their prisoners and took us to... Monkey Island!

When I came to, I was being held captive in a strange, garishly painted gondola lift cabin. LeChuck stood before me and had Elaine tied up. We were in the very heart of the most unusual place in all of the Caribbean. The zombie captain then revealed to me the true nature of the treasure of Big Whoop. Rather than consisting of pieces of gold, it was actually a Voodoo portal leading straight to hell. LeChuck had built an enormous amusement park, the Carnival of the Damned™, around that very portal. He would drag pirates and various other scoundrels through the portal to transform them into zombies, pressed into his service, thus creating a giant army of the living dead, thirsty for blood, glory, and gold. I warned you this story was frightful, didn't I?! To top it all off, LeChuck intended to marry Elaine and make her his zombie queen. I had to take action, and fast. I escaped *from my prison and did away with my assailants. Finally, I jumped on the Roller Coaster of Death to set a trap for my formidable adversary. I had just enough time to whip up a thermo-mojo bomb capable of wiping any "non-living" being off the face of the earth. In an enormous explosion, the bodies of the captain and his henchmen were literally annihilated. I was reunited with my beloved and we left that godforsaken island.*

This story wouldn't be complete without a proper happy ending. I finally slid a (real) wedding ring onto Elaine's finger, and at long last we were officially husband and wife. Mrs. Threepwood and I returned to our ship and took to the sea, hand in hand, and sailed off into the sunset with romantic music playing in the background.

The End

Game design and fun facts

Like good students, Larry Ahern and Jonathan Ackley applied Ron Gilbert's tried and true formula from the first two series installments to a tee. They may even have taken it too far. In any case, *The Curse of Monkey Island* laid all its cards on the table and clearly defined the player's objectives. However, the adventure suffered from a nearly identical repetition of a circuit of challenges, first on Plunder Island, then on Blood Island. This repeat made the player's progression on the second island feel a bit mechanical. Thankfully, the overall production and fantastic work on the ambiance made the game incredible in spite of its faults.

The Curse of Monkey Island is probably the series installment with the most fun facts and interesting references attached to it, perpetuating a certain post-modern tradition that was largely established across all of the studio's titles. However, the effect gets distorted: with so many fun nudges given to the player, the game's overall universe loses depth, becoming a sort of showcase for geek pop culture. In addition, there is a wild number of film references in the dialogue, including, in no particular order, *Apocalypse Now*, *Child's Play*, *Deliverance* (the dueling banjos), *Godzilla*, *The Goonies*, *Highlander*, *Indiana Jones*, *James Bond*, *Star Wars*, and even "Rosebud" from *Citizen Kane*. What's more, LeChuck's ship is called the *Death Starfish*, a reference to, well, you know what!

But rather than endlessly reviewing references that you will easily catch while playing the game, let's instead take a look at the handful of scenes that were cut from the final version due to a lack of time remaining for development.

In the game's official guide,[169] there's a page showing a storyboard for a scene at the end of the adventure while at the Carnival of the Damned. Elaine is forced by LeChuck onto the Roller Coaster of Death. Guybrush then gets into a swordfight with three skeleton soldiers. Amid the mêlée, our hero falls into one of the coaster's cars and the game's progression picks up from there as we know it.

The second major scene cut from the final version was supposed to appear after the credits and featured Guybrush and Elaine singing a song called *Plank of Love*. The lyrics and music were written (and are included in the appendix of this book, on p. 285), but due to a lack of time and funds, the team decided not to actually produce the scene. Additionally, the ending was rightfully criticized by players for its shortcuts and surprising brevity, having fallen victim to forced cuts in the final weeks of production. The production costs for *The Curse of Monkey Island* had already exceeded the most pessimistic forecasts and letting the project become a boondoggle was out of the question, especially since LucasArts had largely been burned by disappointing results for the studio's previous adventure games.

The third episode also marked the return of the iconic insult battles, which received a slight upgrade after having been left out of *Monkey Island 2: LeChuck's Revenge*. Another idea passed down from *The Secret of Monkey Island* resurfaced in volume three: the ship battles. If you remember, Ron Gilbert had planned to incorporate this feature into the first game before abandoning the idea to keep the story flowing well (and to save some time and money). In *The Curse of Monkey Island*, the ship battles are stripped down to a bare minimum, following in the tradition of *Sid Meier's Pirates!* (which was also one of Ron Gilbert's original inspirations). The player controls the ship from a top-down view, with a fairly simple method of dealing with wind direction and the cannons' reload time. There's no health bar, and thus no real strategy or complicated statistics to manage. It becomes clear why Ron Gilbert chose to set the idea aside, and the presence of this phase in the third episode really just serves as a bit of filler rather than actually adding in more fun.

While the game design was nearly identical to that of its venerable forebears, *The Curse of Monkey Island* nonetheless allowed players to visit new places and introduced characters that would become inextricably linked to the saga, most notably Murray. Jonathan Ackley recalls: "Murray was originally designed to be in only one room. He was the disembodied skull supposed to keep you company while you solved the first 'locked-in-a-room' puzzle. When I originally wrote his dialogue, I just made him sarcastic. I showed it to Larry and he gave me one of those 'gee, that's not very good' expressions. So, I took another crack at it

169. *The Curse of Monkey Island: The Official Strategy Guide.*

and this time decided to try the 'lovably pathetic' tack. Larry approved, so the character of Murray was set."[170] The initial feedback from testing showed that the testers adored the character, who they found hilarious. Everyone demanded more of him. "Then Chuck and Chris came to me and asked if they could put Murray elsewhere in the game. I said 'sure,' and soon I was finding him all over the place. I came into the programmers' office one day and they said, 'Come, look at this.' Guybrush walked into the crypt and Murray leapt down from the rafters screaming, 'DIIIIIEEEEEEE!' Then he smacked into the floor and moaned in pain. At that moment, I knew Murray was a star." And, indeed, Murray essentially became one of the series' most popular icons, alongside Guybrush and LeChuck. Given that fact, it's surprising that he really only makes a handful of appearances. In any case, I have to say that his dialogue is well crafted and his voice acting is particularly excellent.

A few more fun facts:

☙ From the start of the game, the menus allow you to select the option "Enable 3D acceleration"; of course, the game is in 2D and any 3D graphics cards available at the time (3dfx, etc.) would have been no help. If you select this option, a message appears proudly announcing, "We were only kidding."

☙ When Guybrush fires a cannon at the skeleton soldiers attacking Elaine's fort, you can type the message "lapostal" to activate a cheat code giving you an infinite number of cannonballs (this is perfectly useless given that the cannon-balls are already infinite). This is a nod to a similar code available for the LucasArts game *Star Wars: Dark Forces*.

☙ During the sea battles, and during the insult combat scenes, I recommend that you press Shift + J on your keyboard to transform Guybrush into a Jedi knight, thus giving you a lightsaber.

☙ When Guybrush manages to enter the crypt of Minnie Goodsoup on Blood Island, if you look through the crack in the wall, you can see the forest from *Monkey Island 1* (with its original, eerie MIDI music). Similarly, again on Blood Island, if you dive into the water near the beach 25 to 30 times, you'll go well below the surface and discover the drowned Guybrush from *Monkey Island 1*.

---

170. *https://scummbar.com/resources/articles/index.php?newssniffer=readarticle&article=1007*

Reception and reviews™

In spite of stiff competition from another heavyweight of the point & click subgenre in that same month of November 1997–the Westwood Studios adaptation of *Blade Runner–The Curse of Monkey Island* instantly became the franchise's greatest success. The title sold a cool 52,000 copies in less than two months in the American market alone, and over double that in Germany. In the end, over the years that followed, *Monkey Island 3* sold almost a million copies, a fantastic figure considering the genre, era, and massive piracy of the game for the only machine it was made for: the PC. As such, for many younger (or less old) players, *The Curse of Monkey Island* is often remembered as their introduction to the series, as the two previous games had already been written off as pixelated antiques. This has contributed to the fact that the visual style of the third opus is often considered the "canonical" artistic exemplar of the saga.

With regard to reviews, in France, the game was praised for its remarkable production and its ambiance, as well as for preserving the series' humor. The magazine *Génération 4* summarized its test thusly: "So, not much to criticize about this third series installment. With impeccable production and a refreshed ambiance, *The Curse of Monkey Island* is an excellent adventure game that won't disappoint veteran gamers and will delight novices!"[171] Still, another comment from the same magazine slightly tempers the overall impression: "First and foremost, I would like to stipulate that, for me, *Monkey Island 2* remains the best adventure game ever created. That is to say, I eagerly awaited its sequel... My first observation: what the series has lost in terms of 'nonsense,' it has gained in innocence. While the humor remains outlandish, it seemed to me to be much more "mainstream" (the French voices have a lot to do with that). In spite of these few reservations, *Monkey Island 3* is undoubtedly LucasArts' best adventure game since *Day of the Tentacle*!" The other leading French video game magazine, *Joystick*, was a bit more circumspect about a genre that was spinning its wheels and happily resting on its laurels: "To summarize, you'll have a very nice time playing *The Curse of Monkey Island.* The only criticisms we can make of the game concern its structure, which doesn't really add anything new and settles for following a path laid out by LucasArts long ago. On the other hand, the scenario is interesting, the vast majority of the jokes are funny, and the game is visually very rich. Fans will not be disappointed; quite the opposite, in fact."[172]

In the United States, the title was named the best adventure game of the year by *PC Gamer*, which came to this final verdict: "If this isn't destined to

171. *Génération 4*, No. 105 (December 1997), Sébastien Tasserie.
172. *Joystick*, No. 88 (December 1997), Seb.

be a classic, I'll swallow a cutlass." In spite of generally positive reviews, the leading website for the genre, *Adventure Gamers*, stood out from the rest by being more critical: "However good the game is, it must be said that it is far too short, and the ending is a little rushed. Two days of gameplay is simply not enough for a modern adventure game. The length also affects the depth of gameplay. You simply do not have enough time to develop relationships with other characters, and get truly immersed in the game's world. After its predecessor, this comes as a big letdown. Also, the ending is an anticlimax, leaving the player thinking he could have done so much more, if only the game's programmers had let him. Minor quibbles, to be sure, for this is a fantastic game, but it's the little details that make the game sparkle... and quite frankly, this game does not."[173] Conversely, the website *MixnMojo*, writing with the benefit of hindsight, talks of the game as a milestone: "Given the high praise and enduring passion, it's fair to ask what makes the game so special. While I wouldn't try to pinpoint it, there is something that continues to strike me about *The Curse of Monkey Island*, and that's that it doesn't seem capable of aging. The reason is simple. There is not one decision, large or small, made about the use of technology in this game that was for any other reason than to support the final vision. [...] Ask yourself the following question: if the game were made this year, with the same vision and intentions, what about it would look different? The resolution would be a bit higher, the cutscenes would be better compressed, and... I can't think of much else. A game composed of scanned illustrations and 2D animation is only ever going to look as good as the quality of the artwork. There might be room for some slight and ultimately pointless bells and whistles but, like an old animated film, we're dealing with something timeless. *The Curse of Monkey Island* is as appealing a game now as it was on its first day of release, and I suspect that another ten years is going to do little to change that." [174]

Legacy and story design™

The game is most definitely magnificent. *The Curse of Monkey Island* is certainly a pinnacle of 2D games. As such, it is an unquestionable success, both technically and artistically. The graphics are refined, colorful, and brilliantly enhanced by a resolution that does justice to the work of Bill Tiller. The game undeniably possesses a certain timelessness that has allowed it to last through the ages without gaining a single gray hair. If you compare it to other games from 1997, from *Tomb Raider 2* to *GoldenEye 007*, from *Dungeon*

173. *https://adventuregamers.com/articles/view/17499*, Tamara Schembri.
174. *https://mixnmojo.com/features/sitefeatures/LucasArts-Secret-History-The-Curse-of-Monkey-Island/1*

Keeper to *Age of Empires*, from *Gran Turismo* to *Diablo*, the LucasArts title objectively remains the game whose graphics have aged the least.

Freed from the constraints of the MIDI format, Michael Z. Land was finally able to deploy his true musical vision for *Monkey Island*. The soundtrack, though very discreet while playing the game, is a real delight to listen to. Hands down the best score of the franchise! Certain songs culminate in pure joys of composition, finesse, and ambiance, with depth never before heard in any adventure game. From the voices to the animation to the interface, everything is perfectly cohesive in this glorious title, which was almost like the swan song of an era, a 2D game thumbing its nose at the world one last time. No failure of taste tarnishes its practically idyllic image from the standpoint of production values.

We also have to recognize that *Curse of Monkey Island* did a great job of continuing the series' tradition of humor. While we can probably say that Jonathan Ackley and Larry Ahern's game went overboard with the post-modern references, the script nevertheless did right by the caustic, sarcastic, and deliciously anachronistic humor deployed in the previous episodes. At its best moments, the third installment proves to be absolutely hilarious, notably thanks to its side characters, particularly Murray, as well as its visual gags. The writing is always well crafted in terms of tone and only suffers from the new characterization work. That last point is, of course, where the game starts to get negative marks. The creators made the radical decision to completely revamp the image of Guybrush Threepwood. Their first mistake was in changing the hero's design. From the wild young man idealized in the illustrations created by Steve Purcell, he evolved into a more childlike version to fit with the new visual style. No more serious, slightly pompous hero following in the legacy of the swashbuckler films of old. Guybrush instead became a guileless, clumsy oaf devoid of sex appeal, always with his head in the clouds. However, what the artists may not necessarily have anticipated was that by making that change a whole part of the ambiance of the first two titles would disappear.

In spite of its ubiquitous humor, up to that point, the series had always cruised along on the popular and retro heritage of the pirate film genre. *The Curse of Monkey Island* dives headlong into a parody of those films, mixing in a cartoon style. And what about how the character of Elaine Marley was handled? The character previously written by Ron Gilbert was an independent, strong feminist; she was a formally progressive element in the story, running counter to other heroines. Gilbert himself has even said about the third episode that he thought the team did great work and managed to capture the spirit of the original games. However, he never imagined Elaine actually falling for Guybrush, and she certainly wouldn't have married him. Indeed, Elaine was relegated to a secondary role and became a run-of-the-mill character, reduced to her status as the hero's love interest, a "damsel in distress" to be saved. She seems to be a far cry from the feminist icon who always swooped in to save Guybrush from the stickiest situations he was incapable of getting himself out of.

Even worse, the overall game design of *The Curse of Monkey Island* at times feels lazy. It very faithfully follows in the legacy of its revered ancestors, but without the ingenuity needed to make proper use of it and to give the game its own identity to match its extraordinary visuals. Thus, unlike *Monkey Island 2: LeChuck's Revenge*, the story design of the third game doesn't come up with anything new and does even less exploration of new possibilities. Curious to know more about this apparent timidness, when, up to that point, LucasArts' adventure games had always strived to be trailblazers, I asked Larry Ahern to explain to me his perspective: "I didn't work much with Ron directly, as I came onto [*Monkey Island 2: LeChuck's Revenge*] halfway into the project and he was juggling the responsibilities of creating the game while also doling out all the art and animation tasks (a job subsequently given to art and animation directors). So, most interactions consisted of things like, 'Here's a list of 5 animations we need,' or 'Looks pretty good, but needs more swashbuckling.' I knew there was a lot I could learn from him, and that motivated me to find another way to learn about making these games and expressing my creative ideas: by bugging Tim and Dave." In 1992, Larry was asked to work with Dave Grossman on *The Dig*, which had been mired in complications. Immediately after that, he joined Tim Schafer to work on *Day of the Tentacle*. "Based on things I've read and heard, I think Ron's wisdom came through pretty much intact, but there was a Tim/Dave spin to it. We went on to make *Day of the Tentacle* and *Full Throttle* after Ron left the company, so I had an opportunity to see a lot of those design tenets put into action. Though we tried to innovate incrementally with each project, this approach probably developed into a bit of a house style, a way of making games that spread through the ranks like scurvy, only more fun and with pixels!" That said, why didn't they try to change the game's structure? "Once we set out to design [*The Curse of Monkey Island*], we weren't going to completely change direction. It needed to follow the style of the previous games to feel like a part of the series. [...] We knew there was a large audience that loved the first two games and wasn't interested in a 3D sword fighting space pirate Guybrush game, so we looked at the tried and true structure and tried to make it an evolution."

The game most likely suffered from being a transitional episode. The creators had to skillfully balance the legacy of *Monkey Island 2*, in terms of storytelling and gameplay, while paving the way for a potential sequel in a different world and with a new identity. As such, the game seems to constantly vacillate between the desire to tell a story and the sense of obligation to longtime fans to remain faithful to the universe established by Ron Gilbert. It was an uncomfortable position to be in, and we have to admit, Larry and Jonathan were able to come out on the other side with their heads held high. I say that because, although *The Curse of Monkey Island* is not the most legendary installment in the cult series, it is still an exceptional game and the last specimen of the pinnacle of a golden age that was swiftly coming to an end.

Can you believe they wanted to replace me with Johnny Depp?!

Chapter 11: *The Curse of Monkey Island The Movie*™

Now, while we're on the subject, let's take a look at the rise and fall of the film project entitled *The Curse of Monkey Island*, a project that was both insignificant and yet revealing of the franchise's value in the eyes of LucasArts.

A few months after the game's release in October 1997, the studio's bigwigs hired a team from ILM[175] to start work on a project to adapt the game into a feature-length animated film. Not very experienced with that sort of work at the time—the official animation branch, Lucasfilm Animation Ltd., wouldn't be created until 2003—a handful of artists worked on an original script blending the different plot lines of the three existing games.

Truth be told, we don't have much verified or official information about the film adaptation, which to this day remains within the realm of possibility for Disney Animation Studios (highly improbable though it may be). Over time, theories and rumors began to form on internet forums and crowd out the official facts provided: "The really interesting thing is that the movie was going to be produced by Steven Spielberg (who is a big *Monkey Island* fan himself). He asked Ted Elliott, a script writer who has worked on several Disney movies (including *Treasure Planet*[176]) and on the *Steven Spielberg's Director's Chair* game, to help with the story for the *MI* movie. The *Monkey Island* movie never got the green light and years later, Ted Elliott wrote *Pirates of the Caribbean: The Curse of the Black Pearl*, which took several ideas from *Monkey Island*. So, basically, the first two *PotC* movies are the *Monkey Island* movie."[177]

We can find no official confirmation from the studio that Ted Elliott was in fact the head screenwriter for the *Monkey Island* movie project, but Elliott himself did confirm it, quite unwillingly and in a very exasperated tone, sometime later in response to invectives hurled at him by fans who accused him of plundering *Monkey Island* to write the two *Pirates of the Caribbean* movies directed by Gore Verbinski. Furthermore, "You should really know your facts before making

175. Industrial Light & Magic: If you recall, ILM is the special effects branch of George Lucas' business.
176. *Treasure Planet* (2002): Disney's modern reimagining of the novel *Treasure Island*, directed by Ron Clements and John Musker.
177. Information from an anonymous source who was supposedly an "insider" and who posted in the forum of a fan website called *WorldofMI*: *http://www.worldofmi.com/comments.php?type=news&id=1259&action=read*

not-so-subtle accusations of plagiarism. [...] Ironically, the creators of *Monkey Island* have acknowledged their inspiration and debt to the 'Pirates of the Caribbean' ride,"[178] stated an angry Terry Rossio, the co-creator of the adventures of Jack Sparrow. That said, the similarities are quite striking, particularly in terms of visuals. There's the overall humorous tone for the writing and development of the main characters, with Will Turner, the hero, making a perfect Guybrush, Elizabeth Swann serving as a doppelgänger for Elaine Marley, Barbossa working as a great stand-in for LeChuck, and Tia Dalma seeming like a perfect copy of the Voodoo Lady. All of these serve as evidence of the similarities between the two universes.

On screen, certain settings of the films perfectly recreate the atmosphere of places like LeChuck's fortress or the pestilential swamps of Scabb Island. Long story short, if there has been any influence between *Monkey Island* and *Pirates of the Caribbean*, I think it's fair to say that it has been reciprocal.

A few years after the *Curse of Monkey Island* project died, in January 2005, visuals of the planned adaptation began to emerge on the Web. First, from artist Anthony Stacchi[179] confirming that the film project was called *The Curse of Monkey Island* and that it was already dead and buried: "The drawing [released by Stacchi] was mine, but the great painting job was done by Steve Purcell. He helped develop the project for a while."[180] Then, the next year, in March 2006, Purcell confirmed: "As far as a *Monkey Island* movie, I'm probably not allowed to confirm or deny in print for numerous, obscure contractual reasons. Although I'd love to share some completely random, unrelated pirate images I have lying around."[181] We know what he means. Years later, in 2011, with the release of the special edition of *The Secret of Monkey Island*, which I will discuss later on in this book, the movie project was finally confirmed. On the game's disc, savvy players can find a package of fantastic visuals produced by Steve Purcell, as well as the Holy Grail: the film's complete set of storyboards.

While many of the characters were taken directly from the games, the characterization and the overall atmosphere of the universe and scenarios were only loosely followed. What's more, the timeline and set-up of the story were totally independent of the canonical games, as if existing in a parallel universe. Given all this, I'd like to offer you a direct translation of the events as told by the storyboards, taken at face value. Even though it adds nothing to the official universe™, it's an irresistible opportunity to imagine that which we will never get to see on the big screen.

---

178. *http://www.oxfordstudent.com/2011/09/23/films-based-on-games-is-there-any-hope/*
179. Director of the 2006 film *Open Season* and the 2014 film *The Boxtrolls*.
180. *https://monkeyisland.fandom.com/wiki/The_Curse_of_Monkey_Island_(film)*
181. *https://web.archive.org/web/20060411121157/http://www.worldofmi.com/features/interview/purcell.php*

The Curse of Monkey Island™: The Script

As the movie begins, the action takes place in an immense, mysterious cavern, with a shot of a statue of a one-eyed monkey head. A pirate hangs nervously from a rope and manages to reach the monkey head. He reaches out to extract the giant idol's sole eye. In fact, the statue's eye, the "Eye of the Monkey," is an enormous, shining orange gem. As the pirate manages to pry the gleaming treasure free, he unfortunately falls and drops the gem. LeChuck suddenly appears in human form, a colossal pirate captain, and snatches the loot. Throughout the cavern, angry voices awaken. An army of infuriated monkeys descends upon the cave and LeChuck is forced to flee. He hands the gem to Murray, his first mate, and orders him to protect the precious treasure.

Captain LeChuck reaches his ship and takes command. However, he now must face the famous "Anti-Pirate Armada" of the equally formidable Captain Elaine Marley. The battle rages on and the pirate's ship is severely damaged. LeChuck fires a trick cannonball and disappears in a cloud of smoke, leaving behind only the ship's Jolly Roger flag. Off the coast of little Mêlée Island, deep in the Caribbean, a pathetic young fisherman named Guybrush Threepwood, living on a houseboat sporting the Jolly Roger,[182] works for a company that makes fishing lures. His boss, Sean Cannery, treats him like a worthless kid. Depressed, our young hero wanders out onto the dock, talking to himself and lamenting his lot in life.

Meanwhile, Elaine continues to pursue LeChuck. The pirate has discreetly repaired his ship, but has to find a way to draw the governor's attention elsewhere. Murray hatches a plan to get away from her. He tells LeChuck and the crew that they should

---

182. The Jolly Roger is the name given to the "official" pirate flag featuring a skull and crossbones.

deceive the beautiful red-headed captain and quickly head toward Voodoo Island. The pirates start belting out a sea chantey and hoist the sails as they pass near the docks of Mêlée Island. Guybrush catches sight of them. As a wannabe pirate, his interest is piqued and he decides to follow them.

Determined to put together a new crew of hardy seafarers to make up for his losses (and carry out Murray's plan), LeChuck pays a visit to the storied SCUMM Bar. There, Guybrush listens to his pitch and feels the call of adventure. The pirate captain declares that he plans to unite all pirates under "one mighty black flag" so that they may make their own laws. After some intense discussions, LeChuck tasks young Guybrush with seeking out the treasure of Monkey Island, offering him the command of LeChuck's own ship. This is an incredible opportunity for the young fisher, who gets a reputation and a solid ship out of the deal. He's totally oblivious to the fact that it's a trap. LeChuck gives Guybrush the map of Monkey Island, and the young man heads out with his new crew in search of the treasure. Meanwhile, LeChuck, Murray, and the band of pirates take possession of Guybrush's old houseboat, and they all cram in together (it's much too small and pathetic for them, but they don't have much choice). The deception seems to work: Elaine pursues Guybrush, while LeChuck makes his getaway to Voodoo Island.

Out at sea, Guybrush's crew proves to be particularly unruly. As the sailors get into yet another argument, Elaine and her armada take advantage of the distraction to board the ship and take everyone prisoner. After a strange series of events, involving a combination of blunders and luck, Guybrush manages to use one of his cannons against Elaine's lead ship. Her vessel explodes and sets off a chain reaction that destroys the entire armada. The roles are reversed and our young hero takes the upper hand.

On Voodoo Island, LeChuck is ready to carry out his dastardly plan. He intends to use the Eye of the Monkey to raise an army of zombie pirates, control them, and become ruler of the entire Caribbean (Classic! Simple, yet effective). However, right when Murray is supposed to complete the Voodoo ritual by placing the Eye of the Monkey into a cauldron, he realizes that he has a walnut in his pocket in place of the gem. Sam, Guybrush's little monkey friend, must have stolen the jewel when they crossed paths in the SCUMM Bar. Enraged, the spirits of the dead punish LeChuck and his crew by cursing them. They are instantly transformed into zombie skeletons. However, the pirate captain has not had his last word: he will find Guybrush to complete the ritual and exact his revenge!

Back to our novice pirate: taking charge, Guybrush announces to his crew that they'll be heading to Monkey Island. The sailors are astonished, fearing the monster-infested waters around Monkey Island. Most of the pirates run for their lives when an adorable little baby monster jumps onto the ship's deck. Then, suddenly, the baby monster's mother appears, in a panic. Guybrush fights alongside the daring Elaine to defeat the enormous leviathan. Our hero, in a last-ditch effort, loads the unlucky baby monster into a cannon and shoots it far into the distance, forcing the mother to leave in search of it. This gives Elaine and Guybrush a reprieve.

They, along with the monkey Sam and the rest of the crew, finally reach Monkey Island. There, they discover an impressive idol of a monkey. When our young captain attempts to approach it, a horde of monkeys (if you recall, the same from the very beginning of this story, in the cavern) appears and threatens our hero. Sam then brandishes the Eye of the Monkey and the crew is welcomed with open arms as saviors. While Guybrush-who is always slow on the uptake-continues to search for the island's treasure, still determined to complete the mission entrusted to him by LeChuck, Elaine urges him to leave the nefarious pirate and come to the side of justice.

Deep down, Guybrush has always dreamed of becoming a legendary pirate, like the heroes of his childhood. And when he again comes face to face with a furious zombie LeChuck, he agrees almost eagerly to go steal the Eye of the Monkey back, at the risk of drawing the ire of Elaine, Sam, and the tribe of ferocious monkeys. He brings the jewel to LeChuck and his living-dead crew. The zombie pirates finish their macabre ceremony and immediately, all across the sea, sunken pirate ships and their zombie crews rise up from the depths, now in the service of the formidable, bloodthirsty Captain LeChuck!

Elaine gathers her troops and the island's army of angry monkeys aboard LeChuck's former ship. Even with all their forces united, they don't stand a chance against the countless living-dead pirates. Guybrush, feeling the weight of guilt, decides that he must take action at all costs. After all, it was his gullibility that brought about this situation. As the battle rages, he gets hold of a fishing rod, his weapon of choice, and uses it to steal the Eye of the Monkey right out of LeChuck's hand. Guybrush brandishes the precious stone and calls for a "captains' duel" to put an end to the massacre.

The improbable fight begins and, very quickly, LeChuck takes the upper hand. Elaine seizes the opportunity to fire a cannon at the zombie captain. However, instead of a cannonball, the little baby sea monster once again comes flying out (he had climbed back aboard the ship and into the cannon because he thought it was fun). Unbeknownst to LeChuck, the baby's mother rises up right behind him and devours him as she rescues her little one.

Finally, Guybrush orders the army of zombie pirates to return to their watery graves. He returns the Eye of the Monkey to its sanctuary. Sam decides to remain with his fellow primates on Monkey Island. And at last, Elaine and Guybrush embrace each other and sail out to sea under a radiant sunset, heading toward Mêlée Island, cheered on by their crew.

While we will probably never see a movie taking place in the *Monkey Island* universe, the legendary aura of this ill-fated project and the many visuals of it that have emerged over the years have kept a futile hope alive in the hearts of fans.

Yet another restructuring of Lucasfilm after the release of the *Star Wars* prequel trilogy[183] and the opening of its own animation studio in 2003, Lucasfilm Animation,[184] definitively killed all hope of one day producing a *Monkey Island* feature film. What's more, the *Curse of Monkey Island* movie was not the only victim of the pivot toward all things *Star Wars*. Another game project, also supervised by Steve Purcell, *Sam and Max: Plunge Through Space*, was canceled too. Another thing that we will get into later in this book: when Disney acquired Lucasfilm on October 30, 2012, the House of Mouse officially gained control of the rights to the *Monkey Island* franchise. Now that the series' "sister" saga *Pirates of the Caribbean* exists, the likelihood of one day seeing Guybrush appear on the big screen seems even more remote.

Controlling pirates with roller coasters and candy shops? Don't remind me, what an embarrassment.

---

183. With the consecutive releases of *Star Wars Episode 1: The Phantom Menace* (1999), *Star Wars Episode 2: Attack of the Clones* (2002), and *Star Wars Episode 3: Revenge of the Sith* (2005).
184. The studio responsible for the series and feature film *Star Wars: The Clone Wars* (2008-2014), the series *Star Wars Rebels* (2014-2018), etc.

Chapter 12: *Escape from Monkey Island*™

The Curse of the Secret of Monkey Island remake: Bill Tiller Edition™

Bill Tiller came out of his *Curse of Monkey Island* experience a different man. After spending hundreds of hours roving through tropical settings with a strong Spanish colonial influence, working Voodoo magic, and fighting ghost pirates, the young artist was able to prove himself and find his own path. Above all, he gained the recognition of his peers. As previously mentioned, the extraordinary praise from critics following the game's release largely focused on the exceptional quality of the graphics and the phenomenal revamp of the series' visual style. And apparently, Tiller has never really been able to cut the cord with his masterpiece. Years later, after leaving LucasArts, he dove headlong back into the same sort of pirate universe with *Ghost Pirates of Vooju Island*[185] and, most notably, *Duke Grabowski: Mighty Swashbuckler!*[186]

However, it was in 1998, just months after receiving several awards for his work on *The Curse of Monkey Island*, that Bill Tiller secretly began work on a remake of *The Secret of Monkey Island* in the visual style of the third episode. Tiller's ambition was to breathe new life into the first game and give the saga graphical coherence. He had zero intention to modify the game design of Ron Gilbert's original opus. He started by preparing three superb visuals, illustrating the SCUMM Bar's dock, the clocktower square, and Governor Marley's mansion, as part of the file that he presented excitedly to the new president of LucasArts, Simon Jeffery. However, Tiller's dreams were immediately dashed. The company had no intention of producing a remake of such a "recent" game, in spite of the undeniable commercial success of *The Curse of Monkey Island* and the popularity of its revamped graphics. It seems that Bill Tiller was just ahead of his time because, as we will see, *The Secret of Monkey Island* was finally updated in 2009.

---

185. Released in 2010 and produced by Autumn Moon Entertainment, a company that Tiller himself founded.
186. An episodic game started in October 2016 thanks to a Kickstarter crowdfunding campaign, then published by Alliance Digital Media.

Again back in 1998, LucasArts continued producing adventure games and supporting innovative licenses. The company was not yet entirely subject to the *Star Wars* diktat. However, the company did definitively turn its back on 2D games. In order to have a future, the *Monkey Island* series would have to explore a new form. As such, unfortunately, Bill Tiller's fantastic idea for a remake of the first episode would never become a reality.

And why not an anti-capitalist, Bolshevist manifesto!™

For their part, the former directors of *The Curse of Monkey Island*, Larry Ahern and Jonathan Ackley, both left LucasArts, for Microsoft and Walt Disney Imagineering respectively. Thus, once again, our favorite franchise was orphaned. However, the company didn't intend to leave things there. You have to understand that while their sales were modest compared to *Star Wars* productions, the studio's adventure games still enjoyed very strong demand at the start of the new millennium, particularly in Germany and Spain (almost 40% of the firm's adventure game sales came from these two countries). The previous *Monkey Island* sold very well, and it seemed like a great opportunity to give it a sequel. Furthermore, LucasArts was aware of the fact that its adventure games gave the company a distinguished, "artsy" image, unlike its mass production of *Star Wars* products, which on their own would make the firm a soulless factory.

Sean Clark and Michael Stemmle, the two directors of *Sam and Max Hit the Road*, jumped on the opportunity. Mike recalls: "After *Afterlife*,[187] most of the (tiny) core team from that game started work on another sim game. The not-so-tentatively-titled *TV Wasteland* was going to be a charmingly offbeat attempt to simulate the life of a television programming executive. [...] While we were struggling with some of the basics of the title, the team had the misfortune of playing *Diablo*[188] and got fatally distracted. Soon, we were convinced that *we* should do a *Diablo*-like game... only with superheroes. LucasArts allowed us to talk them into building this new game we called *Justice Unlimited*, and off we went... for over a year. And then we killed it. After the collapse of *Justice Unlimited*, I took a two-month drive around the country (I'd built up a LOT of vacation time). On the upside, I got an opportunity to see most of the locations we'd ripped-off lovingly homaged in *Sam and Max Hit the Road*. [...] I guess you could call it a low-rent spirit quest capped off by a

---

187. *Afterlife* is a city-building game in the vein of *SimCity* in which the player acts as a "demiurge" who must create a heaven and a hell. Released in 1996 by LucasArts.
188. The famous hack-and-slash game from Blizzard, released in 1997.

bout of ritualistic purging. At the time, I only half-jokingly called it the 'Mike Stemmle Nervous Breakdown Tour of America.' [...] After I came back from my trip, I think LucasArts' management was frankly a little surprised that I didn't resign. I'm not sure how the muckety-mucks decided it was time to do another *Monkey Island*, but I remember Sean and I sitting down with Jack and being told that LucasArts would like another *Monkey Island*. Since we were both big fans (the first game was being finished when we were hired by Lucas), we jumped at the chance."[189] Thus, the new episode would be designed as a sort of outlet for the frustrations of part of the team, who felt stuck in a climate of uncertainty about the future of the company's employees due to the departure of some of the studio's founding fathers and the cancelations of numerous projects.

And, as we will see, their new *Monkey Island*, of all the series' episodes, is without a doubt the most heavily tinged with sarcasm, disillusioned irony, and, for the first time, a significant dose of anti-capitalism. "[The satirical direction was] probably mostly my doing more than Sean's, since I was on a bit of a wild-eyed anti-commercialization bent during those days. In hindsight, making a ham-handed commentary about how commercialization ruins everything in the midst of an opportunistic third sequel of a video game series is probably a little *too* unintentionally ironic," Michael Stemmle jokes self-critically. When the project was launched, the team came together quickly, eventually comprising almost 60 people at the height of the production. He continues: "By the time *EFMI* (note the preferred acronym) got started, the writing was already on the wall for adventure games in [LucasArts]. Most of the people interested in building them were already gone, it was just about impossible to get a non-sequel adventure game started, and the budgets for building them were getting downright unviable. In that environment, *EFMI* was considered a welcome oasis of 'Not *Star Wars*' within the company for a while."

Since the new era seemed to be taking a firm stance in favor of 3D, the new project, named *Escape from Monkey Island*, would also use the GrimE engine developed for Tim Schafer's *Grim Fandango* (see p. 281). Stemmle recalls that: "With Grim Fandango out the door, the company was *really* eager to push things into 3D. Also, they didn't really want to use SCUMM anymore. [...] Design-wise, it didn't provide that much of a challenge (and truthfully opened up a number of design avenues that didn't exist before), but production-wise, things got bumpy from time to time. Lua[190] turned out to be a good (if idiosyn-cratic) programming language to replace SCUMM, but we wrestled mightily with our choice of rendering/animating tool, which probably bled into the finished product in the form of funky animations, glitchy lighting, and texture

---

189. *https://mixnmojo.com/features/sitefeatures/LucasArts-Secret-History-Escape-from-Monkey-Island/8*
190. Lua is a scripting language created in 1993. It is particularly valued in the video game and networking domains for its portability and efficiency (*World of Warcraft*, *GTA*, etc.)

seam issues (none of which were the artists' fault)." Artist Bill Tiller, who had lent his unique style to *The Curse of Monkey Island*, was working tirelessly on another of the studio's projects, *Indiana Jones and the Infernal Machine*.[191] So, it was Chris Miles, a veteran artist who had previously worked on *Outlaws* and *Grim Fandango*, who was given the difficult task of recreating Tiller's style in 3D. All of the backgrounds were first painted conventionally, then scanned in high resolution before being remodeled in 3D. The famous cartoon style introduced by *The Curse of Monkey Island* was mostly kept, even though the characters in episode four were made to look more like the first two games. The characters were modeled in 3D so that they would be able to move around on pre-rendered backgrounds using a controller or directly via the keyboard. No more mouse! And that was precisely one of the problems with the game, but we'll come back to that later.

Regarding the game's sound, for the first time, Michael Z. Land stepped aside, only creating a handful of tracks for the title. It was the very curiously named "Larry the O" (real name Larry Oppenheimer) who filled the role of sound designer. Already comfortable working with iMUSE, having used it for a bevy of *Star Wars* titles (from *Rebel Assault II* to *X-Wing vs. TIE Fighters*), he oversaw a major update to the dynamic music engine, incorporating a system to handle compression of MP3 files. In concrete terms, this gave *Escape from Monkey Island* better optimization of the disc space, as well as the ability to offer a much better range of tracks than a classic audio CD, which had been used up to that point. Interestingly, the excellent soundtrack, mostly composed by Clint Bajakian, offered the same opening theme as its predecessor, *The Curse of Monkey Island*. That was a first for the series, which had always opened with a variation of the original theme composed by Land. In any case, the game's sound and music, from the purely artistic elements to the superb dubbing, were probably the game's greatest technical successes.

Escape from Monkey Island was released for the PC on November 8, 2000, in the United States and two weeks later in Europe. To change things up—as it hadn't happened since *The Secret of Monkey Island* was released for the Sega CD and *Maniac Mansion* for the NES—the game was ported six months later for a gaming console, namely the PlayStation 2. The transposition was relatively easy given the game's original PC controls. What's more, the PS2 version also featured characters made up of a greater number of polygons and better integration of the 3D elements on the pre-rendered backgrounds. While there were many more changes, among the most notable was that players of the console version got access to a few extra mini-games and a treasure trove of concept art created by Chris Miles (spectacular works you absolutely have to see).

---

191. The first 3D game for the adventurous archaeologist, released in 1999.

Finally, thanks to the series' reputation, positive reviews from critics, and, above all, increasing scarcity of adventure games on store shelves, *Escape from Monkey Island* had a respectable run. Still, selling just under 60,000 copies in the year after its release (PS2 sales were kept confidential, but seemingly were catastrophically bad), the game was a disappointment and it became the final nail in the coffin of LucasArts' point & click titles. *Escape from Monkey Island*, to this day, represents the very last member of the long and glorious lineage of LucasArts adventure games. The end of an era...

The statements made in the following extracts from the journal of Guybrush Threepwood represent only the views of their author. The complex political matter of Threepwood's writings may offend the sensibilities of less seasoned individuals. In these troubled times, with the rise of obscurantist ideologies, such progressive notions may prove to be a bit too revolutionary for some.

The Memoirs of Guybrush Threepwood, Part 4™

Spitting the sand of Monkey Island from my mouth, I began to wonder if the life of a mighty pirate was all it was cracked up to be. I'd ignored recent events that should have been warning shots across the bow of my soul, from my wife's brush with death to the anti-pirate ramblings of Australian gazillionaire Ozzie Mandrill. If only I'd chosen a different path, LeChuck might still be dead, and the mystery of the Ultimate Insult might have remained an enigma. If I'd never picked up a sword, the grog-swilling pirates of the Tri-Island Area might be unthreatened by the twin forces of gentrification and demonic backfire. If only... Suddenly, the hairy finger of a familiar monkey tapped me on the shoulder. It was time. Time to stop LeChuck (again). Time to make the world safe for pirates. Time for the biggest battle of my swashbuckling life.

Sometimes, when it's quiet, I can still hear the monkeys. It's hard to believe that it's only been a few years since I first washed up on the beaches of Mêlée Island. Who could have suspected that such a humble pursuit would lead me to cross swords with the evil ghost pirate LeChuck, the slimiest slug ever to plunder the Seven Seas? And who could have guessed that my battles with LeChuck would introduce me to the love of my life, Mêlée Island's Governor Elaine Marley? Or that my efforts to win Elaine's hand would repeatedly drag me to the mystery-drenched shores of Monkey Island? Back then, the only thing duller than my sword was my wit. Now look at me. I'm married to the most beautiful governmental official in the Caribbean. The entire Tri-Island Area shudders [Editor's note: giggles, not shudders] at the sound of my name. My Plunder Bunny (the cute nickname I've given my beloved Elaine) and I were returning to Mêlée Island after the most incredible honeymoon in the history of video games.

Sadly, all good things must come to an end, and Elaine had to return to her duties as governor. Upon our arrival, I was shocked to discover that none of my adoring fans were waiting for us on the dock. Instead, there was just good ol' Timmy, my adopted monkey, who signaled to us that something was not right. We headed straight to Elaine's mansion, where we found a blockheaded union demolition worker who was trying to demolish the mansion with a catapult. We learned that during our three-month absence, Elaine was declared dead at sea, and elections had been called to elect a new governor! Right away, the town elders decided to order the destruction of the Marley family's property to rebuild a new Mêlée. Elaine then set an action plan in motion. She would immediately go and have herself declared "un-dead," take part in the election, and finally reclaim her position as governor. I was tasked with halting the destruction of our humble abode; then, I had to travel to Lucre Island to meet with the Marley family's lawyers and return with a restraining order to stop the demolition. I'm calling it: paperwork and bureaucracy will be the death of piracy one day. But anyway, a new adventure was starting for me—an adventure in 3D!

Just after getting rid of the catapult, I acquired a ship—the only ship still available, actually. The Dainty Lady. A pink ship. Pink. And I was able to put together a crew of my old comrades in arms, who were overjoyed to return to my service. You remember Carla and Otis, don't you? From the first episode? The third scallywag to join our crew was none other than the owner of the famous SCUMM Bar. We sailed off in the direction of Lucre Island. When we arrived safe and sound, I headed straight off to meet with the most renowned law firm in all of the Caribbean. The three sly paper-pushers there handed me a letter from Grandfather Marley, which said: "My dearest Elaine, If you are reading this, then you are married and I am dead. Now that you've finally settled down with a fearless pirate husband, it's time for you to claim the final pieces of your family's heritage. At the Lucre Island Municipal Bank, you'll find a safe deposit chest under my name. Among other things, the chest contains the deed to the Marley Mansion. Never lose sight of this deed. Furthermore, the chest also contains my wedding gifts to you. I'm sorry that I was unable to deliver them in person, but I go to my grave confident that you've chosen a man I would be proud to call 'grandson.' Lastly, and most importantly, the chest contains the keys to the most terrifying secret in the Caribbean, a secret 10 times as terrifying as Big Whoop. The Secret of... the **ULTIMATE INSULT!** If the unholy power of the Ultimate Insult ever found its way into the wrong hands, there's no telling what sorts of heck-spawned mischief could be released upon our fun-loving pirate citizens! Guard these secrets with your life, and know that, no matter where you are, your grandfather is watching over you. With all my love, Horatio Torquemada Marley. P.S. If your deadbeat parents come around looking for a handout, tell 'em to take a long walk off a short gangplank!"

Such a moving letter. And an inheritance is always a nice surprise. So, I headed straight for Lucre Island Municipal Bank. There, I was able to open the family's safe deposit chest and as I searched through the loot inside, a bandit disguised as... well, as me, burst into the vault. The scoundrel pointed a pistol at me and forced me to hand over Elaine's inheritance. He then fled the scene, locking me in the vault. In no time at all, Lucre Island's police came and arrested me. Inspector Canard forced me to wear the Voodoo Anklet of Extreme Discomfort to keep me from leaving Lucre Island. I was free, or at least out on parole, but I had to prove my innocence by finding the real bank robber.

My investigation quickly led me to zero in on a single suspect: Pegnose Pete, a local elusive ne'er-do-well. During my time on the island, I also came across one Ozzie Mandrill, a dreadful Australian who was spreading terror all over the Caribbean. Mandrill was plotting to take possession of every shop in the Tri-Island Area by launching hostile takeover bids against the owners, using insults as a weapon to smash their egos. The old capitalist crook's real goal was to put an end to piracy so that he could launch a chain of luxury hotels and attract tourists from the continent in order to turn a nice profit by exploiting the local residents for their labor. To tell the truth, I didn't understand most of that jibber-jabber, but I got the drift that he was probably the bad guy in this story. I made headway in my investigation, and I was finally able to locate Pete's hideout in the swamp of Lucre Island. There, I overheard a conversation between Pegnose Pete and Ozzie Mandrill. It turns out the Aussie's diabolical plan was to seize the Marley family heirlooms in order to obtain the Ultimate Insult, while framing me for the whole thing. Armed with the evil Voodoo insult, he planned to bring an end to piracy and realize his capitalist dreams. I captured Pegnose Pete, brought him by force to Inspector Canard, and was able to recover the Marleys' treasure. I was once again a free man and had the Voodoo Anklet of Extreme Discomfort removed—and thank heavens for that because, funnily enough, that thing caused me extreme discomfort. I guess I have pretty sensitive skin.

Back on Mêlée Island, I reunited with my beautiful wife Elaine, who was going through a tough time. Her rival for the governorship, Charles L. Charles (what a ridiculous name), turned out to be a rotten populist politician, promising free grog for all those idiot pirates. While Elaine explained the whole situation to me, that good-for-nothing Charles burst into the manor to reveal to us his true identity. In fact, that slimy politician Charles L. Charles was none other than... than... than... LeChuck! That's right: yet again. I know! Shocking, right? My worst enemy had once again returned from the dead. And this time, he intended to win the Mêlée Island election and get his hands on the Ultimate Insult to subjugate the island's poor pirates. I had to stop him. So, listening only to my courage (and Elaine), I again set out on an adventure.

With help from the Voodoo Lady, I soon discovered that the wedding gifts Grandpa Marley had left for us were capable of revealing the mystery of how to create the Ultimate Insult. I have to say, the puzzles in these newfangled adventure games are getting more and more convoluted. However, my dear sorcerous friend also told me that one of the presents was missing, a painting that Meathook, the handless ventriloquist pirate, had created for Horatio Torquemada Marley. I had to figure out what happened to that painting. Purely by chance, while on my way to SCUMM Bar—which had since become Lua Bar, a Tiki-themed restaurant (Ozzie Mandrill was following through on his threats by buying up all of the businesses in the Caribbean one by one, and had gone after the very symbol of piracy by transforming the famous pirate den and slinger of adulterated grog into a tourist trap)—I spotted the missing painting. With all four wedding gifts finally in my possession, I offered them to the figurehead of my ship, The Dainty Lady (that's right, the Dainty Lady in question can speak; she's an enchanted statue who looks like a sexy mermaid). The figurehead came to life and showed me where I could find the ingredients to help me obtain the Ultimate Insult.

The whole thing was totally twisted, but hey, I'm used to this Voodoo magic stuff now. Destination: Jambalaya Island!

Surprise, surprise, once there, I discovered that what had not long ago been a haven for dirty bandits thirsty for gold and grog had become a huge seaside resort owned by Ozzie Mandrill. The resort even had a StarBuccaneers™ and a Planet Threepwood™! I had to collect the three objects that would allow me to build that cursed weapon known as the Ultimate Insult. I'll spare you the details, but I once again needed to use all of my cunning [Editor's note: and incredible luck] to complete the incredible journey. Along the way, I crossed paths with good ol' Stan, who had become a real estate agent, and Murray, who continued plotting to dominate the human race, and I had to complete all sorts of stupid tasks, like a diving competition and a game of Murrayball (don't try it at home!). Once I'd collected all of the ingredients, all I had to do was return to my love on Mêlée Island. In the meantime, Elaine had unfortunately lost the election to Charles L. Charles, a.k.a. LeChuck. And we then discovered that LeChuck and Mandrill had teamed up to achieve their diabolical goals. Elaine was forced to flee. As for me, having just barely set foot back on dry land, I came face to face with the duo of laughable villains. LeChuck explained that Mandrill had rescued him from the ice under which I'd trapped him during our previous confrontation. But more importantly, he revealed that his number-one goal for the Ultimate Insult was to use it to force Elaine, MY wife, to give him her hand in marriage. MY Elaine! But in the meantime, LeChuck and Mandrill decided to take me out of the picture. GULP!

When I came to, I was lying face-down in the sand. The sand of... Monkey Island! Oh no! Once again, I found myself stuck, defenseless and thrown onto that godforsaken island. It was like my whole life was a never-ending series of puzzles! Within minutes, I spotted my little chimp friend Timmy walking out of the jungle. "At least I have a friendly face to help me get through this ordeal," I thought to myself. As I explored the island, I was horrified to discover that a "First Orthodox Church of LeChuck™" had recently been opened, presided over by the ghostly patriarch Father Allegro Rasputin. The immense cathedral had been built on the side of a volcano and was dedicated to my favorite formidable foe. Naturally, the church wasn't there to do any sort of charitable work; it was there to celebrate the future marriage of LeChuck and my beloved Elaine! I absolutely had to put an end to the zombie captain's harebrained schemes once and for all. Even if it meant I'd spend the rest of my days on Monkey Island, I had to go see my old friend, the hermit Herman Toothrot. Perhaps he could tell me how to get a vessel capable of taking me back to Mêlée Island to save Elaine. The poor old fool was just as nutty as always. I had to give him a few whacks on the head with a coconut and a few other things to bring him back to his senses. This unorthodox brain training session jump-started the few neurons the old fool had left. What he then revealed to me was one of the most incredible twists in all of the Caribbean, or even all of pop culture. You may want to sit down for this. "First, let me tell you how I ended up here on Monkey Island with nothing but a broken accordion, most of the clothes on my back, and a head full of broken memories. Like so many stories, it began some 20 years ago in a bar on the other side of the world. I had been lured out of my peaceful retirement in the Caribbean by the thrill of a dangerous sailing regatta off the coast of Australia. The night before the competition, I was steeling myself for the race with several pitchers of grog, when I was joined at the bar by one of the other competitors, an unhappy Australian tycoon with the unlikely name of Ozzie Mandrill. The poor guy seemed so sad, just because no one would do business with him anymore. To cheer him up, I regaled him with stories of my adventures on the untamed Caribbean seas. The next day, as I reached the race's halfway point, I'd already forgotten the grog-induced revelries of the night before. Suddenly, I found myself being rammed by another boat, pushed into a freakish whirlpool. It was none other than Ozzie! But it gets worse: I hadn't just told Ozzie about the wonders of the Caribbean; I'd also told him about all of its terrible Voodoo secrets. Secrets that men would kill to possess. I'd told him about the Gate to Heck known as 'Big Whoop.' I'd told him about the Unbelievable Lineage of the Three-Headed Monkey™. Worst of all, I'd told him about the Ultimate Insult! The Voodoo talisman that could make mice out of men! Strangely, the whirlpool didn't kill me; instead, it dropped me and my shattered ship on the other side of the world. By the time I had righted myself, I had no idea who I was or where I came from. I took the name Herman Toothrot after the remaining letters on my accordion: 'H.T.' That's right: my real name is Horatio... Torquemada... Marley!" Absolutely wild! Elaine had sworn to me that Grandpa Marley had died some 20 years ago. During a regatta. Off the coast of Australia. OK, I have to admit, when I think about it a bit, it all makes sense. Once I had digested the news, Grandpa Marley also revealed to me the existence of a missing fourth ingredient for the Ultimate Insult. Without this information, my adversary would be unable to carry out his plan and the danger was delayed for the moment. To obtain the last ingredient, a bronze hat in the possession of a monkey named Jojo, Jr., I would have to train to master the legendary MONKEY KOMBAT! An incredibly dangerous form of martial arts that I had to use to fight every monkey on the island, including Jojo, their leader. I'll spare you the gruesome details of all the blows and insults I had to suffer before beating the mighty Jojo, Jr. It was horrible, but my drive to win (and to finish this adventure, which had really dragged on for far too long) prevailed. Finally armed with all of the ingredients needed to build the Ultimate Insult, and following the wise advice of Monkey Island's natives, I again plunged into the Giant Monkey Head (you remember it from the first episode, right? You know, the one that you open with a giant Q-Tip) and took control of what actually turned out to be a fearsome war machine: the GIANT MONKEY ROBOT! I was finally ready to take on the bad guys, save my sweet wife, and kick a few zombie butts along the way!

Aboard my Giant Monkey Robot, I traveled across the sea to the shores of Mêlée Island. On an islet, Ozzie Mandrill had installed an Ultimate Insult Amplification Tower. Indeed, Mandrill and LeChuck had succeeded in building a counterfeit copy of the Ultimate Insult. What evil geniuses! It seemed that Mandrill intended to use the amplification tower to exert total control over the fragile minds of my fellow pirates. Following the sage advice of Grandpa Marley, I deactivated the tower.

Through some unknown dark Voodoo magic, LeChuck fused with the enormous statue of Charles L. Charles that had been erected in his honor in the town square. The colossus then recaptured by beautiful wife, and it was finally time for the ultimate MONKEY KOMBAAAAAAT! After an endless battle, about which the bards may one day write epic ballads [Editor's note: doubtful], the giant statue of LeChuck was finally destroyed in a massive explosion. We won! This was followed by a touching reunion between Elaine and Grandpa Marley. We all decided unanimously that Grandpa Marley should return to the position of governor of Mêlée Island, allowing Elaine and I to plunder the Caribbean like real pirates thirsty for gold and glory (and perhaps think about making some baby pirates...). But that's a story for another day.

The End

Game design and fun facts

In order to conceive of the new adventures of Guybrush Threepwood, developers Sean Clark and Michael Stemmle shamelessly plundered material from scenes that had been cut out of the previous episodes. For example, the search for the wedding gifts in the first part of the game was practically copied and pasted from a sequence imagined by Jonathan Ackley and Larry Ahern for *The Curse of Monkey Island*. In the original scenario of the third episode, our wannabe pirate had to free the love of his life from her curse by collecting the cursed gifts from the wedding LeChuck had planned. The incorporation of these puzzles into the Lucre Island sequence was a bit forced in *Escape from Monkey Island*, which probably contributes to the general feeling that the scenario was sort of a mess.

Still in the category of recycling, the big plot twist near the end, in which the Giant Monkey Head of Monkey Island turns out to actually be the exposed portion of a giant robot, can be credited to Dave Grossman, who came up with the idea for *The Secret of Monkey Island*. Originally, it was more of an inside joke within the team than an actual scene they planned to create. The brilliant and ridiculous idea would have to wait until the fourth episode to become a reality.

The construction of *Escape from Monkey Island* follows the classic pattern that has become familiar for us: a series of challenges in which we have to get to know a new island and follow the clues to find the objects that will allow us to progress through the story. All that is colored with a wave of nostalgia when the plot has us return to Mêlée Island or Monkey Island. Where episode four distinguishes itself is its ending. And particularly its legendary, dreaded, and highly controversial Monkey Kombat. An obvious reference to the Midway Games fighting game *Mortal Kombat*, the mini-game was designed to add a bit of novelty and comedic incoherence by replacing the habitual insult battles (even though they didn't entirely disappear from the title). And, of course, it was a totally stupid idea. Horrible to play, repetitive as can be, and totally unbearable, especially at the end of the game when the denouement is so agonizingly slow to arrive, Monkey Kombat is a major fail in a game that was already quite painfully bogged down by its interface and awkward controls.

Another unique feature, *Escape from Monkey Island* had not one, but two antagonists: Charles L. Charles, a.k.a. LeChuck, and Ozzie Mandrill. They both share the spotlight, as well as Guybrush's ire, and they have similar dreams to enslave all of the Caribbean. However, in actuality, the duo doesn't really work. The fact of having these two characters is evidence that the scenario writers tried to do too much. "Our reasoning went like this: if one villain is good, two must be better! Then we laughed maniacally for six or seven minutes," Michael Stemmle explains. But the problem remains that the villain tag team never worked. The LeChuck's and Mandrill's intentions inevitably conflict with each other and their cooperation doesn't seem credible. It's never explained convincingly why the two enemies would team up and why they would need one another. Even worse, the plot lines are mixed together confusingly, whereas the weaving together of different plots had actually been one of the strengths of the previous three episodes.

Of all the games in the saga, *Escape from Monkey Island* is packed with the most Easter eggs and references to other contemporary cultural works. A panoply of references. I would be crazy to try to name them all, but among the cleverest and funniest, there's a colorful scene slyly stolen from *2001: A Space Odyssey*[192] in which Guybrush takes control of the Giant Monkey Robot and all of the monkeys begin to screech and throw the Giant Q-Tip in the air, a shot-for-shot recreation of part of Kubrick's film. And, of course, I'll leave you to hunt for the many film references–*Braveheart, Clash of the Titans* ("Release the Kraken!"), *Dragon Ball, Forrest Gump, Mad Max, Pulp Fiction* ("Everybody be cool, this is a robbery!")–and video game references (covering various contemporaneous point & click titles, from *Broken Sword* to *Discworld*).

A few more fun facts:

    ◎ If you pay close attention, you'll recognize a few, fairly subtle references to the earlier episodes of *Monkey Island*. For example, the title of Act 3, "Guybrush Kicks Unusually Large Butt." In the first episode, the last part is entitled "Guybrush Kicks Butt," and in *The Curse of Monkey Island*, the ending is called "Guybrush Kicks Butt Again."

    ◎ Even more subtle, in the game, Elaine uses the same campaign slogan as the one seen on the poster near the docks in *The Secret of Monkey Island*: "When there's only one candidate, there's only one choice."

    ◎ Jojo the talking monkey sadly informs us that his father died years ago when a stranger taught him to hang from the nose of a totem, but never explained to him how to get down. Of course, Guybrush is the one responsible.

    ◎ The name of the trio of lawyers on Lucre Island is previously mentioned in *The Secret of Monkey Island*. Indeed, in the first game, Guybrush finds a letter on the beach of Monkey Island giving formal legal notice to old Herman Toothrot and listing the initials of the three lawyers.

---

192. By Stanley Kubrick, a cult science fiction film released in 1968.

Reception and reviews™

About two decades after its release, *Escape from Monkey Island* continues to rack up biting critiques and is viewed as the ugly duckling of the LucasArts series. The reception from video game media was lukewarm at best, especially when compared to the game's predecessors. Ultimately, the fourth episode embodied everything that was wrong about that period in video game history: a title opportunistically made in 3D and equipped with intolerable controls, making the long hours spent searching for clues really grueling.

However, English-language media was also not kind to the game's scenario, which they found lacking in coherence and points of reference. They felt like it aimed no higher than to recycle *ad nauseam* the same hackneyed formula. For the website *Adventure Classic Gaming*,[193] Stemmle and Clark's game suffered from the sort of ailments you'd expect from a fourth episode: "As fun as it is to play *Escape from Monkey Island*, it is sad to see that this game is suffering from a severe case of 'sequellitis'—a condition whereby a game license starts to wear out its welcome and can no longer offer any refreshing play to its audience. The characters in this sequel are just not as funny or endearing as they have been in previous games. The humor is approaching infantile and gets nauseating quickly. The series often cannot escape from its own clichés, drowns in its tiresome humor, and spirals down to oblivion. It may even be argued that this game falls nothing short of over-commercialization of an established institution to rip the last drop of profit from its loyal fan base. [...] *Escape from Monkey Island* is not a bad game at all, but it is definitely not the best of the series. If you are a die-hard fan of *Monkey Island*, then this game is a must for you. Otherwise, let us hope that LucasArts takes notice of its recent shortfalls and not gamble any more with the dignity of this celebrated series." Meanwhile, Marek Bronstring of the leading adventure game website *Adventure Gamers* was much kinder: "Judging *EMI* on its own merits, the game is certainly not disappointing. While it does have a few weak spots, it is a well thought-out game, and longer than the previous one. Where *The Curse of Monkey Island* boiled down to undoing a curse and a long and completely unnecessary explanation of earlier events, *EMI* has a sophisticated story with many interesting plot twists. [...] Unlike its predecessor, *EMI* manages to add nicely to the established back-story, without dishing up a seemingly endless flow of mind-numbing minutiae, like we had to endure at the end of *CMI*. Where the story shines, the dialogues fall a little bit short. *EMI* made me laugh out loud many times, but the jokes are sadly not up to the series' standards. The conversations are often tedious and drawn-out, and too many situations feel

---

193. *http://www.adventureclassicgaming.com/index.php/site/reviews/167/*

like déjà vu. For instance, I was not particularly eager to go find a ship and crew, after having done so in each previous game already."[194]

French video game media observed similar problems. The website *Gamekult*, for example, offered a fairly positive test report, but: "The problem is not with the production, but rather with the very principles of the game, which haven't changed since the first installment, released a decade ago. In spite of some notable improvements, we are left with an adventure game that, because it's equipped with an antiquated inventory management system, pushes the player to act in a way that's not particularly thrilling. Indeed, when faced with wonderfully outrageous puzzles (read: 'wildly twisted'), the player quickly resorts to trying every item in their inventory on the various parts of their environment. True, unlike other adventure games, which punish your random attempts with a terribly tiresome 'you can't do that,' *EMI* usually gratifies you with a witty comment highlighting the ridiculousness of your action... but that's a poor consolation prize for the player, especially when they've been stuck on part of the game for several hours. It's a good game, but is really more for die-hard fans of adventure games."[195]

Was *Monkey Island* too old and stale? Was the point & click sub-genre too antiquated? Was the formula worn out? *Escape from Monkey Island* was viewed as a dinosaur in 2000. Its PS2 version even accentuated that feeling, as it was targeted at a different audience that much preferred other console titles that were much better adapted to the machine, in addition to being more ambitious and innovative. *Monkey Island* had been run ragged and would ultimately have to reinvent itself or... walk the plank.

Legacy and story design™

And yet. And yet, *Escape from Monkey Island* made a heck of an effort to keep the series alive. There's no denying that the pattern on which it relied was lamentably conventional and the game showed a lack of ambition, in addition to suffering from the fatal withering away of its entire genre. But what the game does, it does quite well, and it even proves to be a fairly distinguished installment in the series. As such, this "ugly duckling" probably isn't exactly the terrible game that fans love to hate.

Let's just immediately get out of the way all of the production-related items that don't work well in this opus. So, yes, we can say today that *Escape from Monkey Island* is the episode that has aged the worst. The 3D graphics are

194. *https://adventuregamers.com/articles/view/17498*
195. *https://www.gamekult.com/jeux/escape-from-monkey-island-3010000298/test.html*

badly dated and absolutely do not flatter the otherwise very well-made and stylized backgrounds. The modeling of the characters is coarse, even though a lot of care was put into the animation, which was much better than average for the time. Paradoxically, the game seems to be much more anachronistic than its predecessors. And it's quite infuriating when you realize that the 3D was purely opportunistic and aesthetic, adding absolutely nothing to the gameplay. It was a game of its time, just as there was a wave of FMV[196] use in the early 1990s that the *Monkey Island* series thankfully avoided. The game had to be in 3D for it to sell. But the worst part of the game was that, for the controls, the mouse was abandoned in favor of the controller for the very first time, and that change came with a certain level of discomfort. The mouse is essential to the point & click sub-genre, being totally inherent to its game design. The mouse is an extension of the player's arm and hand. It allows you to quickly and effectively search through the entire screen, an action that represents 90% of the classic gameplay of adventure games. Using a controller, the player moves their ~~tank~~ character laboriously in front of each object in the hopes that they'll be able to do something with it. The result is wasted time and a loss of efficiency, which is exactly the opposite of what Ron Gilbert recommended for the genre in order to keep players interested. Furthermore, the GrimE engine made it so that you had to control the camera, not the avatar. When you change screens, the axes get completely inverted and you end up making many false moves. The technical aspects were clearly a fly in the ointment for *Escape from Monkey Island*. But they weren't the only one.

The writing of the fourth installment is a real disappointment. It's not that it's bad; it's just not as good. There were some great new ideas and, as we'll discuss in a bit, an attempt to broaden the spectrum of subtext with the critique of capitalism. But generally, the jokes fall flat, the dialogue is too lengthy, and the plot it poorly conceived. Most of the puzzles make heavy-handed references to objectives completed in the previous games. The narrative structure is abstruse, you swing back and forth between two antagonists with identical ambitions, you're forced to contend with red herrings, and the game is so difficult that you inevitably forget what's expected of you. The character development, which was already seriously deficient in the previous episode, became ridiculously clumsy, taking characters who were previously fun and interesting and making them dull. But then there's the twist with Herman Toothrot, which strangely works quite well, adding welcome depth and coherence.

That said, not a soul will ever be able to forgive *Escape from Monkey Island* for the infamous, odious, appalling MONKEY KOMBAAAAAAT! How is it that

---

196. FMV stands for full-motion video. With the rise of the CD-ROM, many games featured (poorly) filmed (in mediocre picture quality) actors, as in the case of *Gabriel Knight 2, Phantasmagoria*, and *The 7th Guest*.

a commonplace form of repetitive, mechanical gameplay that was already so overused, a parody of a fighting game, could be made even more unbearable? There is absolutely zero interest, in terms of either gameplay or storytelling, to this (long and tiresome) passage in the last third of the game. That leads to a major problem with the rhythm that proves fatal to the adventure, but which also represents an unusual mistake in story design for the studio and the otherwise talented Stemmle and Clark. It's incredible that this passage made it through LucasArts' internal playtests prior to release.

So, what's left after that tidal wave of critiques? *Escape from Monkey Island*, in spite of its countless references and its lack of ambition in gameplay, is still the most ambitious series installment in terms of themes. For the first time, a game in the series made a real critique of society. While that subtext clearly lacks subtlety, it's still relevant commentary. Jambalaya Island, transformed into a hotbed of consumerism, offers some interesting food for thought. It's also the funniest, most inventive, and most successful part of the game, and–dare I say it?–the boldest passage in the entire saga! On Jambalaya Island, the puzzles follow Ron Gilbert's specifications for a good adventure game to a tee, the dialogue is funny, even hilarious, Murray makes a spectacular return, and Stan makes an appearance and is just as obnoxious as ever.

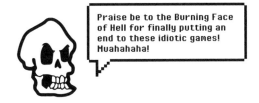

Praise be to the Burning Face of Hell for finally putting an end to these idiotic games! Muahahaha!

Chapter 13: The adventure game is dead!!™

The adventure game is dead! Long live the adventure game! I'm sure you've remarked that over the two decades that we've just reviewed, and for all of the reasons mentioned, the very concept of the video game evolved. From the first explosion of video games in the early 1980s—an objectively very forgettable period of cheap software that flooded stores—to the experimentation and mainstreaming of the medium of the 1990s, we have seen numerous forms, genres, and trends emerge. Technical improvements led pixels to fade into the background and be replaced by polygons. Music produced by the computer's internal buzzer was replaced by symphonic soundtracks using sound technologies like Dolby Digital, THX, and Atmos. Storytelling underwent an equally radical transformation, going from text-based stories to Hollywood-style dramatization. All of those changes led the video game to transition from being a pastime reserved for a select few to a mass-market powerhouse, with widespread adoption of PCs and gaming consoles. All of that has been good in and of itself.

There are a thousand reasons that explain why the adventure game genre gradually rose to become a shining star, only to then fall out of fashion. An article on the website *Gamecenter* (now defunct) had already proclaimed in 1999 that the point & click adventure game was "dead and buried."[197] To summarize the article in question, the journalist dated audiences' gradual abandonment of the genre back to the release of *Myst*.[198] Allegedly, the impressive commercial success of that game led hordes of casual gamers to overwhelm the very perfectionist community of "true" gamers. The same journalist deplored the fact that the throngs of new low-brow players preferred the instantaneity and simplicity of games like *Half-Life* and *System Shock* over the intellectual classics like *Grim Fandango*, *Blade Runner*, and *Gabriel Knight 3*. The author added that the latter, released by Sierra in 1999, probably represented the genre's swan song. Before its resurrection.

---

197. *http://web.archive.org/web/20001002183740/http://www.gamecenter.com/Features/Exclusives/Deadburied/ss01.html*
198. *Myst* is a legendary first-person adventure and puzzle game released in 1993 and developed by Cyan.

The very influential Erik Wolpaw of the website *Old Man Murray*[199] offered a witty response to the Gamecenter editorial in a note entitled "Who Killed Adventure Games?"[200] Wolpaw took the scenic route to illustrate his point by citing a select passage from the walkthrough for the abovementioned *Gabriel Knight 3*, supposedly the ultimate paragon of the adventure genre. For the purposes of a puzzle, the titular character of Sierra's series must disguise himself as someone else in order to get a moped rental clerk to rent him the shop's last moped. But in order to create his disguise, Gabriel must first fabricate a fake mustache. Naturally, obtaining such an item involves a series of totally ridiculous and illogical tasks, particularly in the serious context of the titles by Jane Jensen.[201] To create said mustache, Gabriel has to set up a trap for a cat (using masking tape) so as to steal some fur from the poor animal. Next, Gabriel has to find a second adhesive, of course, to attach the cat hairs to his face. For lack of any alternative, he must do so with maple syrup. "Remember how shocked you were at the end of the *Sixth Sense* when it turned out Bruce Willis was a ghost? Well, check this out: at the end of this puzzle, you have to affix the improbable cat hair moustache to your lip with maple syrup! Someone ought to give Jane Jensen a motion picture deal and also someone should CAT scan her brain." Indeed, Erik Wolpaw's objective with this article was to point out that the point & click sub-genre didn't need anyone or anything else to bring about its demise. It did a perfectly fine job of that on its own. "Who killed Adventure Games? I think it should be pretty clear at this point that Adventure Games committed suicide."

While I wouldn't be as categorical as Wolpaw, the truth probably sits somewhere in the middle of these two explanations. First, the popularization of video games undeniably generated new needs. But contrary to the extremely condescending claims of the website *Gamecenter*, it wasn't that a legion of brain-dead newcomers invaded the exclusive territory of the noble "gamers"; rather, there was a wave of new customers who gave a new boost to the medium. With those new customers, the video game industry acquired new resources—"new" both from a technological and a design point of view—to offer an experience that could better match the artistic ambitions of creators. Ay, there's the rub. Players of classic adventure games didn't disappear with the release of *Myst* or with the arrival of the CD-ROM or PlayStation. They had a choice. A choice between new, revolutionary experiences in terms of

199. A well-respected website in the late 1990s, providing irreverent game reviews that went against mainstream opinions. The website had considerable influence and led to more critical looks at certain influential game designers like John Romero (*Doom, Daikatana*) and American McGee (*Alice*).
200. "Who Killed Adventure Games?": *http://www.oldmanmurray.com/features/77.html*
201. The eminent creator of the *Gabriel Knight* saga and more recently of the games *Gray Matter* (2010) and *Moebius: Empire Rising* (2013).

storytelling (*Half-Life*, *Metal Gear Solid*, and *Deus Ex* each, in their respective genres, offered a radically different way of telling a story while remaining fun to play). For over 15 years (fifteen years!), the point & click sub-genre proved incapable of evolving in any significant way. At best, we can mention LucasArts experimentation in this area. What Ron Gilbert had feared, and looked for every possible means to avoid, continued to chip away at the genre. With puzzles that made you want to pull your hair out, laborious searching through every last pixel, and a lack of attention to crucial aspects like the story design of puzzles, it was inevitable that players would grow weary. And indeed, the genre fizzled out. *Escape from Monkey Island* marked the sad and pathetic ending to a glorious decade for LucasArts, which then decided to go all in on over-exploiting its lucrative *Star Wars* license. The studio unleashed on the world an avalanche of products of frankly questionable quality. *Star Wars: Super Bombad Racing*, *Star Wars: Obi-Wan*, *Star Wars: Starfighter*, *Star Wars: Bounty Hunter*. Don't remember these titles? There's good reason for that.

In any case, in 2001, the heads of the studio, hoping to buy back credibility in the eyes of fans, released that flood of new games. Nonetheless, commercial realities led to the cancelation of sequel projects for *Sam and Max* and *Full Throttle*, marking the end of the road for the studio's adventure games.

That said, the genre was not dead and buried! Certain niche markets, notably in Germany and Spain, had audiences still demanding new games. This allowed a handful of independent studios to continue supplying new adventures to point & click fans. In 2003, the release of *Runaway* caught the curiosity of players. Blending nostalgia with a desire for modernization, titles from the Spanish studio Pendulo took over from there, but without fundamentally changing the eternal formula of the adventure game. Next, the German studio Daedalic and the English studio Revolution Software gave the genre a few shocks with the defibrillator, but without any major success. It wasn't until 2005, with a new studio founded by LucasArts alumni, that a new hope was born.

Can you believe they never even considered me for The Walking Dead? What a bunch of amateurs!

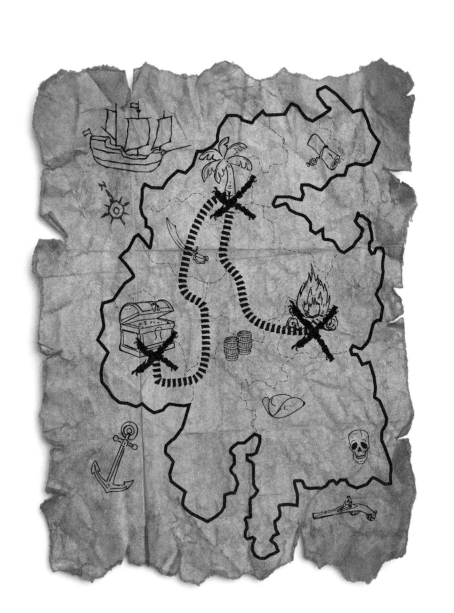

THE MYSTERIES OF
MONKEY ISLAND

Part 3

Chapter 14: Telltale Games™

At LucasArts, the successive changes to internal policy had mixed results. Since Simon Jeffery, a true gamer and fan of adventure games, entered the executive ranks at LucasArts in 1998, levels of sales and production values had been consistently solid. The company was doing pretty well financially, with revenues driven by the successive releases of the *Star Wars* prequel movies. The studio took on one project after another, but the quality objectively declined as they chose to prioritize opportunistic needs of the moment: an action game to put under the Christmas tree, a mediocre spaceship simulator for the release of such and such machine, etc. The old guard of developers were left with doubts about the management of the games division, led by Randy Breen, who came over from Electronic Arts in 2000. Most of the studio's historic game designers—Gilbert, Schafer, Grossman, Falstein, Fox—left to take on new adventures elsewhere, and the development teams who had seen the glory days of the company continued to look back with nostalgia on the firm's ideals of the distant past, remembering an era when employees were driven by the desire to create and tell great stories.

As an ultimate symbolic slap in the face, in 2004, after the quite sudden and disappointing departure of Simon Jeffery, Jim Ward, who had been the Vice President of Marketing, became President of LucasArts and began weeding out the overgrown garden of projects the studio was cultivating. What's more, he confirmed that the company's future was with *Star Wars* and that contracting with external development studios was a viable long-term solution (*Star Wars: Knights of the Old Republic* developed by BioWare, *Star Wars: Battlefront* by Pandemic, etc.). To that point, even in 2002, Ward's predecessor, Simon Jeffery, was already trying to justify that approach: "It's really part of our growth strategy. I read somewhere recently that we were being accused of utilizing outside developers to increase the quality of our games, as if that was some terrible kind of sin. Guilty as charged! The reason we are partnering with people like Verant [*Star Wars: Galaxies*], BioWare [*Knights of the Old Republic*], and more to be announced soon (!) is that we want to build and release the very best quality games possible. We want our current fans, our fans of old, and hopefully some new fans to enjoy every game that we put out. We want the best development talent in the world to build our games—whether those people work at LucasArts, or for a premier developer. [...] We are only partnering with external developers who are as passionate about *Star Wars* as we are. Every 'external' game has a suite of LucasArts personnel working full-time on the project also. We don't view these games as external, we view them as joint ventures. We're heavily involved in the design stage in particular."[202] Still, gradually, between 2003 and 2004, LucasArts almost entirely lost its status as a game developer to become merely a publisher and owner of franchises. Exactly like Electronic Arts, from which the new management drew major inspiration. It was the straw that broke the camel's back for many of the most senior developers at LucasArts, who headed for the exits.

New horizons™

Three of those veteran developers decided to found a new studio in San Rafael, California. On November 14, 2004, Telltale Games, launched by Kevin Bruner, Dan Connors and Troy Molander, opened its doors. All three of them had experienced the glory days of LucasArts, particularly assisting with the development of *Sam and Max*, *Grim Fandango*, and *Escape from Monkey Island*. They shared a common goal: to offer more modest games developed by a small team and which would be targeted at less experienced audiences. What's more, the games would be episodic and fully digital, being delivered through direct downloads. Dan Connors remembers: "I started my career at LucasArts in 1993. The richness of the creativity and the ability to do anything, to do a crazy puzzle about a mummy that you paint red and put spaghetti on his head, [...] just the craziest time-travel-in-a-porta-potty type of stuff: now that was cool. [...] After *Sam and Max Hit the Road*, I started producing on [*Star Wars:*] *Dark Forces*. So, that was my first real shooter story and probably the first time I saw the power of immersive interactive entertainment." Kevin Bruner adds: "I ended up at LucasArts. The game that I was interviewing for there was *Grim Fandango*, and I saw the prototype, and at that point, I was like, 'I'll work for free! It doesn't matter: I have to work on this!'"[203] However, the new team, hoping to blaze a new trail, had a real challenge on its hands. Kevin Bruner explains: "[The idea of episodic games] was, 'how do you bring something to a smaller audience [of mainstream non-gamers] and keep it relevant?'" Connors continues: "In 2000, everybody was thinking, 'how are we gonna get to digital distribution, and once we're at digital, what does episodic look like in that model?' [...] We always felt like story was the key to keep people engaged over five or six months. [...] Digital distribution would give you the freedom to own

202. *https://www.theforce.net/jedicouncil/interview/sjeffrey.asp*
203. YouTube video: Telltale Games: Story Mode (Documentary) | Magnum Opus Games On Complex: *https://www.youtube.com/watch?v=Ozg8O91dqRA*

your own publishing. Episodic would allow you to retain customers over time, and narrative was a way to kind of exploit that. By telling a story over time, you could really make episodic work." They had previously considered using this format for the *Sam and Max: Freelance Police* sequel project, but LucasArts decided to abandon its development in spite of its advanced stage.

Telltale had a modest beginning. The small team was made up of fewer than 15 employees piled into a cramped open-space office. They decided to devote their first three months to developing a game engine (which would be used for almost the entire life of the studio). While their clearly defined goal was to reimagine the adventure game, the first title released by Telltale in February 2005 was a... poker game. *Telltale Texas Hold'em* came out at just the right time, when that particular poker variant was all the rage, even being shown on TV. Strangely enough, that first game combined a number of the studio's interests. It allowed the team to prove that their in-house engine worked, to test their direct-distribution model via PC downloads (through Steam and other such platforms), and to perform some initial tests of integrating storytelling with the player's choices. In a way, the title was almost the first "point & click adventure poker game."

With that initial success under their belts, Telltale negotiated to obtain the rights to the *Bone* comic books from their author Jeff Smith. Following in the footsteps of *Sam and Max*, the studio hoped to use a license for a lesser-known comic book series with a simple design to create their first adventure game. For seven months, the developers worked tirelessly to produce *Bone: Out from Boneville*, a simplistic adventure game without much innovation. The title strictly followed the gameplay of LucasArts' point & click adventures in a 3D environment, much like *Escape from Monkey Island*. The puzzles were simple and the game earned a tepid reception. It was followed by the exploitation of another, more lucrative license: *CSI: 3 Dimensions of Murder*,[204] released simultaneously for the PC and Wii in March 2006. Again influenced by a traditional approach to game design and by an emphasis on storytelling, the perfectly forgettable game nonetheless delivered solid returns for the studio by targeting a broader audience craving simplistic gameplay.

Let's get Sam and Max back!™

In late 2004, a petition circulated on the Web, entitled "Let's get Sam and Max Back!" It garnered over 30,000 signatures, leading certain individuals to

---

204. *CSI*, which of course stands for *Crime Scene Investigation*: a police game set in the universe of the TV series of the same name.

take notice. In March 2005, one Dave Grossman, who had seemingly disappeared since the development of *Day of the Tentacle*, resurfaced. He joined Telltale Games to lay the groundwork for the next big project for an adventure game adaptation, one that had been collecting dust on the shelf for years: a new *Sam and Max*. LucasArts' hold on Steve Purcell's license ended in June 2005 and Telltale immediately scooped it up, announcing a new game shortly thereafter in September 2005. Dave Grossman would be the lead director and Steve Purcell would keep close tabs on the game's preparation and development. The next month, the brilliant author launched a *Sam and Max* web comics series entitled *The Big Sleep*, for which he would obtain a prestigious Eisner Award[205] in 2007. Finally, the first episode of the new adventure game series *Sam and Max: Season One* was released on October 17, 2006. It was entitled *Culture Shock*. For the first time in six years, a piece of the historic LucasArts was revived in the hearts of longtime players, bringing success. The episodic series received respectable reviews from critics and sales were not bad—even if not reaching blockbuster status—confirming for Telltale that they had the right approach. The adventure game had found a new home and would get another taste of the glory days. In 2007, the studio launched a new series called *Strong Bad's Cool Game for Attractive People*, based on a satirical animated web series, bringing back the sarcastic humor and spirit of the golden age of adventure games. In March 2009, Telltale came out with a new adaptation of a famous franchise, *Wallace & Gromit's Grand Adventures*, a successful game series set in the universe created by Nick Park and the studio Aardman Animations.

With the reputation built from *Sam and Max*, and thanks to the reactivation of longtime fans, Dave Grossman felt like the moment was ripe and the stars had aligned to breathe new life into another series that brought fame to the point & click sub-genre in its early days. A series smelling strongly of adulterated grog.

---

205. The Eisner Awards are prizes given each year to figures in the American comics world, presented during Comic Con in San Diego, California.

Chapter 15: *Tales of Monkey Island*™

At LucasArts, there was suddenly renewed interest in old ideas that had been put on the shelf. Was it the new leadership by Darrell Rodriguez, who had also come over from Electronic Arts in 2008, that got the ball rolling again for modern updates to classic series? Or was it the reputational success of Telltale Games and the emergence of a market for games delivered digitally that gave new hope to the studio? Whatever the case may be, it appears that LucasArts began talking about *Monkey Island* again, with the possibility of a remake project.

For Telltale, the esteemed franchise was, of course, always a goal. Since the founding of the studio, its members had made a handful of timid requests to LucasArts in hopes of obtaining the rights. According to Dave Grossman: "You know, we did *Sam & Max*, but we didn't actually go through [LucasArts] to do that, because that belonged to Steve Purcell. There was always somebody over there who was interested in [making another *Monkey Island*], but not always the right people at the right places at the right time. This is fortuitous that we asked the right questions and they had the right answers at the right particular time. They're also doing their own revamp of *The Secret of Monkey Island*, and I guess they thought the idea of having some new games coming out at the same time would be good."[206] However, acquiring the rights was not so simple. Specifically, LucasArts was reluctant to allow Telltale to publish the fruits of its labor on its own. After intense negotiations between February and August of 2008, the two sides reached a deal. In response to a question about who would publish the game, Dave Grossman replied, "We are publishing *Tales of Monkey Island*. We are paying LucasArts money for the use of their characters and license. They are giving us some feedback on how the art looks and stuff like that, but it's basically our show."

A highly anticipated sequel™

Since 2000 and the release of *Escape from Monkey Island*, numerous fan websites had expressed their longing to again cruise through the Caribbean

---

206. *https://www.gamasutra.com/view/feature/132459/back_in_the_water_the_monkey_.php*

in search of the secret of Monkey Island. The leading sites like *scummbar.com*, *worldofmi.com*, and *mixnmojo.com* tracked every little scrap of information, every slightest hint that gave hope for the future of the saga and brought together a lively and passionate community. To spare fans a long wait and generate surprise, Telltale decided to develop its game in total secrecy, preferring to wait until just a few weeks before the official release to make an announcement.

From the beginning, it was clear that *Tales of Monkey Island* would follow the same pattern that had proved effective with *Sam and Max*: a series of five episodes distributed via digital platforms, with a scenario following an overarching plot, but with each individual episode capable of being played independently. In the studio's initial successes (*Sam and Max*, *Wallace & Gromit*), each episode in the series was designed to stand on its own as the developers never knew if the performance of an episode would allow them to produce the next. However, for *Monkey Island*, Dave Grossman was confident and wanted to be more ambitious with the overarching story of the saga. As such, he preferred to design the episodic series like a true new installment in the franchise. "We've left a little bit of mental space between the four games that have come before and this series, basically because we wanted people to take that space themselves to think about it in a slightly different way than they would about something that was meant to come directly after *Escape from Monkey Island*. They might be expecting one story in three acts, with eight billion puzzles that take 20 hours, whereas what we're actually doing is a series. It's more one story in 15 acts; each episode really has a beginning, middle, and an end to it. Then we parcel that out over five episodes in five months, so the mental space is really quite different." As such, the timing of the new story had to be specially managed to account for the time between each episode. What could be worse than the classic episodic format in which the player makes it all the way through the first episode, then forgets everything by the time the second finally comes out? So, each piece had to have a true beginning, middle, and end. And everything would have to fit into a broader narrative. Dave Grossman recollects: "It's [been] almost 20 years, yeah. My last chapter in this saga [*LeChuck's Revenge*] came out in 1991, so that's been 18 years. It's been good, actually. It was a little weird. At first, it was like my old girlfriend just called me out of the blue and wants to see me again, wants to meet for dinner, or whatever. But as we've been working on it, I've been remembering what's fun about these characters and that world–and it really is. Now it's like hanging out with old friends, and it's pretty nice."[207]

---

207. *https://www.gamasutra.com/view/feature/132459/back_in_the_water_the_monkey_.php*

A dream team™

Telltale Games got together a veritable dream team to bring the new adventures of Guybrush Threepwood to life. Under the general supervision of Dave Grossman, the game would be directed by Michael Stemmle (*Escape from Monkey Island*), art direction was entrusted to Derek Sakai, who had previously worked alongside Bill Tiller on *Curse of Monkey Island*, and the music would be handled by the one and only Michael Z. Land. But that's not all. Dave Grossman recounts: "As soon as I was allowed to tell anyone, I called Ron on the phone, because I know the series does mean a lot to him, and he was the original guiding force behind the first games. He looked around and said, 'Could I come down there and brainstorm with you?' And I was like, 'Great! That is absolutely the best thing you could do.'"[208] While the level of his participation would remain confidential, the involvement of Ron Gilbert immediately earned the game credibility in the eyes of fans by showing them that Telltale was doing right by the universe Gilbert had created. "So, he came down and spent the better part of a week with us, just tossing around ideas. We bounced the broad-story stuff off of him; he had some comments about how we were handling Elaine in our first draft that got us to make some changes; and probably a few of his bubbles are in there as well. He had to go back to his regular job as the creative director at Hothead where he's doing his own game, *Deathspank*, which also looks pretty cool. But he did get his chance to put his two-cents in."

While the overall plot was written by Dave Grossman, Michael Stemmle, and Will Armstrong, each of the episodes would be entrusted to different directors so that they could be developed in parallel. Episode two was given to Mark Darin, who had earned his stripes on *CSI: Hard Evidence* and *Sam and Max Beyond Time and Space*. The third episode would be co-directed by Joe Pinney, Jake Rodkin (future director of the brilliant *Firewatch*[209]), and Sean Vanaman (future creator of a spectacular Telltale hit: *The Walking Dead*[210]). Episode four saw the return of Michael Stemmle. Finally, episode five was handled by Mark Darin and Jake Rodkin. It was an all-star team to develop the series, which served as a springboard for these future legends of the adventure game genre. According to Dave Grossman: "We all have slightly different angles on things, which is part of what makes it interesting. I'm just trying to make sure we stay true to Guybrush's core nature. He's a bit selfish, flippant, and unaffected by things, but he's very much in love with Elaine, and their relationship is

---

208. *https://www.eurogamer.net/articles/a-tale-of-monkey-island-interview*
209. *Firewatch* is a "walking simulator" and story-driven adventure game. It is an excellent title from the studio Campo Santo, released in 2016.
210. *The Walking Dead* Season 1 is considered to be Telltale's masterpiece and probably one of the greatest stories ever told in a video game.

actually very important over the course of the season. We want to stay true to the things that are critical."[211]

A casual, dynamic epic™

The in-house game engine was improved for the new game, particularly for the facial animation of the characters, including lip syncing (of note, most of the original cast of voices again returned, adding consistency with the rest of the series). The game's visual style was a blend of all the influences of the previous titles. Thus, Guybrush kept his coat, but his design became slender and lanky like in *Curse of Monkey Island*, and for the first time he was given a pointy little goatee. The backgrounds were largely the same as the last two games, but entirely in 3D this time, with a much more masterful rendering compared to *Escape from Monkey Island*.

In terms of the scenario, Dave Grossman wanted to surprise fans and decided to do away with the saga's "historic" pattern of puzzles (the equation of crew + ship = new island). "Something that I always thought was true about the *Monkey* series was that, while moment by moment it's quite silly and there's lots of slapstick, verbal humor, and ironic pointing out of social dysfunctions, the broad strokes of the story there are actually quite serious. The first one is about this young man who's come to this island to realize his life's dream, and in the quest of doing that, he falls in love and he finds out, 'This is more important to me than my life's dream.' It's actually quite a serious story, despite being a pretty silly experience overall. I've been pushing the team to try and capture that aspect, and when they try and do things in the series that seem baldfacedly hugely ridiculous, I call that into question. Whereas, when the smaller points are ridiculous, that's what I love." Grossman was also fully aware that the adventure game had to change in order to survive. There was no way they could repeat the mistakes pointed out by *Old Man Murray* in his editorial (see chapter 13, "The adventure game is dead!!"). It was this deep reflection on what the very experience of *Tales of Monkey Island* should offer that largely influenced the complexity and logic of the puzzles. No more endless searching for nonsense objects. The adventure game had to transform into a new storytelling experience. And while the metamorphosis was not yet complete (the interactive story adventure game would continue to evolve with titles like *Heavy Rain*[212]

---

211. *https://www.gamasutra.com/view/feature/132459/back_in_the_water_the_monkey_.php?page=2*
212. *Heavy Rain* is a game from French studio Quantic Dream, released in February 2010. It can be considered one of the last evolutionary forms of the adventure game. An interactive experience combining searching for objects with dialogue and moral quandaries, *Heavy Rain* is an almost point-by-point application of Ron Gilbert's commandments written two decades earlier.

in 2010 and *Jurassic Park* in 2011, with the latter also developed by Telltale), *Tales of Monkey Island* was undeniably a step in the right direction. Grossman continues: "Where we've been trying to go with adventures games—maybe someday we won't even call them that anymore, but this style of game story-telling that we do—is towards something that is a more casual experience. The 'sofa experience' is the way I like to think of it. You're going to be sitting on your couch or with your browser, browsing through stuff. You go, 'Oh, look. The new *Monkey Island* is out. I'm going to play that right now.' You download it, play it right away. You might even finish it right in one sitting. And then you move on to something else. You probably have your family there with you. It's a little bit different from the old experience. I remember my own childhood playing these kinds of games—you know, I'm alone, stuck up in my bedroom, and I'm just thinking a lot and banging my head against the wall. 'Curse those designers! What do they mean by this puzzle?' Whereas with this, there are some puzzles in the episodes that I think are hard, but they're not cruel. I think that lack of cruelty is an important feature if adventure games are going to be palatable to a large audience. You just can't be that mean. I'm trying to give people a little fun and let them do some things to make them feel clever, but let them get through the game so that they will be ready for the next one when it comes down."[213]

The puzzles weren't the only aspect to drastically change their orientation. The entire presentation of scenes took a leap forward. No more static dialogue: the 3D engine used by Grossman and his team allowed them to continuously animate numerous parts of the backgrounds and make the production and shots more dynamic. As such, much more than before, the storytelling relied on images, movement, and sound, rather than on text alone. These efforts helped make the game more lively and the experience more fluid and cinematic. The introduction to episode two, which presented a new character dueling with Guybrush, is a perfect example of how this blend of scene-setting, dialogue, and puzzles was put into action.

An episodic success story™

Developed in less than six months, *Tales of Monkey Island* was publicly announced in June 2009 at E3. To promote its release, little animated short films entitled *I Wonder What Happens in Tales of Monkey Island* were featured on the Telltale website. Created by Marius Fietzek, these little comedic gems tried to imagine what might happen in the upcoming episode.

213. *https://www.gamasutra.com/view/feature/132459/back_in_the_water_the_monkey_.php?page=4*

In addition to a PC version, console versions via WiiWare (the Nintendo Wii's download service) and for the PS3 eventually followed, in 2009 and 2010 respectively. Interestingly, in France, the game was released entirely in English, a first in the history of the series. Fortunately for the French, a fan translation in the form of an amateur software patch surfaced on the Web a few months later and was eventually integrated into the game.

For Telltale, the new series became a success that exceeded the studio's hopes in terms of sales. For a few weeks, the game was ranked among the top 10 best-selling titles on Steam, with most players buying the "Season" pack rather than each individual episode–a very positive sign for the studio. In an interview with *VideoGamer.com*, Dan Connors, Telltale's CEO, said: "It was a great launch for us. We're really happy with it. I think it even exceeded our expectations. It's been pretty shocking how much love there is still out there for the *Monkey Island* series. It seems like a generational thing as well." Unfortunately, the sales figures have never been disclosed–the digital market is always particularly sketchy on those details. A "physical" special edition for players who pre-ordered the game was released a few months after the digital release, with an exclusive cover designed by Steve Purcell himself.

Below are the final fragments found to date of the journal of Guybrush Threepwood. These represent the last known days of the legendary pirate, unless we can confirm potential traces of his presence on Libertalia, an island off the coast of Madagascar. But let's not get ahead of ourselves. I now invite you to read these illuminating documents, which challenge everything we know.

The Memoirs of Guybrush Threepwood, Part 5™

When is a sword more than just a sharpened piece of steel used for stabbing a scurvy seadog or trimming a nasty toenail? When it's crafted with a purpose! I've sailed the Seven Seas in search of archaic charms and curiosities, each one rarer than a corked cask of grog on a stranded schooner; I've raided the sunken smelters of Popgowatu for the finest of tools; and I've worked by candlelight in the yawing quarters of my ship to forge together the raw materials into the finest of blades, all to finally put a bloody end to my undead rival and stealer of spouse. It is now that this sword is more than just a sword; it is a covenant! I'm not exactly sure what that word means, but it sounds right. I must make haste for the Rock of Gelato! The seas will sleep soundly tonight, for LeChuck's time is up!

Episode 1: Launch of the Screaming Narwhal

I was off the coast of the Rock of Gelato, deep in the Caribbean. I was going to put an end to the evil Captain LeChuck's diabolical machinations once and for all. LeChuck was planning to sacrifice the legendary Thirteenth Monkey of Montevideo to seize control of the oceans and, more importantly, to seize control of Elaine, whose ship he had captured just hours before. Finally, I arrived on the scene to board the vessel, armed with my brand-new Cursed Cutlass of Kaflu™ that I had so painstakingly assembled. All that was left for me to do to complete the Voodoo ritual was spray the cutlass with enchanted root beer. However, due to the roaring winds of the terrible storm, as well as the belligerence of my many assailants and just darn bad luck, I dropped my only bottle of Voodoo root beer. In hindsight, I probably shouldn't have replaced it with a bit of fizzy root grog—I've always been told to carefully follow instructions on the back of the bottle when dealing with anything Voodoo-related. But I had no other choice. So, I took on LeChuck with my half-enchanted cutlass. And, of course, the results were not what I was expecting. At the end of our fierce battle, I skewered my enemy like a rubber chicken. He had only enough time to grab my hand (but take note of this detail, as it will be very important to my story) before disappearing in a blinding green flash of Voodoo magic... Only to then reappear as... LeChuck! But not the LeChuck that we all know and hate (you know, the one who appears on the cover of every game). No. A real live LeChuck in the flesh. With fresh, rosy skin. A living, human LeChuck! Right as I was about to deal him a fatal blow, my hand refused to obey and flung my Voodoo cutlass towards the barrels of gunpowder laying around on the ship's deck. And just like with most of the other explosions I've experienced, I was propelled way out into the middle of the sea.

When I came to, I was floating aimlessly on a scrap of the ship's hull off the coast of Flotsam Island. The little island, which was constantly buffeted by winds blowing in all different directions, was home to a small community of pirates who were quickly turned against me by my hand, which had turned green, warty, and apparently evil. It seemed to be infected with some sort of Voodoo plague, and I no longer had control over it. A bit awkward, to say the least. Still, I needed to quickly find a ship to return to the Rock of Gelato and find Elaine. The only ship anchored at the island's little dock was called the Screaming Narwhal. A pitiful, haphazardly assembled vessel (beggars can't be choosers) controlled by Reginald Van Winslow. The scoundrel made a deal with me: if I could knock him off the ship, it would be mine. I've had tougher challenges in my day, and after some clever work with explosives—my specialty!—I won my ship. However, the inward-blowing winds of Flotsam Island prevented any ship from leaving. I had to figure out how to reverse the winds using some magical mojo machines. And who knows more about mojo than the Voodoo Lady?

I told my old friend about my most recent misadventures. She informed me that I had contracted the Pox of LeChuck. It was a terrible curse that had jumped from the rotten body of my enemy to make its new home in my hand. Once freed of his curse, LeChuck returned to being human. Still, I would need to destroy the dreadful curse once and for all. And there was only one artifact capable of treating my monstrous magical malady: "La Esponja Grande." A legendary sea sponge with incredible Voodoo exfoliating abilities, capable of absorbing an unlimited amount of Voodoo mojo. And to get my hands on said sponge, the Voodoo Lady sent me to look for her ex-boyfriend, Coronado de Cava, who had spent many years searching for it. De Cava had last been seen in the Jerkbait Islands.

I had a ship and a goal: I just had to get off that darn island. Outside, the sky grew darker. The Pox of LeChuck was beginning to form a cloud. The entire Caribbean was in danger! Since I didn't have the magic sponge, a French doctor, the Marquis de Singe, offered to cure my hand of its affliction. However, that rapscallion proved to be not just an insufferable aristocrat, but also a real nascent psychopath prepared to chop off my member (I'm still talking about my hand: don't get any ideas...). I escaped at the last second and plunged deep into the jungle of Flotsam Island in search of an ancient temple that would supposedly allow me to reverse the direction of the winds. After an absolutely absurd series of tasks, in keeping with LucasArts tradition, I activated the machine, which then reversed the winds. I could finally sail off on the Screaming Narwhal and head to the Rock of Gelato to reunite with my dear Elaine...

Episode 2: The Siege of Spinner Cay

As I approached the Rock of Gelato, I spotted Elaine's ship in the distance. But just as I was finally going to see her again, a sword barred my way. At the end of that sword was the formidable Mighty Pirate Hunter™, Morgan LeFlay! She had hunted down pirates from Mêlée to Zanzibar and was sent after me by the nefarious Marquis de Singe. She then boarded the Screaming Narwhal. With a cruel swipe of her sword, she cut off my hand! Granted, my pox-cursed hand, but nonetheless, I'd grown attached to it after all these years! We entered into a fierce battle, in which my sharp wit and sword led me to victory. Morgan LeFlay fled, but not before stealing my hand.

From there, we set a course for the Jerkbait Islands, where it appeared Elaine's ship was headed. The little Jerkbait Islands were mainly inhabited by a strange tribe called the Vacaylians. They generally lived under the sea, but over time had established their administrative headquarters on the surface. I needed to repair the mast of the Screaming Narwhal, which had been severely damaged by Morgan LeFlay. I also had to find Coronado de Cava so that he could tell me how to find La Esponja Grande. Finally, I had to get back my Elaine and kick LeChuck's butt. A long to-do list, but I intended to get it all done within a day.

I found Elaine in the island's throne room. She was parleying with the queen of the Vacaylians when I arrived. After our touching reunion, she explained to me that she intended to find the three golden artifacts hidden by the Vacaylians that would allow us to find La Esponja Grande: the Wise Turtle, the Noble Sea Horse, and the Cranky Fish. The Pox of LeChuck had already contaminated much of the ocean; the situation was serious and we could no longer flee.

In no time at all, I took one of the golden artifacts, which was in the possession of those idiot, pox-plagued pirates in McGillicutty's crew. Then, deep in the jungle of Spoon Island, I spotted LeChuck in the flesh—and I mean in his human, non-rotting flesh. I still think I may have preferred when he would spit fire and stunk of regurgitated grog. With his haughty attitude, he claimed that he wanted to help me find the second artifact. With MY help, we discovered it.

Back on Spinner Cay, the main hub of the Jerkbait Islands, I was surprised to hear the far-off sound of cannon fire. McGillicutty's pirates had no intention of letting La Esponja Grande slip through their fingers and were trying to get back the summoning artifacts for themselves. They had set up a blockade, preventing all ships from leaving the port of Spinner Cay. While LeChuck created a diversion using the cannons on the beach of Spoon Island, I was able to slip past the blockade on my little raft and get back to the Screaming Narwhal. I then prepared to board McGillicutty's ship and, using a clever ruse, managed to sink it, saving the queen of the Vacaylians in the process.

To thank me, the queen combined the three summoning artifacts into one ultimate summoning item. Then all I had to do was throw the ultimate artifact into the sea and pronounce the magic incantation: "Oh Great Legendary Creatures of the Sea! Come on! Come on, boys! Get the ball! You want the ball? Huh? You want the ball? Come get it!" I must admit, the ritual words turned out to be a bit less grandiose than I had imagined, but whatever. I did as instructed and the goofy sea creatures appeared. My first mate Van Winslow and I returned to the high seas aboard the Screaming Narwhal, following the strange monsters. Off to find La Esponja Grande!

Episode 3: Lair of the Leviathan

Ah, the sweet pirate life! Out in the deep blue with your best ship and crew, searching for the world's rarest treasures... Which just happened to be a giant, Voodoo-sucking sea sponge in this case. It makes you wonder why anyone would consider any other life. Of course, the pirate life isn't always so rosy. While we followed the strange sea creatures, the beautiful and fearsome Morgan LeFlay reappeared with her usual theatrical flourish. My hand wasn't enough for her: she had been hired by the Marquis de Singe to capture me alive. But right when I was about to send her packing once again, a humongous, gigantic manatee (did I mention he was big?) swallowed us all whole: the Screaming Narwhal, Winslow, LeFlay, and me.

Inside the dark belly of the Leviathan, I was shocked to come face to face with none other than Coronado de Cava, Mighty Explorer. The poor sucker had been held prisoner inside the giant manatee for years. He was ingested while out searching for La Esponja Grande. And I feared that his long imprisonment had made him a little crazy: I had to prove to him that I had never had any extramarital relations with the Voodoo Lady (yikes!) to finally get him to agree to help us. He informed me that La Esponja Grande was supposedly hidden inside the "sacred manatee mating grounds." To get there, we would have to "motivate" our host to head that way (double yikes!).

In the course of our search in the bowels of the Leviathan, we encountered the rest of Coronado de Cava's crew. The survivors had founded the Democratically United Brotherhood of the Manatee Interior. It was a sort of hippie community in which the former pirates lived an idle life of self-indulgence. I had to use every bit of my cunning to take advantage of the frat bros and... Murray! Who had to hit pause on his plans to destroy the Spanish armada with a demonic army when he got locked away in a treasure chest. Once the inner ear of our giant manatee was fixed, the manatee returned to its mating grounds and expelled the Screaming Narwhal from its body via... Well, never mind, I'd rather not say how he expelled us. In any case, we were finally a few fathoms from the ancient manatee mating grounds, home to La Esponja Grande.

Thanks to my incredible talents as a freediver—have I ever mentioned that I can hold my breath for a whole 10 minutes?—I was able to descend to the bottom of the ocean to find the cave of La Esponja Grande. I was so close to the prize! But a big obstacle sat in my way. A ferocious female giant manatee prevented me from going any farther. Subduing the female was no easy task. Her fickle mind was the greatest of all riddles. Complex, confounding... beautiful. But I digress. I had to use de Cava's invention, called the Tongue of the Manatee, to communicate with the lady manatee. After a little manatee courtship, I was finally free to seize the legendary Esponja Grande. I could feel its power siphoning off my pox infection. It was working! I returned to the ship, but since nothing ever goes as planned, de Cava, in a supreme fit of jealousy, fomented a mutiny against me and I was imprisoned with Morgan LeFlay. After a fierce battle (and with the opportunistic help of a hungry giant manatee), we were finally safe and sound.

Episode 4: The Trial and Execution of Guybrush Threepwood

I was so close to my end goal; the only thing that could stop me was betrayal by a close ally. And apparently, that was precisely Morgan LeFlay's plan: she chose that fleeting moment of happiness after we had managed to free ourselves and maintain possession of La Esponja Grande to knock me out and take me back to her patron, the evil Marquis de Singe. The Marquis believed that he could find the secret to eternal life within my

THE MYSTERIES OF MONKEY ISLAND. PIRATES AHOY!

veins. I know that my bodily fluids have often helped me get out of tricky situations—like winning a spitting contest on Booty Island—but I had no idea that I possessed such power. LeFlay brought me to Flotsam Island, where the Marquis de Singe was not the only one anticipating my arrival. A whole crowd of cretinous corsairs was there, waiting to drag me to the court of pirate law. I was to be put on trial! And for what, you might ask, my adoring audience? For no less than four despicable charges brought by the brand-new prosecutor... Stan. Good ol' Stan. His first charge: that I supposedly started a bar fight at Club 41 that led to terrible injury to the adorable cat of the pirate elder Hemlock McGee. Second charge: during the same fight, I supposedly spilled boiling nacho sauce on the exposed leg of Bosun Kathryn Krebbs, hideously scarring her. Third charge: that I allegedly conspired with one Joaquin d'Oro to craft and sell counterfeit Porcelain Power Pirates™. And finally, the fourth charge: that I supposedly damaged the X symbol marking the spot where treasure was to be found, but which was actually protected as a historic landmark belonging to Killick Hardtack. It was a sham trial!

After a few bouts of verbal sparring—my specialty—I was able to have each of the charges against me dropped. However, I wasn't entirely in the clear yet: those four were just civil charges. As it turns out, the court had a much more serious criminal charge against me as well, for "the creation, incubation, dissemination, proliferation, and mastication of a pox or pox-like affliction." In other words, I was accused of spreading the terrible Pox of LeChuck across the entire Caribbean. And I have to admit, I was not entirely innocent of that one. Luckily, my beloved Elaine chose that very moment to burst unexpectedly into the courtroom looking absolutely terrifying. I thought that I was saved; boy, was I wrong. My sweet, pox-afflicted wife threw a fit of jealousy when she smelled Morgan LeFlay's perfume on my clothing. The court was momentarily adjourned. I was taken back to a jail cell, from which I escaped and went to Club 41, where Elaine and Morgan were fighting fiercely over me. It was so romantic! But I had not a moment to lose. Elaine had to appear as a witness; otherwise, it would be straight to the gallows—or worse—for me. I arranged to have Elaine "dragged" before the court in spite of the pox and the unhealthy jealousy she was feeling. I then had an incredible verbal battle in which I had to muster up every bit of my cunning to get Elaine to say that I was in no way responsible for the pox and that it was that pathological liar LeChuck who was responsible for the accursed virus. But to no avail. Even La Esponja Grande couldn't bring my sugar plum back to her senses.

Things were looking dire, when LeChuck suddenly entered the courtroom. He revealed to the stunned audience that I was not the one to blame for the curse that had struck so many pirates; he was the main culprit. He told the court that they should instead honor me for my heroism. Can you imagine? LeChuck. My LeChuck. My habitual enemy over the last five games! And what he revealed next left the entire courtroom aghast. You may want to sit down for this. It appears that an unknown, silent power had urged LeChuck down those darkened Voodoo corridors. A power far more insidious than LeChuck could ever hope to be. He produced a journal—the journal of the Voodoo Lady! LeChuck explained that she had been manipulating his insatiable hunger for power since the very first episode released in 1990.

I was in complete shock, but was immediately freed. LeChuck: my sworn enemy or my savior? I could no longer say which. He was thrown in jail. However, that gave me time to clear things up with the Voodoo Lady. OK, "clear" might not be the best word. She explained to me that each of our lives fit into a greater plan, but she never meant to do me harm. She told me to find six ingredients scattered across Flotsam Island to "nourish" La Esponja Grande in order to bring it to maturity so that it could cure the great plague of pox. I had my doubts about the Voodoo Lady, but I absolutely needed to save Elaine from the curse.

Following the Voodoo Lady's instructions, I obtained all of the ingredients and then stumbled upon Elaine fighting with the Marquis de Singe. The mad scientist had set his sights on the love of my life in hopes of obtaining the original pox strain, which he believed would allow him to complete his experiment. In the midst of a fierce battle, the wretched Marquis de Singe was pushed inside the complex machine that controls the winds on Flotsam Island. It was a horrific death, but a fitting one for him. Once again reunited with my sweet Elaine, all we had to do was use the machine ourselves to spread the power of La Esponja Grande 2.0. Right then, my pal LeChuck appeared. The strapping fellow had escaped from jail to come meet us. I was just about to give him a hug when he ran his sword straight through my chest.

There he was, the LeChuck we all know. Human, but still diabolical. He was yet again carrying out a plan to seize both power and Elaine's heart. His true nature had returned with a vengeance, and he aspired to once again become an evil being. Sigh... I could feel my strength failing me. I was dying; I was dead; I was buried.

Episode 5: Rise of the Pirate God

When I awoke, I really was dead, a hole through my chest. I guess you could say I was a "holy" spirit (hehe, "holy...holey"...see what I did there?). My mouth was full of dirt. I had been buried in a ghostly cemetery in the middle of nowhere. It felt so strange to be dead. I've always been pretty transparent, but this time I was even more so than usual. After climbing out of my grave, I went to get information from a zombie skeleton wearing a black cloak, working as a ferryman. I got in his boat and the sinister fellow took me to a sad place, the "Crossroads," a sort of gateway to the underworld, wedged between the world of the living and the world of the dead. There, I met a kindly living-dead resident of the Crossroads by the name of Galeb. He told me that LeChuck had already passed through, but had carried out a Voodoo ritual allowing him to open a portal through which he returned to the land of the living. He had hidden the formula inside a chest that he buried at the Crossroads.

With my latest dead friend at my side, a good doggy named Franklin, I eventually managed to get my hands on the magic spell and performed the ritual. Unfortunately, my new friend Morgan LeFlay, who was disgracefully stabbed in the back by LeChuck, had to sacrifice her soul to help me. Once the Crossroads portal was open, I jumped through it and was flung directly into LeChuck's infernal galleon. LeChuck was waiting on the other side of the Crossroads portal, attempting to open it. How could I have known that I would allow him to return to the land of the dead and become the zombie god of pirates? What's more, he had kidnapped my plunder bunny Elaine and planned to make her his goddess of the dead! Before my very eyes, he used the evil power of La Esponja Grande 2.0 to transform Elaine into his demonic bride. I tried desperately to grab the Cutlass of Kaflu to do away with my enemy, but being a ghost, I couldn't handle any physical objects in the land of the living. Before I knew it, I was sent back through the portal.

I had completely lost control of the situation. I reviewed everything that had happened with the Voodoo Lady during a magical "telephone" conversation. To stop LeChuck, I would have to return to my physical body in order to take the cutlass and have the ultimate showdown with my worst enemy. It turns out that the sacrificial ritual had opened up multiple portals, one of which could take me to Flotsam Island to recover my beautiful body and permanently reattach my soul to it using Mix n' Mojo brand Spirit Gum™. I'll spare you the unpleasant details of how I recovered my body, which was being used as a dartboard at Club 41, or of how I got some old, chewed-up chewing gum from the jail. In any case, I was able to get back my mojo and confront LeChuck once again.

At the gateway to the land of the dead, the situation was getting worse. Elaine had gone completely over to the dark side. Thankfully, a whole armada of pirates arrived on the scene, led by my old friend Winslow. The ferocious corsairs entered into a fierce battle with the army of the dead. It was like something out of a Hollywood blockbuster! Still, LeChuck was able to send me back through the portal to the Crossroads. I had to find a way to diminish the power of La Esponja Grande by putting it on a diet in order to prevent LeChuck from entering the underworld. Once I had finished preparing the various ingredients, I performed the ritual on La Esponja Grande.

Immediately, the incredible sea sponge shrank down to become so small it could barely be used to do the dishes. I was once again propelled through the portal and onto LeChuck's galleon in the middle of the battle between good and evil. It was epic and beautiful. Elaine was restored to her usual self. After a final, insane struggle (in which I suffered countless blows), we managed to get LeChuck stuck in a portal between the lands of the living and the dead. On each side, Elaine and Morgan simultaneously dealt him fatal blows with their swords. LeChuck perished with a long cry of agony.

Then, everything went black. I found myself alone at the Crossroads... dead. Dead for good this time. That is, until I remembered the words to the magical spell: "Courage, Anchor, Direction, Sacrifice. Place these things in a Ring at the center of the Crossroads." Of course! Elaine's wedding ring! As soon as I placed the ring at the very center of the Crossroads, I found myself once again under blue skies aboard a brand-new ship, sailing across the Caribbean Sea. And Elaine was there. My beautiful Elaine. Back to being the woman I always loved. After this improbable adventure, we were finally reunited, as if it had all been nothing more than a dream. Or just one giant act of Voodoo mind-control!

The End

Game design and anecdotes™

Tales of Monkey Island was not simply a modernized "best of" the *Monkey Island* series. Each episode has its own unique personality and tone. It includes direct tributes to classic point & click games in episodes two and five, particularly with the court "simulation," inspired by Capcom's *Phoenix Wright: Ace Attorney* saga, with long narrative sequences in which a particular emphasis is placed on the dynamics of the dramatization. Each of the episodes also has its own distinct personality in terms of writing. That's the genius of *Tales of Monkey Island*, a sort of ensemble adventure in which, for the first time, the writing outshined all the game's other qualities. Sean Vanaman, the brilliant writer who would go on to write Telltale's *The Walking Dead*, was responsible for giving "Lair of the Leviathan" its very particular style, in which you can see the beginnings of what would become his famous hit zombie series. The fourth episode, "The Trial and Execution of Guybrush Threepwood," is a marvel of scene-setting thanks to the work of Michael Stemmle. Once again, it brought in a heavy social, tragicomic subtext to the sham trial. It was a social critique that was already present on a more subtle level in *Escape from Monkey Island*, with its dishonest, corrupt, and crooked lawyers. It was thanks to *Tales'* ambiances and the quality of its writing that Telltale's episodic game excelled and entered the pantheon of the franchise. In spite of its comedic tone, the focus always stays on the plot, infusing the game with its apocalyptic atmosphere, with numerous betrayals, dramatic characters, and a return to form for Guybrush, who once again became the hero originally created by Ron Gilbert.

What's more, the overall level of difficulty of *Tales of Monkey Island* was very clearly revised downward compared to its predecessors. The puzzles are more obvious, there are fewer objects to be found, and the lack of multiple verbs in the interface makes the story flow more smoothly. As was mentioned in previous chapters, Telltale offered a critical look at the video game medium in general and at the traditional adventure game specifically. While competitors (*Broken Sword*, *The Longest Journey*, *Runaway*) continued to follow classic gameplay to a tee, Dave Grossman and his team took a risk by aiming to attract a broader audience. And one has to admit that what *Tales of Monkey Island* loses in pure gameplay, it gains in quality storytelling. No other game was able to so successfully juggle multiple sub-plots, numerous side characters, and a final climax that was wrapped up so nicely. While *Monkey Island 2: LeChuck's Revenge* remains the heart of the saga, the episode that gave the series its form and personality, *Tales of Monkey Island* is its one true heir, the only one to be equally captivating.

It was also an opportunity for Telltale to experiment with cinematic production. The sailing phases, like the opening scene of the first episode, make use of dynamic lighting, continuous movements simulating waves and collisions, flash effects, and sound design that matched the epic feel. All of that helped make *Monkey Island* more "real" and immersive than ever before.

Of course, Telltale's game held to the sacrosanct rule of offering parody and post-modern references. Even if, globally, the lightness of the third game disappeared, *Tales* eased up on the hysterical and zany tributes of the fourth. *Tales of Monkey Island* has some truly hilarious comedy bits. You won't want to miss a single second of the riotous end credits of the third episode, hosted by the great Murray, who delivers a fantastic roast of the entire cast and crew. Or a single detail of the delicious dark humor delivered throughout the game's poetic and tragicomic epilogue. Among the more subtle references, Club 41 on Flotsam Island owes its name to the technical limitations of games distributed through WiiWare, Nintendo's online service. To digitally distribute the game through WiiWare, Telltale was forced to delete an entire scene from the first episode in order to stay under the store's maximum limit of 40 MB. Hence the name of the exclusive pirate club.

Originally, Adam Harrington, the human voice of LeChuck, also did the voice of the captain's demonic version. However, after the game's release, the feedback on internet forums was terrible. The Telltale team decided to have all of that dialogue re-recorded with the voice of Earl Boen, the original voice of LeChuck in *Curse of Monkey Island* and *Escape from Monkey Island*, starting in episode four. As such, the CD version is the only one to feature the original voice of demon LeChuck, since the digital version was modified. Finally, most of the pirates you come across in the underworld in episode five are actually people met in the first two episodes, and there's a good reason for that. According to Mark Darin, the director of the final episode, quite simply, budget cuts forced the team to reuse existing assets, hence why we see these pirates again. They just had to twist the scenario a bit so that it all made sense.

Throughout the season, Guybrush, in typical fashion, bumbles from one situation to the next without ever really being in control. He discovers the dark side of LeChuck like so many other insane revelations and finds himself flabbergasted when he discovers that the Voodoo Lady seems to be the mastermind behind it all. However, one character never loses her cool and always seems to be one step ahead. Indeed, Elaine is a beacon of intelligence in the sea of stupidity that is the pirate world of *Monkey Island*. Michael Stemmle offers an explanation of the real motivations of the characters and the highly complicated positioning of Elaine, who is at once strong and in the background across the five episodes: "Elaine has long suspected that the Voodoo Lady has been putting Guybrush and LeChuck through a never-ending cycle of conflict for mysterious purposes. This annoys the heck out of Elaine, who is ultra-protective of her hubby and chafes at the notion of being manipulated by forces beyond her control. But Guybrush trusted the Voodoo Lady too much for Elaine to simply say, 'Hey, I think this nice lady that has helped you on umpteen previous occasions is using you like a puppet.' Besides, she didn't want to get on the Voodoo Lady's radar. When LeChuck suddenly became human at the start of the first episode, Elaine intuitively realized that LeChuck was also playing some sort of long game against the Voodoo Lady, so she went along with it, keeping an eye on LeChuck all the while, and nudging Guybrush in ways both small ('trust me') and large ('take the ring'). Of course, she didn't plan on being overwhelmed by the Pox or on LeChuck actually managing to kill Guybrush. That's why she's so forlorn at the start of the final episode; she's played things too close to the vest, and now her snuggle bunny is dead."[214]

A few more fun facts:

◉ The shrine in the Voodoo Lady's house is dedicated to the dreadful god Nor Treblig. Try reading that name backwards...

◉ In episode two, for a time, the designers considered making it possible to switch out Guybrush's hook hand for various other items in the inventory.

◉ Episode four could have had a totally different ending. Originally, Michael Stemmle had planned for Guybrush to absorb the Pox of LeChuck and become an immense demonic creature. However, in the end, that didn't really fit with the overall atmosphere of the game or with the studio's desire to have a cliff-hanger before the final episode.

◉ The enigmatic Galeb, the guardian of the Crossroads, is a direct reference to Papa Legba, a figure from Haitian folklore who's a master linguist, warrior, and personal messenger for fate. He stands at a religious, spiritual crossroads and grants or denies permission to speak to the spirits. Furthermore, Galeb is an anagram of Legba.

Reception and reviews™

To say that the fifth installment in the adventures of Guybrush Threepwood was expected would be a bit of a lie. The game's announcement was even dubbed by IGN as the "biggest surprise" of E3 2009. *Tales of Monkey Island* took home a handful of awards after its release, including best PC game, best adventure game, and best return of a franchise, honors given by *Gamasutra*, *PC Gamer US*, and *OC Weekly* respectively. However, French video game media were not kind and the reception was lukewarm at best. For *Gamekult*, Telltale's series didn't give fans much to be enthused about: "Insipid side characters and

---

214. *https://web.archive.org/web/20110720000237/http://talesofmi.net/?p=823*

humor that repeats itself and overuses the typical devices, thus struggling to make us laugh. The offbeat humor and absurdity are still there, but even the homage to the insult fighting isn't enough to bring out a chuckle. It seems that Telltale's eyes were a bit too big for its stomach, as we can see from the ending, which aims to be epic, but which has a cruel lack of breathing room due to lackluster directing and a lack of any real stakes. [...] Thankfully, the game has the studio's customary high-quality writing and dubbing, some clever anachronistic ideas, backgrounds that are often excellent, and off-the-wall puzzles using that very peculiar logic that generally makes lovers of the genre fall head over heels."[215] For *Jeuxvideo.com*, which was slightly more enthusiastic, the game failed to distinguish itself: "*Tales of Monkey Island* has all of the positive qualities of a Telltale game. Well-paced, quite varied, and funny, it offers excellent dubbing and a whole host of colorful characters. Still, it's a shame that Telltale never totally let loose on the scenario or on the level of difficulty, which is generally quite low."[216] *Gameblog* at least was mostly more positive: "Unless you're completely immune to the charms of this legendary saga or, worse, if you have absolutely zero sense of humor, there's no reason to deny yourself this pleasure. *Tales of Monkey Island* is a great success that undeniably deserves to sit proudly alongside the first two installments in your collection of adventure games."[217]

In America, reviews were much more favorable. *Tales of Monkey Island* was almost unanimously viewed as a real return to the exceptional quality of writing of the first two games: "*Tales of Monkey Island* harks back to the heyday of adventure gaming with a great story, engaging characters, and a lot of entertaining puzzles. Though the solutions generally aren't as tough as their predecessors were, you'll still feel a rewarding sense of satisfaction as you think your way through this game. Infrequent performance hitches and occasionally slow pacing are minor issues compared to the hours of humor, intrigue, romance, and insult sword fighting you get for the very reasonable price of $34.95. If you've got a hankering for adventure, then get your hands (or hooks) on *Tales of Monkey Island*."[218] And another take: "Whatever the minor failings may have been, *Tales of Monkey Island* as an entire work has been a comprehensive and grand story on a scale that might be able to compete with any previous *Monkey Island* game—not a statement I make lightly, but ultimately a reflection of how incredibly strong a final impact this game leaves and how well it ties everything together. In spite of this chapter's sometimes

215. *https://www.gamekult.com/jeux/tales-of-monkey-island-chapter-5-rise-of-the-pirate-god-3010006698/test.html*

216. *http://www.jeuxvideo.com/articles/0001/00014833-tales-of-monkey-island-test.htm*

217. *http://www.gameblog.fr/tests/499-tales-of-monkey-island-pc*

218. *https://www.gamespot.com/reviews/tales-of-monkey-island-review/1900-6244163/*

bland early tone and uneven puzzle mechanics, 'Rise of the Pirate God' and the series as a whole both come with my highest recommendation as a modern adventure genre must-play."[219]

In the Curse of Monkey Island Special Edition™, you can marvel at my full demonic power in HD!

219. *https://adventuregamers.com/articles/view/18375*

Chapter 16: *Monkey Island Special Edition*™

After a wave of disappointments at LucasArts, with the relative failures of non-*Star Wars* products like *Thrillville*[220] and the mediocre *Fracture*,[221] the studio's leaders felt that in order to save the company, they needed to take a step back and finally consider why they had fallen out of favor with players. For the studio's in-house developers, *Monkey Island* and the old characters from the glory days of the point & click adventure game represented a massively valuable and untapped resource. In 2007, under the guidance of Craig Derrick, a producer brought over from Vicarious Visions,[222] a team began imagining a *Monkey Island* sequel in the form of an old-school 2D point & click adventure. During their lunch breaks and evenings after work, they planned out a direct sequel to *Monkey Island 2: LeChuck's Revenge* that wouldn't deprecate *The Curse of Monkey Island*. However, the team's vain attempts to sell the project to management ended in definitive failure.

At the beginning of the previous chapter, we saw how a new leader, Darrell Rodriguez, arrived at LucasArts in 2008. Well, in summer 2008, Rodriguez delivered a surprise. Unlike his predecessors, who had put all of their eggs in the *Star Wars* basket, he finally understood the importance of the image LucasArts had lost and of the nostalgic appeal of 1990s franchises. Furthermore, the recent success of online distribution platforms like Xbox Live Arcade (on the Xbox 360) and Steam (on the PC), as well as the growing importance of the digital media market, ultimately convinced him that it was possible to produce games at a minimal cost for a niche market while simultaneously restoring some shine to the studio's reputation as a creator. While Telltale Games had already begun developing another installment in the saga, in June 2008, Rodriguez assigned Craig Derrick to study the possibility of reviving an old treasure of an adventure game. As the saga approached its twentieth anniversary, Derrick immediately chose *The Secret of Monkey Island*.

220. A theme park management game developed by Frontier Developments and released in 2006-2007 for the PS2 and Xbox.
221. A third-person shooter (TPS) whose unique feature is the ability to deform the game's terrain. It was developed by Day 1 Studios for the PS3 and Xbox 360.
222. A studio on the East Coast of the United States, mainly specializing in porting titles to other consoles.

Respect your elders™

With that choice made, LucasArts decided to not take any risks and to produce a true remake of *The Secret of Monkey Island* while being as true to the original as possible. A team formed around Craig Derrick. Adam Bormann and Dominic Robilliard would focus on reworking the game design. They didn't change one bit of Gilbert's masterpiece, but, for budgetary, practical, and nostalgic reasons, they decided to once again adapt the SCUMM engine, which apparently will live forever (20 years for a game engine!). How could they offer an original experience from a style of game that had nearly gone extinct due to its lack of inventiveness? That was the challenge faced by the small team. They would have to satisfy longtime players while attracting a new audience. According to Craig Derrick, "As great as the original is, we knew that a generation of gamers may never have heard of *Monkey Island* or be familiar with the classic LucasArts point-and-click adventures. Plus, the game was very dated graphically (which is also, of course, part of its charm), had no voiceover dialogue, and at times is very challenging to a novice."[223]

These were the three major pillars of change in the remake: a contemporary makeover for the graphics, the addition of well-crafted voiceover, and an overall reduction in the level of difficulty. To draw in a new audience, LucasArts didn't plan to simply re-release the original title as-is on digital platforms, but rather decided to modernize the game's appearance by drawing inspiration from the major successes of *The Curse of Monkey Island*. "We knew if we wanted to bring new gamers to it, we had to update all of these areas and focus on accessibility to the new player via updated controls and an in-game hint system. At the same time, we knew we couldn't alienate our original fans," he explains.

To satisfy everyone, Bormann and Robilliard also decided to make the new features adjustable. The game allows the player to choose whether or not to activate the hint system and voices. What's more, they even made it possible to switch from the modernized graphics to the original graphics, with their inimitable VGA style, simply by pressing a button on the controller (or a key on the keyboard). In a way, it was the best of both worlds. Derrick continues: "Early on, we knew we wanted to include the original game with the special edition in one form or another, stay true to the original composition of the background art, establish some continuity in the character designs based on their appearances throughout the series and bring back as many of the original voice actors from the very first *Monkey Island* 'talkie,' *The Curse of Monkey Island*. We thought if we could do all of that then we may just be able to appeal and balance enough features for both new and old fans alike."

---

223. *https://www.theguardian.com/technology/gamesblog/2009/jun/28/games1*

However, the remake didn't aim to position itself as a "revival" of an old glory from days gone by. "Today's gamers are more diverse and broad than I would say even the audience of point-and-click games was back in the '90s. When we started this, however, I always told the team that this wasn't necessarily about getting people excited about a point-and-click game, but about getting people excited about a game with great storytelling, characters, and humor. The *Special Edition* adds a unique, whimsical art style and gameplay pacing and mechanics that I think will stand apart from many of the games available on Xbox Live," says Craig Derrick. It was making something new out of something old while keeping in mind that *The Secret of Monkey Island* held a status as an untouchable cult game and that the "community" of players was not the easiest to contend with.

Take a pirate by the hand™

The player of 2008 was very different from the player of long ago in the heyday of EGA screens, the Amiga, and Sound Blaster sound cards. As such, the integration of the hint system available to the player on demand would help them more easily solve many of the game's puzzles. Truth be told, some of the puzzles were so absurd that they could inhibit the flow of the game's story, in spite of the attention Ron Gilbert had paid to that exact detail at the time. For many years at that point, "modern" games had taken on cinematic storytelling, with the pacing that goes with that. Difficulty based on "blind" searching was no longer going to work. And the adjustments that Telltale Games had made, for example, clearly went in that direction. Of course, this didn't mean that "modern" players were stupider or more impatient than their forebears; it simply meant that they weren't accustomed to the old style of gameplay. "Modern" players were more interested in a sort of immediate gratification, putting less and less emphasis on observation; instead, games needed to put extraordinary effort into guiding players along. With all this said, *The Secret of Monkey Island: Special Edition* managed to skillfully avoid spoon-feeding players. Craig Derrick explains: "We considered adding new puzzles, but no, we never wanted to tamper with the original game or make puzzles less obscure in nature. What we did do, however, is create an in-game hint system that will help new players solve those more obscure puzzles without having to consult an online hint doc." The hint system is gradual. The first hint requested simply reminds the player of the objectives. If the player clicks again, the hint will get a bit more specific, then mention an object or a combination to be made, and will finally give the full solution as a last resort. Simple, smart, and effective.

The very idea of making a classic adventure game with gameplay entirely based on puzzles and refusing to guide the player along seemed totally absurd by that point. With the exception of a few marginal counterexamples, who made their difficulty a selling point, creating such a challenge was just not an option. Did the classic point & click adventure game lose all of its appeal simply because of our laziness? Today, as video games tend toward a shorter, more intense, more fast-paced format, are we no longer capable of using our brains to solve puzzles requiring the slightest bit of patience?

Indeed, the adventure game, in its most classic form, went extinct because of the internet and *GameFAQs*[224] and, above all, because of us. The lifeline for a player in the 1980s or 1990s was to buy a magazine offering the solution or, even worse, to call a hotline advertised on a flyer (at the risk of drawing your parents' ire due to a hefty phone bill). All that to say that finding the solution was an adventure in its own right. Then, the internet came along. Initially, text files of early solution manuals were exchanged covertly, but before long, certain specialized websites saw walkthroughs as a way to draw in visitors. The rest was history. All sorts of help resources became widely available and frighteningly easy to access: all you had to do was a quick search online for the solution and presto, there it was. Today, almost no one plays a classic adventure game without ever seeking help online, to the point that all those adventure game gems have become ordinary commodities. You can find a whole slew of detailed, step-by-step walkthroughs on YouTube, even for the most obscure of games.

Given that fact, today, what's left for game designers to offer us a great video game adventure? Well, thankfully, game designers have no shortage of original ideas to try to prevent us from going online to look for the solutions to their games and thus keep us immersed in the adventure. Jakub Dvorský, in *Machinarium*,[225] offers us hints in exchange for solving relatively simple little puzzles. The solution is then delivered in the form of a comic strip. In *The Legend of Zelda: The Minish Cap*,[226] at any time, you can talk to a secondary character, Ezlo (a chatty little green cap), who gives you somewhat vague indications of which way to head in order to continue your adventure. In *Secret Files: Tunguska*[227] (and many others), simply pressing a button reveals the "clickable" locations and thus allows you to avoid the need to go "pixel hunting" when you miss a poorly visible object. These different systems share a common goal: to maintain focus on the puzzle and the interest of that type of

---

224. *GameFAQs* is a famous website where players can publish solutions and complete walkthroughs, which are often of great quality.
225. *Machinarium* is a superb 2D point & click game independently developed by Amanita Design and released on October 16, 2009.
226. The *Zelda* games are not representative of the point & click sub-genre, but part of their gameplay is puzzle-based. As such, the developers of those games have also had to put some effort into reinventing themselves and guiding players along.
227. *Secret Files: Tunguska* is an adventure game released in 2006 and created by Jörg Beilschmidt.

challenge while keeping the player immersed in the story. Why? Because when the player jumps over to *GameFAQs* or YouTube to find the solution, they lose a bit of their connection with and emotional investment in the game's universe.

Going over Guybrush with a fine-tooth comb™

Filling the shoes of Steve Purcell and Mark Ferrari to reinterpret the universe of *The Secret of Monkey Island* was a daunting task. Especially after the proposal made a decade earlier by Bill Tiller to reimagine the game in the distinctive, acclaimed visual style of *The Curse of Monkey Island*. In the position of art director, Jeff Sangalli surrounded himself with talents capable of holding their own, like Andrea Rhodes and Molly Denmark for the backgrounds, and Dela Longfish for character design.

Early conceptual drawings show that the overall design choice was not an easy one to make, both for the backgrounds and for the characters. From realistic to dreamlike, with numerous other styles in between, the team finally chose a fairly unremarkable design, putting forward solid colors and aiming to stay true to the original visuals. A lot of criticism was leveled against the game for this lack of inspiration that gave the *Special Edition* the appearance of a simple high-definition update, imitating the visual style of a lackluster "Flash"[228] rendering while failing to do right by the original idea. Fans were particularly disappointed when the first visuals of Guybrush's new design were leaked during E3 in 2009. Our favorite hero was seen wearing a ridiculous hairstyle, with a strange sort of pompadour sticking straight up from his head. Craig Derrick defended the team's choices: "We've remained very faithful to the original art and the composition of the pieces, but we wanted to embellish them with storytelling, obviously rich color, and our art director Jeff Sangalli wanted to capture the feel of an illustrated storybook."[229] If we're being nice, we can say that the style is fairly original, but it was far from earning unanimous praise.

The monkeys are back™

Officially announced for the first time in Los Angeles during the 2009 edition of the famous E3 trade show, *The Secret of Monkey Island: Special Edition* was

---

228. Flash (from Adobe, formerly Macromedia) is software offering an easy way to animate vector graphics. The format became widespread thanks to its small size, giving a visual style to an entire generation of animated videos and 2D video games.
229. *https://www.youtube.com/watch?v=5UDrXP3qM2Q*

released shortly thereafter on July 15, 2009, initially for the PC, iPhone, and Xbox 360, then later for the PS3, Mac, and iPad in February 2010. In addition to the aforementioned "improvements," the new edition added a few Easter eggs for those in the know, changing visual details here and there in the backgrounds, or even adding Spiffy the dog back into the SCUMM Bar, as there hadn't been room for him on the floppy disks in the original version.

And you have to admit that the charm of the original is still there. *IGN* praised the remake, saying, "Almost 20 years after its release, it remains a blast to play." The French website *Gamekult* concluded its playtest review thusly: "A legendary point & click title, *The Secret of Monkey Island* is making a big comeback in style with this *Special Edition*, which sensibly adapts to all audiences. [...] There may be a group of malcontents who will refuse to pay €8.99 for a game released nearly two decades ago, but when you look at what sells for a premium these days, and the annoying tendency of certain unscrupulous publishers to ask top dollar for remakes in which they've barely changed a thing, we won't be listening to those naysayers."[230] Finally, the website *Jeuxvideo.com*, like its fellow French sites, praised the high quality of the remake: "With *The Secret of Monkey Island: Special Edition*, LucasArts is not trying to hoodwink its players. The publisher didn't simply re-release an old title after blowing the dust off; they carried out a massive redesign that commands respect and truly deserves it."[231] And the sales were apparently good, for both the PC and in Xbox Live Arcade, inviting a new generation of players into the universe of *Monkey Island*.

The masterpiece™

For Craig Derrick, starting with the first game was an obvious choice. Two decades later, the series needed a new beginning; but the whole time, he had his heart set on *Monkey Island 2: LeChuck's Revenge*. The combined successes of *Tales of Monkey Island* and the special edition of the first game gave him the carte blanche he needed to finally tackle the greatest masterpiece, the point & click game that, for him, had always stood well above the mêlée (haha). However, given the size of the LucasArts team dedicated to the project in San Francisco, and considering the fact that the second episode was five times bigger than the first, Derrick would have to seek help from outside this time: "I believe that leveraging all of the skills, technology, and tools developed for the first [special edition] was the ONLY way we could have even possibly created a special edition as complex and large as *Monkey Island 2* while adding NEW

230. *https://www.gamekult.com/jeux/the-secret-of-monkey-island-special-edition-3010006693/test.html*
231. *http://www.jeuxvideo.com/articles/0001/00011181-the-secret-of-monkey-island-special-edition-test.htm*

features in the same time it took us to create the first game. The distributed nature of the teams between San Francisco and Singapore introduced some new challenges, but since some of the first special edition was created there, they understood what to do and I'm very proud of the amazing job they've accomplished."[232] It was a bigger and longer project, and naturally one that required greater care in order to preserve the spirit of the original. Jesse Harlin had the tough job of reinterpreting the original music of Michael Z. Land. He speaks of the seriousness of that undertaking: "The *Monkey Island* games have a very vibrant fan community, and 20 years on, they regard *Monkey Island 2* to be not only the best *Monkey Island* game, and not only the best LucasArts adventure game made, but they regard *Monkey 2* as the best adventure game ever made. There's definitely pressure there to live up to their expectations. Add on top of that the added pressure that this game was so much larger than the first one. Then add on top of that the challenges of recreating the functionality of iMUSE. It was a big set of shoes to step into."[233]

The new features in *Monkey Island 2 Special Edition: LeChuck's Revenge* were, in the end, quite similar to those added to the previous SE. It got a new graphic design, this time making sure to give Guybrush a less extravagant hairdo, high-quality dubbing, a hint system, and a reorchestrated soundtrack. Interestingly, while like the first special edition, players had the choice to play with the original graphics from 1991, this time, they also could get the original voices and subtitles. However, the greatest interest of the remake for *Monkey Island* scholars like ourselves was the addition of one very important new feature.

Developer commentary™

It was a dream come true, a real gift to fans: the developers of the special edition added in audio commentary from the original developers. The game commentary gave the trio responsible for the hours we spent exploring the Caribbean (Ron Gilbert, Dave Grossman, and Tim Schafer) the opportunity to talk about the game's development. "The commentary is an optional feature that works very similar to those found on film DVDs. After turning the option on from within the bonus features menu, the player will be given a choice to listen to select scene commentary while playing through the game," Craig Derrick explains. "On most occasions, the commentary appears as you enter one scene or another, but it will also appear after a particular moment has occurred providing further commentary or anecdotes about the scene."[234]

232. *https://kotaku.com/monkey-island-success-could-mean-more-adventure-from-lu-5549234*
233. *http://www.audiogang.org/interview-with-lucasarts-jesse-harlin/*
234. *https://kotaku.com/monkey-island-success-could-mean-more-adventure-from-lu-5549234*

And even though none of the original three creators was part of the team responsible for the special edition, Ron and his friends played along perfectly, providing a wealth of humor and anecdotes. Ron Gilbert commented on how funny it was to look back 20 years later and take stock of all the goofy things they'd come up with while making the *Monkey Island* games. For him, one of the things that made the special edition so "special" was the chance to sit down and reminisce about all of those wacky ideas. Tim Schafer echoed Ron's sentiments. He enjoyed trying to remember all of the puzzles. To his surprise, he even got stuck at certain points. That was in spite of the fact that there were places in the game where he knew every single pixel by heart after spending a ridiculous amount of time fixing a whole host of bugs. He remarked how fascinating it was to see how much the game had stayed with him after all those years.

More of an informal laugh fest among old friends than a feature of actual historical interest, the commentary nonetheless shows us the humor, laid-back attitude, and good nature that are the essence of the three creators. In any case, the game commentary is something you won't want to miss if you're the kind of fan who wants to know everything about the game—which you probably are if you're reading this book.

The last of the Mighty Pirates™

Monkey Island 2 Special Edition: LeChuck's Revenge was released almost exactly a year after the first SE, on July 7, 2010, for the PS3, Xbox 360, PC, iPhone, and iPad. Sometime later, a bundle of the two remakes received the honor of a release on physical media (PC, PS3, and Xbox 360). Once again, the game was praised by critics. It's also worth mentioning that the SE came with a rich gallery of artwork.

Sadly, *MI2SELR* (its cute little acronym) is to date the last *Monkey Island* game to be released [Or is it...]. In spite of pretty decent sales, adventure games remained marginal in the market and another major shake-up was being prepared behind the scenes at LucasArts. The damage had already been done and the prestigious studio had fallen from grace.

Chapter 17: The life and death of LucasArts™

From 2004 to 2008, under the tutelage of Jim Ward, LucasArts made the questionable choice to shrink its in-house team and instead have its games be developed by external studios. In spite of some commercial and artistic successes, like *Star Wars Galaxies* (developed by Sony Online Entertainment), *Star Wars: Battlefront* (Pandemic Studios), the excellent *Star Wars: Knights of the Old Republic* (by BioWare in 2003 and its sequel by Obsidian in 2004), and *Lego Star Wars* (Traveller's Tales in 2005), the studio's image began to tarnish, slowly but surely, as the company appeared to lose its identity and creativity. Darrell Rodriguez had tried to chart a new path, as we saw in the previous chapter. In spite of the feeble shock from the defibrillator, administered via the studio's fabled games of yesteryear, LucasArts' policy remained the same. The massively multiplayer *Star Wars: The Old Republic* had a successful launch, and the new *Clone Wars* TV series was to be accompanied by a constellation of games, without much regard for quality.

However, inside the company, things went off the rails. The development of *Star Wars: The Force Unleashed*, the firm's next AAA blockbuster, proved to be a nightmare. Many team members threw in the towel and left the company. In 2010, Darrell Rodriguez, after spending only two years at the helm of the studio, also turned in his resignation letter, handing the reins to Paul Meegan. Mr. Meegan was riding high at the time. He came over from Epic Games, which had just scored a major hit for the Xbox 360 with its new series *Gears of War*. He declared to employees: "In recent years, LucasArts hasn't always done a good job of making games. We should be making games that define our medium, that are competitive with the best of our industry, but we're not. That has to change."[235] Two years later, on April 3, 2013, LucasArts ceased operations for good after a wild ride that had lasted 31 years.

On its deathbed™

In those last two years, the many hopes of bringing back point & click games and originality to the studio were squashed for good. For example, a remake

---

235. *https://www.mcvuk.com/business-news/lucasarts-eyes-return-to-form/*

THE MYSTERIES OF MONKEY ISLAND. PIRATES AHOY!

of *Day of the Tentacle* was killed before it could see the light of day. The game was being developed in Singapore and was nearly finished. It used 3D characters on remodeled backgrounds and revealed a number of scenes that had been cut from the original game. But that wasn't the only victim of LucasArts unraveling.

In 2009, LucasArts launched a project called *Star Wars: Underworld*, initially envisioned as a clone of the successful series *Grand Theft Auto*, but set on the planet of Coruscant (which lovers of the prequel trilogy know well). The designs looked promising and attracted the curiosity of George Lucas himself. Lucas, in spite of being such a talented filmmaker and storyteller, didn't fully understand the issues inherent to video game development. He would periodically insert himself into the production and completely changed the overall vision for the project, forcing the team in charge to reconsider all of the work they'd accomplished. *Underworld* became a clone of *Gears of War* before finally, under the direction of Meegan, becoming an intriguing copy of *Uncharted*. It then took on the name *Star Wars 1313*. From 2012 to 2013, and then from 2013 to 2015, the game, directed by Dominic Robilliard (who had previously worked on *The Secret of Monkey Island Special Edition*), became a sort of phantom menace.

At the same time, several other projects were almost entirely developed before getting the chop. *Star Wars: Outpost*, a management simulation game in the tradition of *Farmville*; *Star Wars: Death Star*, a space station simulator for the iPhone; *Smuggler*, a multiplatform game in which players would take part in interstellar trade via social media; then there was the more ambitious *Star Wars: First Assault*, which was supposed to compete with *Call of Duty*. Meanwhile, the studio was also planning to create an online platform for digital distribution of games, much like Steam or EA Origin.

According to Jason Schreier, a respected journalist for the website *Kotaku*,[236] there were many reasons behind the decline of LucasArts. The leadership of Micheline Chau, President of Lucasfilm until September 2012, seems to have progressively plunged the company into a quagmire. She approved the almost cult-like organization of the firm around George Lucas, whose divine intervention could make or break decisions or projects. The side effects—including demotivation, constant managerial changes, sudden departures, and numerous sources of pressure—transformed LucasArts from a dream machine into a nightmare meat grinder. As an individual connected to the studio told Jason Schreier: "The [San Francisco] Bay Area is filled with people who have had their hearts broken by Lucasfilm or LucasArts. The sad legacy of multiple presidents, multiple layoffs... There are a lot of people out there who've been treated badly by the company."

---

236. *https://kotaku.com/how-lucasarts-fell-apart-1401731043*

The Disney empire strikes back™

At LucasArts, everything seemed to be strangely on hold, notably the monumental production of *Star Wars 1313*. Then, news came out that hit the employees like a ton of bricks. On October 30, 2012, The Walt Disney Company acquired Lucasfilm (and thus LucasArts) for over $4 billion. It was a merger of two titans. George Lucas sold his empire to Mickey Mouse. Disney thus gained control over the rights to two of the most lucrative movie franchises in history: *Star Wars* and *Indiana Jones*. It also added to its portfolio LucasArts' classic adventure games: *Maniac Mansion*, *Day of the Tentacle*, *Grim Fandango*, and, of course, *Monkey Island*. The studio's official line was that all was well. Disney would help sustain productions in progress and even–probably–provide additional financial support. LucasArts continued hiring and employees felt reassured.

Then, on April 3, 2013, Disney sounded the death knell of LucasArts. The studio officially closed its doors and its 150 employees were all laid off. It was the end of a 31-year dream. The *Star Wars* video game license was given to the publisher Electronic Arts, which was supposed to continue production of *Star Wars 1313* and launch another project developed by Visceral Games and directed by the eminent Amy Hennig.[237] An entire piece of video game history went up in smoke. *Star Wars 1313* was canceled once and for all in 2015; Visceral Games closed its doors in 2017; the only legacy that players had to look forward to was *Star Wars Battlefront 1 & 2*.[238] Doing nothing to help the studio's place in history, the last two LucasArts games were the very forgettable *Kinect Star Wars* and *Angry Birds Star Wars*. A pretty pitiful final act for the company.

With great nostalgia, Ron Gilbert offers his thoughts on Lucasfilm as it existed in another age: "Working there was like being part of a creative Cambrian explosion. We fed off the creativity of each other and dreamed whatever we dared. We were free of market pressures, yet we all wanted to make games that sold well. We wanted to make games that a lot of people played and loved. We were passionate and naive and idealistic. Maybe Lucasfilm Games was just a perfect storm. The right people in the right place at the right time. Whatever it was [and whatever it became as time went by] I am proud, honored, and humbled to have been a part of it."[239]

237. The brilliant game designer of the series *Uncharted* and *Legacy of Kain*.
238. Developed by the studio Dice and released in 2015 and 2017, respectively.
239. *https://kotaku.com/how-lucasarts-fell-apart-1401731043*

The knives come out at Telltale Games™

On September 21, 2018, the employees of Telltale Games working to produce the second episode of the final season of *The Walking Dead* sat down at their desks like they did every day, not knowing that a few hours later, they would all be sent packing.

Since we last saw them in July 2009, with the release of *Tales of Monkey Island*, Telltale Games had taken off like a rocket. From classic adventure games, their productions had gradually evolved towards a more story-driven format, with puzzles pushed to the side. This evolution was particularly realized with *Jurassic Park: The Game* in 2011, but also, most notably, with the episodic saga of *The Walking Dead*, directed by Sean Vanaman (who had previously worked on *Tales of Monkey Island*, episode 3). That colossal success seemingly made the studio's management giddy. Quite simply, the adaptation of *The Walking Dead* comic books by Robert Kirkman, Tony Moore, and Charlie Adlard redefined an entire genre. With its masterful storytelling, exceptional writing, and the captivating moral choices forced upon players, *The Walking Dead* became the new gold standard for video game storytelling and won the prestigious title of Game of the Year at the 2012 Spike Video Game Awards.

Of course, Telltale Games was delighted by the flood of money that came in, and the studio went all in on the game's strategy. The zombie series was developed into five seasons and the studio no longer had any trouble at all getting contracts for big-name franchises. *Game of Thrones*, *Stranger Things*, *Guardians of the Galaxy*, *Batman*, *Minecraft*, and *The Wolf Among Us*, the new market niche was mercilessly exploited for nearly six consecutive years. The more money the games brought in, the more the studio's management made commitments and launched new projects, enticed by the potential profits and confident in what they believed to be a proven formula.

However, within the studio's teams, the rigor imposed so that they could produce so many titles within tighter and tighter deadlines became absolutely untenable. From 50 employees, the company doubled, then quintupled its staff to eventually reach around 350 people.

In November 2017, the first signs of the company's impending fall began to appear on the horizon. Around a hundred employees were summarily laid off. The studio's toxic management, or rather its lack of proper internal project management, meant that it had to hire a whole bunch of drone workers to finish projects on time, then had to let people go almost as quickly in order to "manage costs." Telltale faced a growing number of complaints and lawsuits—evidence of a broken system. Video game development had evolved to look nothing like the idealistic and creative dalliances of Lucasfilm's early days, instead becoming a perpetual rat race in which every single choice could destroy a project, in which fierce competition had to be fended off from all sides, in which costs (and losses) became prodigious. Gangrene set in and began to destroy the sector as practices like brutal "crunch times" and mental abuse of employees became widespread. Some Telltale employees even reported that for weeks at a time, in order to meet impossible deadlines and maintain an insane pace of releases, they had to work for 20 hours a day, 100 hours a week, over several months. An anonymous source from the company told the news website *The Verge*: "You'd get a lot of people coming right out of school, going, 'Oh, I really want to prove myself, and I really want to make sure that they see that I'm contributing.' The thing that broke my heart the most was seeing new team members that were just so gung-ho and optimistic and excited to be at Telltale get overused and abused because they did not feel comfortable drawing the line in the sand to say, 'This is my limit.' They either worked themselves out and would get sick or would become bitter."[240]

Faced with this radical change in atmosphere, most of the studio's most brilliant creatives jumped ship, including Dave Grossman, Mike Stemmle, Chuck Jordan, Sean Vanaman, and Jake Rodkin. Having lost so many crucial people and totally incapable of reinventing itself, Telltale Games kept churning out titles according to *The Walking Dead* model, which was starting to get old in 2018. Finally, only the most aggressive, the wiliest, and the least empathetic (and not necessarily the most talented) managers were left to pilot the company's many projects. Again according to *The Verge*, a former Telltale employee told them, "'I think a lot of the insecurity [for CEO Kevin Bruner] came from *The Walking Dead*.' The game's success had significantly raised the profiles of [Jake] Rodkin and [Sean] Vanaman and earned them widespread praise. 'I think that that really irked [Bruner] a lot,' says the source. 'He felt that... he deserved that. It was his project, or it was his company. He should have gotten all that love.'" Bruner became CEO of Telltale in 2015 and systematically dashed the creative dreams of new designers, fearing that others would outshine him.

In addition to the misguided ways of the studio's managers, poor financial management of the company put it on the road to bankruptcy. In September 2018, without warning, all of Telltales employees were let go. In shock, people lost their fear of speaking up and began denouncing the entire system of the video game industry, not just Telltale. The press and social media happily spread their claims far and wide.

---

240. *https://www.theverge.com/2018/3/20/17130056/telltale-games-developer-layoffs-toxic-video-game-industry*

The adventure game declares its independence™

I think it's fair to say that the closures, one after another, of LucasArts and Telltale Games signaled the end of an era for the heirs of Lucasfilm. The classic business model of the big studios could no longer support fresh, original projects like *Monkey Island* or *Grim Fandango*. I've mentioned this previously, but there is still a market for classic point & click games (but also for adventure games more broadly, in all their different forms). And it was Tim Schafer, at the helm of his own studio, Double Fine, who was able to prove to the entire gaming community that the world still wanted more from the old glories of LucasArts.

In 2012, the brilliant game designer launched a crowdfunding campaign on Kickstarter to fund the development of *Double Fine Adventure*. The campaign was a huge success: with nothing more than a promise from Schafer, the project raked in over $1.2 million in less than a week. That was almost as much as the original budget for *Full Throttle*. On March 13, 2012, the Kickstarter campaign ended and Double Fine was able to rely on an incredible budget of over $3 million to develop *Broken Age* (the official name given to the game), with a release planned for 2014. A true heir to an era that refused to die, the game is a dyed-in-the-wool point & click adventure, set in a totally original universe, making it a worthy successor to the great LucasArts classics. Schafer and Double Fine didn't stop at that big comeback: they went on to produce remastered versions of LucasArts classics, obtaining the rights from Disney. Thus, Double Fine released *Grim Fandango Remastered* in 2015, *Day of the Tentacle Remastered* in 2016, and *Full Throttle Remastered* in 2017.

Schafer was not the only one wanting to revive the energy and feeling of LucasArts' golden age. Ron Gilbert, who had never stopped developing games, also planned a triumphant return to the point & click sub-genre with a crowdfunding project. As early as 2014, he and Gary Winnick (*Maniac Mansion*, if you remember!) began working on a scenario combining the ambiance of the TV shows *Twin Peaks*, *The X-Files*, and *True Detective*. On November 18, 2014, they launched a campaign on Kickstarter and brought in exactly $626,250. The game *Thimbleweed Park*, as it was named, was then developed using a game engine very similar to SCUMM to deliver pixel art graphics in the style of *Maniac Mansion* and *The Secret of Monkey Island*, and almost identically replicating their interface. "The point of this project was very much to build a game that was evocative of how you remember the old adventure titles," explains Ron Gilbert. "We've used pixel art less as a retro thing, and more because we just love it. [...] We just went with what felt right. [...] I want to expose all of the great things about point and click adventures to a new audience. I think younger players get caught up in a little bit of nostalgia when they hear about the Nintendo era, the point and click era, the mystique of these games. It's interesting to them, but when they go back and actually play those games, they realize how crude they were. So, *Thimbleweed* is about letting them relive and understand what those games were, but through a game that has all of the stupid stuff removed from it. It's challenging, but without the confusion. We give you all the pieces you need to solve any puzzle in this game, and nothing is too obtuse. We specifically removed all that. Everything is logical."[241] To program the game, Gilbert enlisted the services of another famous Lucasfilm Games alumnus: the one and only David Fox. And Mark Ferrari, the creator of the fabulous pixel art backgrounds of the first *Monkey Island*, lent his talents to the game's backgrounds. They put together a little dream team that went on to create a game that was as fantastic and funny as it was referential and intelligent. "With the exception of certain technical aspects, like the parallax, the lighting, and the digital music, there's nothing in the game, from a creative standpoint, that we couldn't have done back in the day. I think that over the years, when I look back on the design work I've done, I feel that it's gotten a bit darker. It's like I'm attracted to more mature, deeper, or richer stories, unlike *Monkey Island*, which is purposefully innocent, colorful, and cartoonish."[242]

So, there remains a future for the legendary licenses of LucasArts, and probably also for our Mighty Pirate, who, as I write these lines, has been in hibernation for over a decade. We can say without a doubt that said future will be written without LucasArts, but we can still hope that it will involve the avant-garde, wacky, and genuine minds of these video game pioneers.

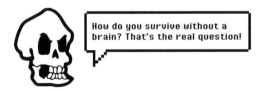

How do you survive without a brain? That's the real question!

241. *https://waypoint.vice.com/en_us/article/qkxda7/ron-gilbert-talks-thimbleweed-park-crowd-funding-and-funny-bones*
242. *Translation of interview from https://www.gamereactor.fr/articles/516203/Entretien+avec+Ron+Gilbert/*

Chapter 18: The secrets of Monkey Island™

"What is the secret of *Monkey Island*?" Few mysteries have been the subject of such extensive speculation. No other question has spawned so many hypotheses and interpretations, or stirred such passion, as this one posed by Ron Gilbert's series.

Three decades later, this secret continues to intrigue us, with Ron Gilbert happily fanning the flames while remaining tight-lipped on the subject. At one point, Gilbert told fans that if he didn't make another *Monkey Island* sequel, he would take the secret to his grave. So, WHAT IS THE SECRET OF *MONKEY ISLAND*?

When Guybrush himself poses the same question to a sinister-looking pirate the first time he sets foot in the SCUMM Bar on Mêlée Island, the response he gets is: "Only LeChuck knows."What's more, I'm sure that you excitedly opened this book with that same question in mind (in addition, of course, to being attracted by the beautiful cover art and the renown of the author), certain that the answer would finally be revealed to you. So, if you don't feel like burdening yourself with the various hypotheses and details of this great mystery, I invite you to skip directly to chapter 22 of this book: it contains the ultimate revelation, straight from the mouth of Ron Gilbert in exchange for a handful of Pieces o' Eight and a few good zingers.

The Mysteries of Monkey Island™

The first common misconception with regard to the secret of *Monkey Island* is that there's only one secret. You have to understand that initially, the first game in the series was designed as a stand-alone game. While writing it, Ron Gilbert wasn't planning to create a whole series. *The Secret of Monkey Island* was his second game and thus the commercial success of the title was far from guaranteed. The project went through four or five different names (*The Pirate Game*, *Mutiny on Monkey Island*, and even *The Pirates of the Caribbean game* because it was easier to present to the studio's leaders that way). In the end, he only added the word "secret" because he needed an original and mysterious title. Once the game was released in October 1990, the Hint Line quickly saw that the titular "secret" had become an inexhaustible source of curiosity among players. On *CompuServe*, players speculated about the true reason behind the title, and that confusion became a running joke at Lucasfilm.

Naturally, the more twisted minds of the troublemakers Ron, Tim, and Dave were all too happy to exploit the confusion. As we will see, the answer to the "secret" of the first episode is really quite obvious; but from the second installment onward, the genius creators sowed doubt in the most masterful, frustrating, and unfair way possible. Particularly, as mentioned at the beginning of this book, the second opus introduced new themes for a Ron Gilbert trilogy that would go unfinished, for reasons well beyond simple amusement. The episodes that followed were nothing more than attempts to deal with the complications of *Monkey Island 2: LeChuck's Revenge*.

It turns out that there are actually as many "secrets" as there are games in the series. And the answers are hiding in plain sight; there's no need to wait for a hypothetical *Monkey Island 3* by Ron Gilbert. For example, in the first episode, the titular secret is really just LeChuck's hideout, the infernal cave where the fearsome zombie has been keeping his ship and which Guybrush accesses by inserting a giant Q-Tip into the ear of the Giant Monkey Head. But there are many more mysteries to explore...

The Carnival of the Damned™

The reason why I chose to start with the third game is to immediately dismiss its famous attempts to explain away the true mystery that endures with regard to the meaning of the second game. I discussed this in extensive detail in the chapter on *The Curse of Monkey Island*, but finding a way around the enigmatic open ending of *Monkey Island 2: LeChuck's Revenge* was no easy task for Larry Ahern and Jonathan Ackley. Still, the two creators were able to offer a wealth of explanations in the scenario of the third opus, as if to fill the void or make up for players' frustration. Thus, Big Whoop became a portal between the land of the dead and the land of the living. An element that connects directly to the Fountain of Youth in Tim Powers' *On Stranger Tides*, the novel that inspired Gilbert and his universe. The infamous Captain LeChuck had an amusement park built around the portal on Dinky Island to hide it and deceive all bandits and pirates who might venture there. He thus created his army of the dead in hopes of conquering the Caribbean and Elaine's heart. This new "secret" of *Monkey Island* was an elegant pirouette around the ending of the second game, even if the purists who swear by the word of Ron Gilbert weren't so happy about it. A pirouette that even managed to fit into the bigger picture of the saga without sticking out like a sore thumb. While it artificially eluded the trap set by the ending of the second opus by totally inventing Guybrush's amnesia, it still respected both the spirit and the primary influences of the series. However, it lost that incredible mystical substance.

The Ultimate Insult and giant robots™

Displaying incoherent one-upmanship, *Escape from Monkey Island* can be seen as the most over-zealous of the entire series. Some of the references to the previous games are poorly executed and sometimes even betray the true reasons and motivations of certain characters while brushing past the dead ends they create in the story. The fourth episode also offers not one, but two equally outrageous "secrets." First, there's the famous "Ultimate Insult" that would supposedly allow the terrible Ozzie Mandrill to dominate the pirate world. Then, for the second, ultimate "secret" of *Monkey Island*, we got an explanation for the presence of a Giant Monkey Head (the entrance to LeChuck's secret hideout in the first game) on Monkey Island: it's the cockpit of a giant robot, a sort of Voodoo *kaiju*![243] Sure, why not? As funny as the idea may be, it's nonetheless a hard pill to swallow and doesn't fit very well with the bigger picture painted by the saga (even though we have to admit that there have never been any real limits to the series' colorful universe).

Big Whoop and the mystery of Monkey Island 2™

When it comes to *Monkey Island 2: LeChuck's Revenge*, the situation is, of course, much more complicated. I'll remind you, the game's epilogue was thought up and written at the last minute, at the very end of development. As such, it was in no way premeditated, making all doubts about it perfectly valid and raising a panoply of questions ("Sam, is 'panoply' a real word?" *Sam and Max©*). After going through hundreds of videos and pages of online forums, I've reached the conclusion that the wild imaginings of fans in search of the "truth" fall into two categories. First, there are those who believe that the world of *Monkey Island* isn't real and is merely in the imagination of a child from our own time, who sees himself as the hero of his own story. There are, of course, many factors to support this theory. The anachronisms peppered throughout

---

243. A giant Japanese monster, two of the most well-known being Godzilla and Gamera, the friendly ancient turtle.

the first two games, the repeated references to Disneyland (including the supposed treasure of Big Whoop, which proves to be nothing more than a Disney E Ticket), the shipping company that comes to the Voodoo Lady's place to pick up the crate for delivery to LeChuck's fortress, and, obviously, the confounding ending: all of these are clues that the game's universe is totally imaginary. That said, the world of *Monkey Island* was originally created to be a video-game recreation of the Disney Pirates of the Caribbean theme park ride, a stylized universe whose rules differ from those of the real world. Seriously: have you ever tried to fly somewhere by climbing into a cannon (even while wearing a pot as a helmet)?

However, there are two facts that irrefutably prove that this theory does not hold water. First, the final, mid-credits scene of *Monkey Island 2: LeChuck's Revenge* shows Elaine, still in the jungle of Dinky Island, wondering where the heck that big goofball Guybrush might be. On its own, this frivolous scene serves to insert doubt into the player's mind. The other element that seems to prove that the contemporary amusement park of Big Whoop is an illusion is the final look at the camera given by Chuckie, with his diabolical, red, glowing eyes, as the first notes of the end credits begin to play. However, the detail that plunges a wooden stake into the heart of this theory, one that few players have discovered (and which almost singlehandedly justifies the money you had to fork over for this book), can be found in the official guide for *Monkey Island 2*. In a series of drawings by Peter Chan showing the game's various islands, an easily overlooked drawing (on page 48) gives us a totally decisive clue. Simply entitled "Dinky Island Underground Map,"[244] it reveals to us a secret room. A room that contains "vast amounts of unobtainable wealth." As such, there is, in fact, pirate treasure to be found in the underground of Dinky Island, which proves as undeniably and officially as possible that the contemporary world we see is nothing more than a trick, and the "pirate reggae" world that we and Guybrush know and love really is the "true" world of *Monkey Island*. With the almost pathological rigor with which Ron Gilbert thought out every detail of his universe, it appears likely that this seemingly insignificant detail is actually a major clue pointing at the truth.

The second category of fans believes that the presence of the Big Whoop amusement park is nothing more than a Voodoo illusion devised by LeChuck (which appears to be confirmed by the evil look from Chuckie at the end) or –Why not?–by the Voodoo Lady (the theory advanced by *Tales of Monkey Island*). In any case, there is almost zero tangible evidence to support this theory or to allow us to further speculate on it. Ron Gilbert and Dave Grossman (who

---

244. Dinky Island Underground Map: *https://archive.org/details/Monkey_Island2_HintBook/page/n47/mode/1up*

is apparently privy to the truth) have long muddied the waters with regard to what they may have planned to do after development of *Monkey Island 2*. Certain jokes, and maybe even some sketches, pertaining to a hypothetical third opus were circulated, but the departures of Gilbert and Grossman killed –at least temporarily–all hope that we might learn more.

Our greatest mistake may be believing that we have to choose one camp or the other, while it's very likely that both theories are at once partially true and partially false. Let me explain...

Introspection™

"The ending to *Monkey Island 2* should not be taken literally. It's a metaphor. Or is it simile? I confuse the two."[245]

Ron Gilbert

If we set aside the desperate attempts by Larry Ahern and Mike Stemmle in the last two games to mollify players, what continues to intrigue us and raise questions is the famous secret guarded by Ron Gilbert himself. It's a true stroke of genius given that the frustration that he maintains among players again positions him as the only person capable of pulling the strings of the *Monkey Island* universe.

The contents of the following paragraphs are pure speculation. Still, I offer a theory based on careful observation of the game and its creators. It is the result of analysis relying on a year of research involving the viewing of numerous videos and the reading of countless references, including over a hundred interviews. Of course, yours truly is not infallible and may have had a bit too much adulterated grog, but the combined evidence I present to you below will undoubtedly arouse your curiosity. It may even lead you to completely change the way you look at the first two games in an inoffensive (on its surface) point & click adventure game series from the early 1990s.

We know, without a doubt, that Ron Gilbert had ultimately decided to make his series a trilogy. *The Secret of Monkey Island* created the universe and introduced it to players, *Monkey Island 2: LeChuck's Revenge* began to insert plot elements and clues suggesting the existence of a "bigger secret" than what we had imagined up to that point, and the third episode (*Monkey Island 3a*, and I'll explain the reason behind that name in the next chapter) was supposed to solve the mystery and explain the exact nature of the game's universe and the

245. *https://twitter.com/grumpygamer/status/1961348177*

reality of the key characters, namely Guybrush and LeChuck. However, in the end, the third episode–the one imagined by Ron Gilbert–was never created and the cliffhanger of the second game, along with the cryptic clues it provided, barely give us a glimpse of what Ron had in store for us.

It's also undeniable that the world of *Monkey Island* is a stylized fantasy universe. The reality of Caribbean pirates of the 16th and 17th centuries was actually nothing like the fun, romantic, glamorous image conjured up by LucasArts' universe, or even by the Pirates of the Caribbean ride at Disneyland. It's quite obvious that, from the very beginning, everything points to the backgrounds, ambiances, and various other elements of the two games being straight out of the mind of a child. We've already discussed this. But what about Guybrush? Where does he come from? How did he arrive on Mêlée Island? If it weren't for Ron Gilbert's early design documents, which allowed me to provide the extracts of Guybrush's journal found in this book, we would know absolutely nothing about our hero's background.

Monkey Island represents a world of fun and play, like a schoolyard. What's more, you can't die in the game's universe. The battles between pirates are totally inoffensive, and in spite of the incredible dangers faced by Guybrush, he always comes away totally unscathed. That's in spite of the fact that he deploys superhuman effort to get himself into perilous situations... The pirates depicted in the series are a bunch of kids more interested in procrastination, tanning, and having fun than in chests full of Pieces o' Eight. *Monkey Island* is the very embodiment of an enchanted kingdom, seen through a child's eyes, in the form of attractions, where there's no place for parents and other grown-ups.

When Guybrush pays a visit to the Voodoo Lady in the first game, she gives him an enigmatic warning: "Now go and find the one that loves you, but be warned... Not of LeChuck... of yourself and what you will find! What you will find out about yourself and your world. It will terrify you!" As a character who's both cryptic and omniscient, the Voodoo Lady seems out of sync with the broader context of the game. But in any case, what is this terrifying personal secret that Guybrush should beware of? In the second game, our hero falls and hits his head, the world becomes tinted with red, and a vision appears: two adults walk toward Guybrush... they're his parents! "We came looking for you!" The young pirate is dumbfounded: he had always believed that he had been abandoned as a small child. "We are such loving parents," his mother reassures him. This is the first time that Ron Gilbert gives us some clues about the deeper end of Guybrush's personality. He has apparently grown up without his parents, without a mother's love, which LeChuck himself confirms when he tortures Guybrush inside his fortress and Guybrush asks, "Where do babies come from?": "In your case, the orphanage." This reveals a more complex psyche and a more fully-fledged character than the intrepid novice pirate ever suggested previously. What if Ron Gilbert was subtly trying to give us clues? The "secret" of *Monkey Island* may exclusively concern Guybrush (not the world around him) and his past. A terrifying secret, as the Voodoo Lady foretold. A suppressed memory of the past, dead parents, an idealized universe... It all starts to look like a case of childhood trauma.

So, could the world of *Monkey Island* represent a post-traumatic delusion resulting from an unhappy childhood? A metaphor in which a child's mind prefers to wander rather than face its own internal demons? In that case, the ending of *Monkey Island 2: LeChuck's Revenge*, in the underground passages of Dinky Island, where Guybrush sees the skeletons of his parents in an infirmary, has all the hallmarks of a deep trauma tied to the loss of loved ones. Could it be that Guybrush's parents died a violent death? The reincarnation of his own mother seems to suggest as much at the very end of the game when she says, "I wish you wouldn't run off like that, young man. We were worried sick. You don't know what kinds of murderers and ne'er-do-wells might be hanging around a place like this!" It may be that Guybrush felt a sense of abandonment after the tragic loss of his parents, grew up in an orphanage, and developed a psychological syndrome in which he retreats into an imaginary world in order to escape from his terrible reality. A world in which people don't die. A fantasy world shaped by happy memories from his childhood, a world in which he reconnects with the things that sparked his imagination as a kid. As if he was finally getting up to walk around in his favorite theme park ride. Doesn't that remind you of a certain quotation from our dear Ron Gilbert?

If not, let me give you a refresher: at one point, Gilbert studied psychology. That period may not have lasted long, but in any case, it was an area of interest for the young game designer. It may be where he got the inspiration for his vision of the consequences of childhood trauma. Experiencing or witnessing such trauma can lead a child to feel like the world around them is no longer safe and predictable. It gives them a frightening viewpoint and makes them fear that the traumatic event will be repeated. Reactions to such trauma vary from one person to the next depending on, for example, the child's age. Quite often, those reactions include a desire to bury all memories of the event, but also may include repeatedly reliving the event through nightmares, imaginary recreations, etc.

As such, could the universe of *Monkey Island* be purely imaginary? A fantasy allowing someone to escape from reality? And could the objective of the game be to gradually bring Guybrush to come to terms with reality and the terrifying "secret" of his past? This explanation may be a bit hard to swallow. And yet... As you already know, *Monkey Island 2: LeChuck's Revenge* was written by three men: Ron Gilbert, Dave Grossman, and Tim Schafer. Let's now take a closer look at the latter of the three.

Tim Schafer is a creator of universes, an author in the traditional sense, and has a very distinct style. In 2000, he left LucasArts to found his own studio,

Double Fine, and began production of the game *Psychonauts*, a concept he'd had at the back of his mind for... a decade or so. "Making *Psychonauts* has been the longest and craziest experience of my life,"[246] he told IGN. Released in 2005, the game is a true gem. In it, the player controls a character named Razputin, a child with supernatural powers who has been rejected by his father and wishes to become a "Psychonaut," a spy with psychic abilities. In order to fight back against an evil professor who's stealing brains, Raz has to literally enter the psyches of his classmates and defeat their various traumas. Filled with humor and originality, this brilliant game from Tim Schafer brushes aside all taboos to tackle deep and serious subjects like loss of identity, rejection of reality, the prison of one's mind, and childhood trauma. Sound familiar? Still not convinced? Allow me to continue.

Let's go back to San Francisco in 1991. *Monkey Island 2* was written and produced between the months of January and August. At the same time, Lucasfilm became LucasArts and moved its offices to be next to those of Industrial Light & Magic, the prestigious studio specializing in special effects. Post-production of the most recent Spielberg film was underway. It was an adaptation of J.M. Barrie's *Peter Pan*, a movie called *Hook*. As I'm sure you know, Peter Pan is a character who shuns the real world for an imaginary one; he creates his own adventures filled with pirates and other ne'er-do-wells, including the diabolical Captain Hook. Barrie's original play and novel featuring the Peter Pan character, as well as the film derived therefrom, all deal with a child's thanatophobia—the fear of death—and the hero's name has even been famously used to describe a psychological syndrome theorized about by American psychologist Dr. Dan Kiley in 1983. The same year that a young Ron Gilbert spent studying psychology... According to multiple accounts, Gilbert went at least twice to visit the teams working on the movie's special effects, notably the scene in which the main characters fly over the island, which looks eerily similar to Monkey Island.

Analyzing the work of Ron Gilbert through the lens of *Peter Pan* offers a dizzying new perspective. Barrie's character refuses to grow up, and death plays an important part throughout the story, embodied by the terror caused by Captain Hook and the fear of oblivion and abandonment. We also see in the story the theme of sexual awakening for Wendy and the Freudian feelings of Peter Pan toward a maternal figure, which is very similar to the relationship between Guybrush and Elaine (I'll remind you that for Gilbert, the two characters were never supposed to get married as he viewed their relationship as being more complex than that). Guybrush, like his alter ego Peter Pan, is not really the naive and jovial young man that he first appears to be. And

---

246. *https://www.ign.com/articles/2005/03/07/tim-schafer-interview*

Guybrush, again like Peter, seems to be inextricably tied to his universe, as if he existed first and the universe came after.

All this can even lead us to look differently at Steve Purcell's illustration on the cover of *Monkey Island 2: LeChuck's Revenge*. In it, we see a close-up of LeChuck, holding up a Voodoo doll, while Guybrush stands behind him with his hands on his head, clearly experiencing terrible suffering. A literal reading of this scene tells us that the zombie captain is torturing our poor hero. But an alternate reading through the lens of the information I've just provided can give the scene a very different meaning. What if Guybrush, in this pose, is trying to fight off his inner demons—his trauma and nightmares? What if Guybrush is simply trying to fight back against Monkey Island and the sad, terrifying truth?

In 2016, during a question and answer session with fans, Ron Gilbert revealed that he wouldn't agree to work under a license with Disney. For him, the only real way to be able to work unfettered and create his own *Monkey Island 3* would be to acquire the intellectual property from the House of Mouse. Why this stubbornness on his part? After all, Tim Schafer was able to revive his old treasures (*Day of the Tentacle*, *Full Throttle*) with his studio Double Fine, so, why not Ron? What if the main reason is simply that what Ron Gilbert has in mind is so wild that Disney would never agree to it? What if the third installment in the adventures of Guybrush Threepwood, the story we've all fantasized about for years, doesn't take place in a good-natured pirate universe? What if Ron's sequel takes place in a totally different setting and a totally different timeline? That of the real Guybrush? Let me remind you that previously, during development of *The Curse of Monkey Island*, Larry Ahern said that there was no way that the new game could take place outside of a pirate universe—that such a drastic change of ambiance would be too destabilizing for players.

Now, that's just speculation and we can't jump to too many conclusions. We don't know, and we may never know, the true nature of the "secret" of Monkey Island. But that's precisely what makes this incredible series so powerful. It fosters infinite fantasies, like no other video game has done before. And that's what matters most.

A video game without Murray is like a ship without a rudder!

Chapter 19: The Legacy of Monkey Island™

How ironic that, at the time, Ron Gilbert and his teams didn't get to enjoy the benefits of the *Monkey Island* saga's cult following and the incredible critical success that it has today. "*Monkey Island* was never a big hit," Ron Gilbert recalls. "It sold well, but not nearly as well as anything Sierra released." To underscore that point, LucasArts took advantage of the series' cult status when it produced the remake known as *The Secret of Monkey Island: Special Edition* in 2009. The nostalgia factor was enough to briefly place the SE at the top of the sales charts. Journalist John Walker, of the eminent website *Rock Paper Shotgun*, even declared that, looking back on the 1990s, it seemed to him no other studio in the history of video games had created such a superb series of titles.

What if the secret to that strong legacy was simply the fact that LucasArts' games, and the *Monkey Island* series in particular, told good stories? "If any type of game is going to bridge the gap between games and storytelling, it is most likely going to be adventure games. They will become less puzzle-solving and more storytelling, it is the blueprint the future will be made from,"[247] Ron Gilbert predicted. After all, spectacular though they may be, the greatest scenes of blockbuster action games have done the same things over and over for decades (car races, goals in *FIFA*, and the slaughter of innocent mushrooms in *Mario*). But a good story stays with the player, leaves a mark on them, and shapes them as a human being. And of all the stories told through video games throughout our youth, the adventures of Guybrush Threepwood, Mighty Pirate, have stayed with us for longer than others. "It amazes me that people still play and love *Monkey Island*. I never would have believed it back then," Ron Gilbert confides. "It's hard for me to understand what *Monkey Island* means to people. I am always asked why I think it's been such an enduring and important game. My answer is always, 'I have no idea.' I really don't."[248]

While writing this book, I endeavored to find an answer to this question. There are some clear historic milestones in the series that influenced the video game medium, like major innovations in game design, the dogma of video game

---

247. *https://grumpygamer.com/why_adventure_games_suck*
248. *https://grumpygamer.com/monkey25*

storytelling, the careful attention to detail in the graphics, the timeless humor, the musical themes, etc. But you can find all of that in other great games. Putting nostalgia aside, how can a mere title prove to be so evocative? There are probably as many answers to the question as there are players who have wandered the warm, shaded streets of Mêlée Island.

"There are two things in my career that I'm most proud of. *Monkey Island* is one of them and Humongous Entertainment is the other. They have both touched and influenced a lot of people. People will tell me that they learned English or how to read from playing *Monkey Island*. People have had *Monkey Island* weddings. Two people have asked me if it was OK to name their new child Guybrush. One person told me that he and his father fought and never got along, except for when they played *Monkey Island* together. It makes me extremely proud and is very humbling," Gilbert adds.

Quite simply, I think that Ron and his band of 1980s hippies managed to capture a certain creative energy at the right time and turn it into funny jokes, iconic phrases, and dialogue that has become part of the collective unconscious. They created a well-crafted universe; they took their work very seriously while not taking themselves seriously at all. There is no magic formula for creating a game that will earn a cult following; it's just a matter of the stars aligning. "I was very fortunate to have an incredible team. From Dave and Tim to Steve Purcell, Mark Ferrari, an amazing testing department, and everyone else who touched the game's creation. And also a company management structure that knew to leave creative people alone and let them build great things," Ron Gilbert concludes.

The mark of Monkey Island™

It would be impossible to list every instance, but there are numerous references to the series in other games, a testament to the popularity of and mark left by Guybrush and his crew on the collective imagination. From 1990 to the present day, every game developer on the face of this planet (maybe I'm exaggerating just a hair) has slipped subtle references to the saga's humor into their games. Among the more recent examples, Guybrush made a notable appearance in *Uncharted 4: A Thief's End*[249] as one of the most famous pirates of the legendary Libertalia; in *The Witcher 3: Blood and Wine*,[250] a character curiously named Mancomb battles the Witcher himself, Geralt of Rivia, with a barrage of insults. Among the older examples, in the fantastic game

---

249. Naughty Dog (2016).
250. CD Projekt (2016).

Discworld,[251], Rincewind looks Lady Ramkin up and down, and says: "That's the second largest woman I've ever seen!"; in the RPG *Fable*,[252] a tomb bears the epitaph: "No man can hold his breath for ten minutes"; in the Pixar movie *Finding Nemo*, a yacht anchored in Sydney harbor is named *The Sea Monkey*. I could also mention *Ultima 8*, *Quest for Glory*, *King's Quest 6*, *Psychonauts*, *Grim Fandango*, *Icewind Dale*, *Simon the Sorcerer*, *The Longest Journey*, and more.

Then, of course, there's the countless fan-fiction stories and comics, tributes to the game's music, and fantastic artwork created by fans all over the world. Among the most impressive, someone created a stage play! Indeed, a man named Martin Kreusch used a crowdfunding campaign to produce a theatrical adaption of *The Secret of Monkey Island* in 2015. The campaign reached its goal, bringing in €12,000, and several performances were given in Germany.

Monkey Island, Guybrush, Elaine, and LeChuck have all become true pop culture icons.

---

251. A point & click game developed by Teeny Weeny Games and published by Psygnosis in 1995. It is an adaptation of the famous universe created by author Terry Pratchett.
252. Lionhead Studios (2004).

Chapter 20: Ron Gilbert vs. Disney™

When Disney acquired Lucasfilm in 2012, the company had no plans for what to do with the video games division. Four years later, it was officially announced that there would be no more in-house video game production and that the studio was already pursuing a policy of simply managing franchises (*Star Wars*, *Indiana Jones*, *Marvel*, etc.). It was the end of an era.

Naturally, with the new policy, *Monkey Island* and the other LucasArts adventure game licenses were locked away in the Disney Vault, with dim prospects for their future. As for Ron Gilbert, for a number of years, he has dreamed of reviving the adventures of Guybrush Threepwood. On May 23, 2016, he published on his Twitter account @grumpygamer a tweet that went out like a message in a bottle: "Dear @Disney, now that you're not making games, please sell me my *Monkey Island* and *Maniac Mansion* IP. I'll pay real actual money for them."

Of course, there was radio silence from the House of Mouse. Disney has remained silent on the fate of the point & click classics, and apart from the HD remakes of *Day of the Tentacle* and *Full Throttle*, the company doesn't seem interested in giving up a single Piece o' Eight from the hoard of treasure it acquired.

A few weeks after Gilbert's tweet, someone with the username Thaddeus Sharpe started a petition on the website *Change.org* entitled "Disney, please sell the rights to *Monkey Island* back to its creator Ron Gilbert." Over 20,000 signatures later, it still doesn't seem like the rights to Guybrush Threepwood will change hands so easily. Sadly, the petition may have actually been counterproductive. By showing Disney that the *Monkey Island* franchise remained popular and in demand, the petition proved the value of the license and how it would be detrimental for Disney to sell it. Ron Gilbert confirmed as much in a forum for the game *Thimbleweed Park*: "While these petitions are nice, they don't help. This is about the fourth one that's appeared. Disney is paying no attention, and even worse, if they do, the more interest these petitions get, the more Disney might think the IP has value and not sell it back. The best thing to happen is for everyone to forget about *MI* and for Disney to think it has no value."

Monkey Island 3a: The Secret Revealed or Your Money Back™

The malicious gossips of the world will say that Ron Gilbert's career has not gone as well as he would have liked. Others will say that the relative flops of *DeathSpank* (Hothead Games, 2010) and *The Cave* (Double Fine, 2013) seriously dimmed the eternal aura of respect surrounding the creator. Others still will cynically criticize Ron Gilbert for clinging onto his past glories to continue drawing attention to himself. However, Gilbert has never stopped showing his love for his characters and universe. He has always, very respect-fully, watched the evolution of the series with a benevolent gaze and has made himself available to help out in any way he can, even when LucasArts gave him the cold shoulder while making *The Curse of Monkey Island*.

When he left LucasArts in 1992, Ron Gilbert intended to part ways on good terms as he founded Humongous. He even said in an interview given in 1993 that Lucas could bring him back as a contractor to direct *Monkey Island 3*. However, the studio's managers at the time couldn't forgive him for continuing to use the SCUMM engine to make his own games. While the divorce between the two sides was never made official, it took years and major changes at the top of the studio for LucasArts to bury the hatchet. All the while, as explained in chapter 18 of this book, Ron Gilbert kept hope alive among his fans that he might one day create a sequel and potentially reveal the much vaunted secret of Monkey Island. According to him, the original series was always supposed to be a trilogy, and while he has great respect for *The Curse of Monkey Island*, it's not at all what he had in mind for the third episode. *Monkey Island 3a*, as he has dubbed it, has long been one of the greatest phantoms of the video game world, alongside *Half-Life 3* and *Shenmue 3*. But that hope is not futile: after all, the third *Shenmue* is set to be released in 2019 after an 18-year hiatus.

On April 13, 2013, on his blog, Ron Gilbert published an article explaining the broad strokes of what he imagined for *Monkey Island 3*. "It would be a retro game that [hearkened] back to *Monkey Island 1* and *2*. I'd do it as 'enhanced low-res' [a style he would eventually use for *Thimbleweed Park*]. Nice crisp retro art, but augmented by the hardware we have today: parallaxing, depth of field, warm glows, etc. All the stuff we wanted to do back in 1990 but couldn't. *Monkey Island* deserves that. It's authentic. It doesn't need 3D. Yes, I've seen the video, it's very cool, but *Monkey Island* wants to be what it is. I would want the game to be how we all remember *Monkey Island*."[253]

He then details the game design he envisions: "It would be a hardcore adventure game driven by what made that era so great. No tutorials or hint systems or pansy-assed puzzles or catering to the mass-market or modernizing. It would be an adventure game for the hardcore. You're going to get stuck. You're going to be frustrated. Some puzzles will be hard, but all the puzzles will be fair. It's one aspect of *Monkey Island* I am very proud of. Read this." He then continues to fantasize about his hypothetical sequel: "Full-on inventory. Nice, big, juicy icons full of pixels. The first version of *Monkey Island 1* had text for inventory; a later release and *Monkey Island 2* had huge inventory icons and it was nirvana. They will be so nice you'll want to lick them. That's a bullet-point for the [game] box. [...] There would be a box. I imagine most copies would be sold digitally, but sometimes you just want to roll around in all your adventure game boxes. I know I do. Besides, where would you store the code wheel? [...] I would rebuild SCUMM. Not SCUMM as in the exact same language, but what SCUMM brought to those games. It was a language built around making adventure games and rapid iteration. [...] It would be made with a very small team. Not 30 or 20, but 10 or less. It means the game would take longer, but it would be more personal and crafted with love." A bit later on, he adds: "It would be called *Monkey Island 3a*. All the games after *Monkey Island 2* don't exist in my *Monkey Island* universe. My apologies to the all talented people who worked on them and the people who loved them, but I'd want to pick up where I left off. Free of baggage. In a carnival. That doesn't mean I won't steal some good ideas or characters from other games. I'm not above that. [...] It won't be the *Monkey Island 3* I was going to make in 1992. I'm not the same person I was back then. I could never make that game now. It is lost to time. Hopefully this one would be better." Finally, he concludes: "The game would be the game I wanted to make. I don't want the pressure of trying to make the game you want me to make. I would vanish for long periods of time. I would not constantly keep you up-to-date or be feeding the hype machine. I'd show stuff that excited me or amused me. If you let me do those things, you will love the game. That, I promise."

However, since then, we've had zero indication that *Monkey Island 3a* might become a reality. *Thimbleweed Park* has, in some ways, fulfilled a number of Ron Gilbert's wishes that he intended to realize in his legendary third opus. Hoping that the brilliant game designer doesn't take his secret to the grave, we cross our fingers that we will one day get the chance to discover the true

253. *https://grumpygamer.com/if_i_made_another_monkeyisland*

meaning behind the mysterious look from Chuckie, Guybrush's brother, at the very end of *Monkey Island 2*.

Chapter 21: Conclusion: So long...™

Well folks, we have arrived at our final destination. I now write the final lines of this book after nearly a year of archaeological digging through the archives of LucasArts. A year of imagining what daily life was like at the studio that produced probably the most emblematic game of my childhood. A year of hunting down information, raising questions, making repeated contacts, and tirelessly harassing all of the important names I found in the credits of *The Secret of Monkey Island*. This is the moment for me to get nostalgic, to look back on the long hours I spent in front of my computer screen, to the point where my vision began to blur (speaking of which, I need to go put on my glasses!), to remember just how much the world of Guybrush inspired me–to an irrational degree, if I'm being honest, more than any other artistic work has ever inspired me. And to that point, for me, the eternal debate over the question "is a video game a form of art?" was resolved long, long ago. *Monkey Island* inspired in me a fiery passion for pirates, for the novels of Robert Louis Stevenson, for a certain kind of humor; it may have even, in a way, inspired in me a way of relating to others, a combination of passive naïveté and ingenuous observation. *Monkey Island* even helped me learn English! I was so obsessed with the game that, almost 30 years later, I decided to spend a year of my life writing a book about it.

When I started thinking about this book, I had several objectives in mind. I felt a need to understand why I, personally, was obsessed with the game, but also, above all, why it resonated with so many people. What was the rational explanation for why we continue to talk about a humble adventure game developed by a bunch of hippies in *Star Wars* T-shirts in the late '80s? Granted, there's the unquestionable, scientifically proven quality of the game design, which, in its own way, made important contributions to video game history. There's also probably the quality of the writing and the game's quirky humor, which has often been imitated, but never equaled. Of course, we can explain it as a convergence of events, an alignment of the stars, and probably a bit of Voodoo magic in the mix. To tell the truth, not even the original developers understand it. Dave Grossman, Tim Schafer, Larry Ahern, Mark Ferrari, Khris Brown–practically all of them commented to me that they can't explain the series' staying power. Still, it's funny that *Monkey Island* seems to have resonated with so many people, don't you think? Some even confided to me that the series' legacy could be intimidating at times, that it was hard to do better or move forward. However, I discovered that each of them has had an exceptional career. It's as if the words *Monkey Island* on a résumé automatically lead to success. So, still, the question remains.

Quite frankly, we will probably never be able to answer this question. Why *Monkey Island* and not some other game? As I said before, there are probably as many answers to the question as there are players who have wandered the shaded paths of Mêlée Island. My answer is that I am convinced the series owes its lasting legacy to this brilliant title: *The SECRET of Monkey Island*. It's a *secret* we are obsessed with and that gives the series that special something. A *secret* that we delight in trying to discover, but which we know all too well will probably always remain a mystery. A *secret* that was probably the most brilliant idea ever to come from an equally brilliant man. Ron Gilbert.

Chapter 22 - Return to Monkey Island™

Sometimes, life takes us by surprise.

Since the 2019 French release of this book (the writings of a neurotic, obsessed fan), I've gotten the impression that the "world of *Monkey Island*" was spinning differently on its axis. Perhaps it was just my own totally biased perception? After so many years of watching the franchise gradually fade away in the annals of video game history, I was happy to see the abundance of love that remained for the series: first, kind words about the book; then, passionate, in-depth discussions about certain nuances; the emergence of historical treasures and brand-new revelations; an anthology published by Limited Run; and a progressive return to social media for the handful of artists who worked on the games, sharing their fond memories of their swashbuckling days. Then, without warning, this brief message was published on the blog of our favorite Grumpy Gamer on Friday, April 1, 2022: "For 18 years, the Grumpy Gamer blog has been April Fools' Day-free because it's a stupid tradition. So, to mix things up a little, I'm taking this opportunity to announce I've decided to make another *Monkey Island*."[254] And the world—our world, my world—was set ablaze...

With the release of *Return to Monkey Island*, I have my own opportunity for a return: a return to this book that's so near and dear to my heart, for a re-release alongside a new English edition. Of course, it was too good of an opportunity to pass up. After a brief discussion with my publisher, we agreed to create an "extended edition" with this new chapter written almost four years after the original publication. I decided not to revise certain details that were debated by the keenest fans—nothing serious or spectacular. I also decided not to change the original ending. As such, the book takes on this new, special form, as if jazzed up with one of those post-credits scenes you see in some movies, in which a new twist is revealed. Without further ado, after our conclusion in 2019, I now invite you to return to Mêlée Island and the adventures of Guybrush Threepwood. Anchors aweigh!

254.. *https://grumpygamer.com/april_fools_2022*

A stupid tradition 31 years in the making

Everyone was familiar with Ron Gilbert's unpredictable and facetious nature, but in the moment, there was total confusion. And yet, the *Monkey Island* creator had warned us years previously in a tweet dated September 20, 2013: "If I ever get to make another *Monkey Island*, I'm going to announce it on April 1ˢᵗ."[255] It just goes to show that perseverance pays off. An amusing anecdote revealed by Dominic Armato,[256] the irreplaceable voice of Guybrush Threepwood: "Ron told me that was his plan early on, to do the April 1ˢᵗ announcement, and I knew about the whole background with his distaste for April Fools' jokes and all that. I was like, 'That's brilliant! That's fantastic!' But he didn't realize that date fell on a Friday! So, originally, the plan was he was going to do the announcement on his blog, and then–boom!–the next day, they were going to drop the trailer, like, 'No, no, no, this is really a thing!' But then, because of the timing, they didn't want to drop the trailer until Monday, so it ended up being this extended, long weekend of torture for a lot of people! That was never his original intent! [...] It only made it harder for me too because I was like, 'Just drop the trailer! I want to see it!' My heart goes out to the folks who spent a whole weekend in agony wondering if it was true or not."

In this age of social media and instant gratification, the impact of the message was explosive. It once again showed fans' love and passion for the series. Ron Gilbert, Dave Grossman, the original trio of musicians, and others would all be returning with a brand-new installment! Thus, on Monday, April 4, 2022, after 72 hours of endless speculation about the veracity of the announcement, the first teaser for *Return to Monkey Island* finally appeared on the Web. "Social media existed the last time we did this, for *Tales* and the special editions, but not like now," Dominic Armato continues. "Because I've been out of voiceover for so long, this is the first time I got to do a game release firmly in the social media era. And I've wondered for years, and I'd think about it, like, 'Gosh, what would it even be like now to launch a *Monkey Island* game these days?' Because there would be so much insanity online. [...] I try to respond to everyone that I can, and I know that I miss people, but I just want to be there, I want to be talking to people, I want to be in the middle of it because that's who I am. [...] Because I know how much these games meant to me and I know how much it means to them."

The sound of waves; a nighttime scene on the docks of Mêlée Island; a ghostly figure holds a violin as Murray sits by her side, waiting.

255. *https://twitter.com/grumpygamer/status/380819751208902656?s=20&t=c5Z3PbgKeEy-5DMeapfS01w*
256. Interview conducted specially for this book.

The first notes of LeChuck's theme play as a burly sailor drops a crate on the dock labeled "Lucasfilm Games"; then a second crate drops, labeled "Devolver"; finally, a third labeled "Ron Gilbert's Terrible Toybox." Murray is unable to contain his surprise: "Ron Gilbert told me he'd never make another *Monkey Island* unless…" But before he gets a chance to finish his sentence, he's thrown into the sea. *Return to Monkey Island*, one of the best-kept secrets in the world of video games, was preparing for a release in 2022. Such a secret is particularly hard to keep these days, with just about all projects being leaked on the internet. Yet another "secret" of *Monkey Island…*

For me, my own return to *Monkey Island* came a few months later in late August 2022, just a few weeks before the game's official release on September 19, 2022. My new journey to *Monkey Island* began on a particularly hot and sunny afternoon in Paris, just steps from the Louvre pyramids, on a café terrace. No menacing clown in sight (*Broken Sword*, anyone?); instead, sitting across from me was a happy man. "When I joined LucasArts, I had a dream: to make a new *Star Wars* adventure game, an *Indiana Jones* game, and a new *Monkey Island…*" A hat trick for Craig Derrick. The last time we saw the Lucasfilm executive producer (LucasArts at the time) was in 2010 with the special edition of *Monkey Island 2: LeChuck's Revenge*. "*Star Wars Eclipse* is in development at Quantic Dream,[257] here in Paris, and it's going to be the most incredible adventure game ever made; *Indiana Jones* is underway at Machine Games;[258] and *Return to Monkey Island* is coming out soon," he tells me with an almost palpable feeling of accomplishment. "The *Monkey Island* sequel, Ron's project, has been a long time coming. Much longer than the general public knows." The waiter interrupts him to serve us a pair of espressos and Craig takes his time as he sips his coffee. Meanwhile, I stare at him, hungry for more information. "… And maybe one day we'll be able to tell the whole story."

Let's go back in time: the year is 2011 and LucasArts, the game development studio, still exists. Then, on December 21, 2012, Disney officially acquires Lucasfilm, along with all of the teams falling under that umbrella. "Almost overnight, I got a new boss and just about all projects were canceled." The weeks went by and Disney decided, at first, to hit pause on the projects *Star Wars: 1313* and *Star Wars: First Assault*, before officially shutting down the game studio on April 3, 2013, laying off the vast majority of the employees, with the exception of a small handful of people, including Craig, who was then put in charge of managing the company's licenses. Any potential for a new

257. Quantic Dream is a French video game studio responsible for the titles *Heavy Rain* and *Detroit: Become Human*.
258. As I write these lines, the *Indiana Jones* game does not yet have an official title, but is being developed by MachineGames, the Swedish studio responsible for *Wolfenstein: The New Order*.

Monkey Island was dead in the water; however, the seed of an idea was planted in the brain of Ron Gilbert, who put out a note on his blog on April 13, 2013: "If I Made Another *Monkey Island*."[259] And you already know the rest of that story. Ron asked Disney several times to sell him the franchise, repeatedly refusing the possibility of collaborating with the House of Mouse. He also made a wish list: a retro game using classic pixel art, fitting directly into the lineage of SCUMM point & click games of the 1990s. Those same specifications would more or less be applied to *Thimbleweed Park*, which came out on March 30, 2017, and was followed by a free standalone game called *Delores: A Thimbleweed Park Mini-Adventure*, both developed by Terrible Toybox, the studio co-founded in 2014 by Ron Gilbert and Gary Winnick. "That article was just this weird stream of consciousness," Gilbert later told *Ars Technica*[260] concerning his blog article. "I don't remember the exact incident, but I remember I was feeling a little depressed that I wouldn't ever get to make another *Monkey Island*, and that really kind of spawned that article. [...] I think if I could redo that article, I would probably cage it a bit differently because these aren't things that absolutely will happen or absolutely things I'll do," Gilbert continued. "Anybody who's involved in any creative process knows that as soon as you start, everything changes. Coming up with ideas, you change the story, you change characters, you change puzzles. Everything is not written in stone." That could have been the end of it if it wasn't for a chance encounter. "I was working on a little RPG game that I was just doing solo, just me," he tells *IGN*.[261] "That was kind of a hobby project more than anything. [...] And then came PAX 2019."[262]

PAX Vobiscum

"Well, I bought Disney, that's how this all happened," Ron Gilbert jokingly tells Emily Morganti of the website *Adventure Gamers*.[263] Ron stated it publicly many times: he could not possibly imagine working for Disney. The biggest reason why he left LucasArts in 1992 was to gain creative independence, and he wasn't about to give that up nearly three decades later for any project, no matter how important to him. "Yeah, I said I wouldn't do it unless I owned it,

259. *https://grumpygamer.com/if_i_made_another_monkeyisland*
260. *https://arstechnica.com/gaming/2022/04/in-rare-interview-monkey-island-designers-tell-ars-about-long-awaited-return*
261. *https://www.ign.com/articles/return-to-monkey-island-ron-gilbert-dave-grossman-how-it-became-reality-monkey-island-3*
262. PAX (Penny Arcade Expo) is a series of gaming events, tournaments, concerts, and keynote speeches held in the U.S. since 2004.
263. *https://adventuregamers.com/articles/view/ron-gilbert-dave-grossman-return-to-monkey-island*

and I certainly kind of poked around Disney trying to figure out whether there was any interest in that. What was very obvious was that they really liked *Monkey Island*, that *Monkey Island* meant a lot to the people, at least in the Lucasfilm group of Disney. And that was just never going to happen. It's not like Disney needs the money, and I could slip them some money, and yay, they can make their quarter or something. It's just not a reasonable possibility for me to do. And I think the more important thing, rather than owning it, was that I really wanted to have creative freedom. I didn't want to be making a game and having somebody tell me what I should make. It's not a work-for-hire gig. So, what was probably more important than actually owning it, was being able to make the game we wanted to make."

So, that brings us back to the PAX 2019 conference: Gilbert was approached by Nigel Lowrie, one of the co-founders of Devolver, a prominent American game publisher founded in 2009 and particularly known for its hit games *Hotline Miami*, *Enter the Gungeon*, *Shadow Warrior*, and *Broforce*. Lowrie told our dear Grumpy Gamer that he was in contact with John Drake, the manager of licenses for Lucasfilm Games who had just joined Disney and was tasked with assessing their existing partnerships, particularly with Electronic Arts (*Star Wars*), Square Enix (Marvel), and Warner Bros. (Pixar). But that wasn't all... Interestingly, in February of that same year, Disney's Supreme Leader, Bob Iger, lamented: "We're good at making movies and television shows and theme parks and cruise ships and the like, we've just never managed to demonstrate much skill on the publishing side of games." Given that fact, John Drake was directly tasked with breathing new life into game publishing, which, barely two years later, led to a series of announcements (including for the aforementioned *Star Wars Eclipse* and *Indiana Jones* games). Returning to December 2019. "I told Nigel [Lowrie], 'I need to think about this. I need to make sure that we have a good idea.' It's obviously–it's a game that's just fraught with problems, just because of the historicalness of it, and I just wanted to make sure that we had a good idea. That's when I called Dave [Grossman], before that, and Dave flew up here [to Seattle], and we spent a couple of days just hammering out, 'Okay, if we were going to make another one, what would it be?' We just thrashed all sorts of ideas and talked about what are the themes, and what do we want to say in the game, all that stuff. And it was after that discussion with Dave that I felt confident–'All right, I think we can make a good game.' And that's when the discussion started up for real," Ron Gilbert tells *Adventure Gamers*. In January 2020, things officially began to fall into place.

Return to secrecy

"By coincidence, Dave [Grossman] and I were working on a project about four months before Nigel contacted me. It was a project that never came to fruition but, you know, we were in contact and working together and designing stuff. [...] He was very enthusiastic about a new *Monkey Island*, probably more than me," Ron explains to journalist Laura Cress.[264] "I was still a little bit nervous about doing a new *Monkey Island*." After a few days of brainstorming over pints of grog, coming up with ideas that they might put into a new installment in the adventures of Guybrush Threepwood, Ron went back to Nigel Lowrie to confirm his interest and get the ball rolling with Disney.

From January 2020 to that fateful day of April 1, 2022, we didn't hear a peep about *Return to Monkey Island*. Outside of the people directly involved in the project—about 25 artists and a handful of producers and other folks in the production's orbit—no one knew a thing. No news, no leaks, no curious musings—not the slightest hint! And this is coming from a particularly obsessive nerd. Only a few brief tweets from Craig Derrick could possibly have put us on the scent, but the anthology of previous games released by the publisher Limited Run dispelled any suspicions. The project team maintained a culture of secrecy, an age-old recipe guarded by the small coven of *Monkey Island* developers. "I don't know if it was hard necessarily to keep it secret," Ron Gilbert tells Marius at the website *MixnMojo*.[265] "It was something we had to be very, very careful about. Everybody who came on the project, with maybe the exception of Dave, actually, had to sign an NDA. A pretty strict NDA. So, everybody knew that we were very, very serious about the confidentiality of this game. We just had to be very careful."

Paris, August 2022. The server brings us a second round of espressos and Craig Derrick watches the constant hustle and bustle of people strolling down Rue de Rivoli. "I can't even tell you how great it is just to see so many people on the street. Of course, back in February 2020, no one suspected that a global pandemic was coming that would turn everything on its head. The streets became deserted and everyone at Disney had to work remotely. But I have to say that worked remarkably well." *Return to Monkey Island* is a game of "the pandemic era." Development started at the same time as the COVID pandemic and essentially ended at the same time as well. "I think in some ways, having the pandemic hit right as we started the game actually helped us, because people were really kind of confined to their homes," Ron Gilbert explains to

---

264. *https://www.youtube.com/watch?v=LHmnvnfhHjw&ab_channel=Cressup*
265. *https://mixnmojo.com/features/interviews/Ron-Gilbert-and-Dave-Grossman-talk-Return-to-Monkey-Island*

MixnMojo. "They didn't have a bunch of people coming into their homes, their friends. They weren't out with their friends. So, that probably helped us, in that regard. But I think the whole team was just amazing at keeping the secret. I think everybody on the team really bought into how important that was. They all wanted this to remain a secret as well." Thus, each member of the team worked from their own space, wherever they were in the world–in the United States, of course, but also in Europe–sharing as much as possible with each other while ensuring that no information leaked. "I have not worked in an office since around 2012," Ron tells *AdventureGamers*. "Whenever *The Cave* came out, that's the last time I worked in an office. So, working remotely–I mean, I feel bad in some ways, because this whole pandemic has been meaningless to me. It's like the same old world; I don't have kids, I don't have to deal with school, I don't have to deal with any of that stuff. I do like working at home. I am somebody that works very well alone. I'm self-motivated, I don't need that. But I do miss being able to walk into Dave's office or David's office and just start chatting about something and hashing out stuff. We kind of do that on Slack calls or whatever, but it's not the same thing. It's not the same as being able to just sit down with somebody or walk down to the coffee shop and drink your coffee." The messaging platform Slack thus became the communication tool that was crucial for the success of the project, even allowing the team to organize "chill times" in which anyone could talk about whatever was on their mind, as long as it wasn't about *Monkey Island*. "I went to PAX this past year, in 2022, in the fall, to do some promotional stuff for the game and just hang out with everybody," Dominic Armato tells me. "It was a little weird because, for me, I'm thinking like, 'Oh, this is going to be a little strange. I'm kind of jumping in for the first time with this team,' but *they* were all meeting each other for the first time in person! You know, it was an international crew and, you know, almost the whole crew was able to fly in, and they were all meeting for the first time and hanging out. We rented a big house there, an Airbnb, and they were all kind of camping out together. So, [...] I think that was a really cool thing for them."

Back to early 2020. It was now time to put together a team. Ron Gilbert and Dave Grossman would share the duties of writing and general management of *Return to Monkey Island* while maintaining total independence. As such, they could draft an all-star team from LucasArts point & click adventures. First, David Fox, a well-known veteran of the studio and creator of *Zak McKracken and the Alien Mindbenders*, would head up the technical side of development, with support from another specialist, Robert Megone, who notably worked on *Thimbleweed Park*, as well as Leigh Graner, a former Lucasfilm Games developer. Next, there were the great "Three Stooges," as I've dubbed them, the inimitable Michael Z. Land, Clint Bajakian, and Peter McConnell, who would compose yet another masterpiece of a soundtrack for the new game. "It's weird when you get back together with people like that, who you haven't worked with or seen in thirty years," continues Ron Gilbert for *Adventure Gamers*. "It's like, we all look older, but we're all the same people. The same conversations I remember having with Michael about the music and the *Monkey Island* theme and all this stuff, it's the same conversations we have right now. That's a lot of fun." Jenn Sandercock, who had previously been a producer for *Thimbleweed Park*, would be in charge of scheduling and coordinating the team of artists spread all over the world. Veteran artists Rhonda Conley and Dev Madan, who had worked with Ron Gilbert as far back as the time of Humongous Entertainment's *Pajama Sam*, would handle the designs for the backgrounds and the game's many objects. *Return to Monkey Island* wasn't just the opportunity of a new adventure for the thousands of players eagerly awaiting it; it was also, above all, an opportunity for a small group of trailblazers to reunite and make magic once again, to infuse 30 years of acquired maturity into a new project, the likes of which has rarely, if ever, been seen in the history of video games. However, still to come was a decision that would contrast sharply with the heavy involvement of veteran creators. And that decision singlehandedly marks a break with the past and can probably sum up the artistic intent of *Return to Monkey Island*. The game is not just an ordinary sequel, nor an homage, nor a throwback, nor a retrospective piece. It is all of that and more.

Monkey Island 3b, or "Consistency is the last refuge of the unimaginative"[266]

"So, Ron contacted me because of a piece of fan art that I'd done, probably back when I was doing, maybe *Tearaway*, I guess?" recalls Rex Crowle in an interview with Marius of the essential fan site *MixnMojo*.[267] On July 7, 2009, to celebrate the release of the special edition of *The Secret of Monkey Island*, the British artist drew his own version of Guybrush and posted it on his personal blog, commenting: "One of my favourite games from childhood, *Monkey Island*, is getting a re-release next week, all smartened up for the HD generation. Personally, I'm not a fan of the new HD visuals, probably because I grew up with the old version. I'm a big fan of pixelly retro-ness, and the youngsters shouldn't listen to old salty dogs like me. But in the meantime, I couldn't resist a sketch of the games' sometime-hero Guybrush Threepwood as he exists in my world of doodles and piratey memories."[268] This is the first time I've mentioned the name Rex Crowle in this book. And there's a good reason for

266. Thank you, Oscar Wilde.
267. *https://mixnmojo.com/features/interviews/Rex-Crowle-talks-Return-to-Monkey-Island/1*
268. *http://hairyteeth.blogspot.com/2009/07/guybrush-threepwood.html*

that: he was not involved in the early days of the Lucasfilm Computer Division, nor did he work at LucasArts, nor even at Telltale! He discovered Guybrush and company in exactly the same way as you and me, probably in his childhood bedroom. Crowle cut his teeth in the video game industry working at Lionhead Studios on *Black and White* (2001) and on *Fable* (2004). He then joined Media Molecule for the development of *LittleBigPlanet* (2008). Some years later, he rose to prominence when he became the lead designer on *Tearaway* (2013), showing off his very peculiar artistic style. Finally, he founded Foam Sword Games to develop *Knights and Bikes* (2019), which was published by Double Fine, Tim Schafer's company. Small world.

In early 2020, as the team was coming together, Dave and Ron still didn't have any hard and fast ideas for the game's overall artistic design: "I joined the project initially for a month, just to experiment with this," Crowle tells *MixnMojo*. "I worked very closely with Ron, as kind of like a side project, almost, to iterate on this style for–it was Guybrush, Elaine, and LeChuck–and see how the characters would look in a sort of progressed version of this style. One that would have a bit more nuance, be able to show emotional range in the characters, and not be quite as bold as that original image. And then also work on the backgrounds, and figure out a style that would get a good contrast between the characters and the backgrounds behind them. I think the initial locations I did were the lookout, the kitchen at the back of the SCUMM Bar, the Monkey Head on Monkey Island, and also another location."

After that first month of experimentation, in September 2020, the artistic direction in which Rex Crowle was heading matched Ron Gilbert's first impressions. "When we started, I was kind of the only artist and *kind-of* animator. And as soon as we had professional animators on the project, it was really interesting to see what they were trying to do with Guybrush. And that suddenly throws up a bunch of new iterations that you wanna do. So, I think it's so important with game development to... You have schedules, and you're sticking to those, but having a little bit of wiggle room and freedom to react to what other members of the team are doing–whether they're from the same discipline or a different one. Like, when we finally–we didn't hear Dominic's voice on Guybrush 'til, like, years later, after doing it. And as soon as you hear it, you're like, 'Okay, right. I want to go back and make some changes to his mouth,' because this is the first time we've heard him talk. And I think it's really important to have those little moments that you can squeeze into the schedule and manage to be informed and inspired by other people's great work." Taking inspiration from, among other things, the energy of *Samurai Jack* and, more generally, from the work of Genndy Tartakovsky (*Star Wars Clone Wars*, *Hotel Transylvania*), the new team officially turned away from the original artistic vision of *Monkey Island 3a*. No pixel art and no retro-nostalgic vibes.

It seems that Ron Gilbert and Dave Grossman came to the realization that their potential audience and that audience's expectations for a new *Monkey Island* essentially fell into two distinct camps. On the one hand, there was the small group of nostalgic forty-somethings—alas, a group to which yours truly belongs—who had been with the saga pretty much since the beginning, who dreamed of once again setting foot on Mêlée Island and randomly digging holes in a lush jungle, and who had sharpened their swords so many times over so many years that all that remained was a flimsy metal wire. On the other hand, there was a group of curious, probably younger, players who had heard of this mythical saga and who might be tempted to give it a try, but who wanted nothing to do with antiquated game design rules or big, juicy pixels. *Return to Monkey Island* found itself stuck in this particularly modern conundrum, having to strike a balance between its status as a franchise near and dear to the hearts of longtime fans and its desire to draw in a new potential audience. Let's be clear: the attempt to balance those competing visions was not a purely profit-driven consideration; it was, above all, an artistic one. *Return to Monkey Island* is both a return to an old adventure and an invitation to depart on a new one. "Legacyquels," the sequels tacked onto legendary series from the 1980s and '90s like *Star Wars*, *Jurassic Park*, and *The Matrix*, in an attempt to reinvigorate their audiences 20 or 30 years later, are generally terrible at doing just that. It's a matter of striking a balance between paying tribute to the old while reinventing the series. A balance between tradition (Michael Land, Clint Bajakian, and Peter McConnell) and modernity (Rex Crowle). Between continuing the longstanding heritage of the point & click narrative design, which we've discussed extensively in this book, and revising the very foundations to fit with the habits of modern players (for example, offering a built-in hint book so that players never get stuck in the adventure).

Return to Monkey Island had to pull off a complex acrobatic act: between two flips, it would attempt to catch a trapeze. As such, *Return to Monkey Island* perpetuates certain traditions: it attempts to advance a medium by constantly blazing new trails, while also evolving its artistic style by fully entrusting its design to new, talented trailblazers. Following in a prestigious lineage of designers that includes Steve Purcell, Mark Ferrari, Peter Chan, and Bill Tiller, it would now be Rex Crowle's turn to dazzle us and bestow a new identity upon a universe we know and love.

Look behind you!... A return to childhood

Strange though it may seem, Ron and Dave began replaying the first few *Monkey Island* games before writing a single line of the new opus. "We did have to do a little research, 'cause it's been a while. We definitely played the games again," Dave Grossman tells the website *Shacknews*.[269] "It's weird to research yourself, but it's good to do actually, just to kinda remember what was charming and funny in *Monkey Island*. Which is why I wanted to go back there again. [...] I'd forgotten almost everything. I have a terrible memory. I think we sort of knew what we wanted to do before we went back into *Monkey Island*." Ron Gilbert, in a blog entry, gives a few more details: "July 18, 2020 - Played *MI1* again. Taking a lot of notes about what made *MI MI*. After *TWP* and fast walk and other almost invisible improvements, it's painful to play a 35-year-old adventure game. I was surprised at how many objects didn't have custom default responses. A large number of objects just said 'That doesn't seem to work.'"[270] Dave and Ron started by roughly sketching out their vision for the new game's overall story, incorporating wherever possible the series' most iconic characters. "We chose our favorite characters from *Monkey 1* and *Monkey 2* because those were the games we had done," Ron explains to Laura Cress, "but Murray is such a wonderful character, we both absolutely wanted to have him in the game." Ron Gilbert's guiding light, which had remained the same since he first mentioned a hypothetical new *Monkey Island*, was to be able to pick up the story where he'd left off 30 years earlier, in a mysterious amusement park. That meant setting aside the contrived solution devised by Larry Ahern and Jonathan Ackley with the Big Whoop in *The Curse of Monkey Island*. In response to the question of why he chose to start the new game right where *MI2* ended, Gilbert replies: "It was important to me. [...] It really was the one thing that I absolutely wanted to do. [...] When Dave came up to Seattle, when we first started talking about the game, that was a big point of discussion. How do we start this thing? We probably spent a good day just hashing out different ideas and talking about different things and figuring out what we wanted to do with it. It wasn't a tricky problem; it was a fun problem." Before long, the idea to start the game by deceiving the player with Guybrush's son, endearingly named "Boybrush," gained traction, to the point that, for several reasons, it became a given.

First, there was the imperative of narrative consistency with *Monkey Island 2: LeChuck's Revenge*. I imagine that by this point in this book, you've realized that consistency and continuity are quite abstract notions in the *Monkey Island* universe. Still though, it's interesting that the player is duped at the beginning of the new game, believing that they're controlling a juvenile version of Guybrush himself before realizing that the real Guybrush—now an older, wiser, more mature father—is sitting on a bench with that familiar head-in-the-clouds look. The creators thus maintained continuity with the second game.

269. *https://www.shacknews.com/article/132200/return-to-monkey-island-ron-gilbert-dave-grossman-interview*
270. *https://grumpygamer.com/dev_diary*

From there, we encounter the obligatory twist, intervening from the start of the game to subconsciously make the player suspicious of everything they see going forward. The player knows they can expect more subterfuge and charades. Finally, there's the nostalgic dimension. That's an element aimed at you and me, the old-time players, the fans, the forty-somethings who anchored in the harbor of Mêlée Island as far back as 1990. The players now passing down their old memories to their offspring, like Guybrush to Boybrush. The players who launched into *Return to Monkey Island* with a whole group, gathering the family around the computer screen, ready to introduce a whole new generation to the colorful world and wacky, nonsensical adventures of our favorite pirates. This aspect is probably one of the game's most brilliant ideas, properly illustrating the way to approach this return with an elegant mirror effect.

Thus, old Guybrush sets about recounting to Boybrush and his friends his adventures from the good old days, while, of course, indiscriminately blending exaggerated truth with flat-out lies, calling the player to discover a new installment in his story with a mix of laughter, surprise, and skepticism. This mise en abyme plays a big role in infusing *Return to Monkey Island* with a light, nostalgic melancholy. We travel through a world of memories; we return to Mêlée Island, where things have changed, much in the same way that we and our perspective have changed. The parallel is striking and the metaphorical dimension of the return becomes apparent.

As a whole new adventure begins, the game simultaneously establishes a dialogue between Dave and Ron on the one hand and the player on the other. "Dave and I really [talked] about storytelling, nostalgia, and unreliable memory. These were all things that Dave and I talked about at the very beginning of the game because we knew we had this huge nostalgia thing that we had to deal with," Ron Gilbert tells Laura Cress. "Storytelling is obviously very important to both Dave and I. As things developed, we kind of realized that we really had something just with that issue. We didn't want to just brush it under the carpet or deal with it in an abstract way. It really became the focus of the story that we were trying to tell because we knew we had to deal with those issues with fans, and it just seemed like the most interesting story to tell in a way, but tell it indirectly through Guybrush and his son."

Returning to the issue of continuity in storytelling, I'm sure you've noticed that the title *Return to Monkey Island* makes no mention of the number three. The game isn't called *Monkey Island 3: Guybrush Strikes Back*. We find two ideas consciously intertwined within the title. The first is to detach from any sequential numbering so as to make a place in the series for the new game while respecting all the episodes that came before it. From the moment the game's trailer was released on April 4, 2022, Ron Gilbert was clear that the new story would not wipe away the existing sequels, *Curse*, *Escape*, and *Tales*, and that he and Dave had taken care to not fall into that trap. The second idea is to use the title to present a very literal theme of the game. As I said earlier, the game is an invitation to leave on an adventure. An invitation particularly aimed at those who have previously wandered the narrow streets of Mêlée Island. In response to a question about how Mêlée Town looks older than it did in the original game, Gilbert says, "It's kind of the theme of the game, and it's part of going back to *Monkey Island*, it's part of that memory that people have towards things and how it's not really accurate." The creators made Mêlée Island "very familiar, but not familiar. It's familiar, but has also changed over time, just like Dave and I have changed over time, just like players have changed over time, and so that's really what we were trying to do by having Mêlée Island be similar, but not." Stan's Shipyard is particularly indicative of this position. In front of the abandoned lot that was once home to Stan's new used ship business, Guybrush reminisces about better days: "It was such a bright and lively place back then." *Tempus fugit*. We encounter old, familiar faces, as well as young, insolent pirates. The old council of pirate leaders has been scrapped in favor of a new trio led by a pirate named Madison, who claims that she knows more about the ways of piracy than the old guard. In this, we can almost hear Gilbert, Grossman, and the like metaphorically and a bit cynically calling out the host of young developers who came up behind them. The backgrounds tell a story of change. The old timers who we met in previous games have followed different life paths. That said, certain places like the SCUMM Bar haven't changed much at all. While the entire first part of the game verges on graceful, nostalgic reverence—even offering cards from a trivia game (a fantastic idea) that you can find in the backgrounds to test your level of nerdiness—the rest of the adventure turns in a totally different direction.

Obsessions

Guybrush's quest to finally discover the secret of Monkey Island is interspersed with scenes of Boybrush, who regularly questions his father about the story. This is another brilliant and adorable idea, beautifully metaphorical of the way that *Monkey Island* has become a classic that parents lovingly share with their children. But at a certain point, we slowly come to a realization. Is it all really worth it? Elaine is the first to pose this question. Why are we so obsessed with this elusive secret, of which we really know very little? Guybrush and LeChuck, his longtime antagonist, share this same obsession with finding... well, truth be told, we don't even know what. A treasure? Knowledge? This obsession to which the main characters cling is, of course, a reflection of our own. Our obsession that has led some to harass Ron Gilbert and his loved ones over years and years with the same question: "What is the damn SECRET????" And the thing is that it's pointless to fixate on that elusive secret as we know perfectly well, deep down, that the truth will inevitably be a disappointment. It's an obsession that has completely changed the way that fans and the creator perceive the game's universe. Ron Gilbert himself has admitted that he really didn't have any sort of well-formed master plan to answer those questions when he left LucasArts in 1992. Just a few vague ideas for some jokes and characters... In the end, *Monkey Island 3a* became *Return to Monkey Island*, a metaphorical reflection on the blind obsession of the fandom.

"That theme of obsession in the game spilled over into the real world maybe a little more than anybody intended," Dominic Armato told me. "Whether that's a matter of happenstance or whether that's a matter of design, I'm sure the fellas [i.e., Dave and Ron] were addressing that, at least a little bit." Here, Dominic is referring to the events that took place in the few weeks after the announcement of *Return to Monkey Island*. Enraged by the radical change in art direction, a minority of players flooded Ron Gilbert's blog with their criticisms. On May 1, Gilbert published a post that concluded thusly: "*Return to Monkey Island* may not be the art style you wanted or were expecting, but it's the art style I wanted. When I started this game, my biggest fear was Disney wouldn't let me make the game I wanted to make, but they have been wonderful to work with. It's ironic that the people who don't want me to make the game I want to make are some of the hardcore *Monkey Island* fans. And that is what makes me sad about all the comments. *Return to Monkey Island* is an incredible roller coaster. Get on and have some fun, or stomp out of the amusement park because it's not exactly the roller coaster you wanted. I hope you'll jump on with the rest of us."[271]

A few days later, disgusted by certain responses, Gilbert announced that he would stop communicating outside of official channels, ~~raising~~ a new debate about toxicity in the fandom. "It's weird for me," Dominic adds. "I'm sort of in this between space because I'm part of the team but I am also, and before all, a huge fan. And it's interesting to me to kind of see that back and forth. I feel like I understand both perspectives. On the internet, it's very easy for a very small number of people to seem like a massive horde. There certainly was a contingent that was very upset about how some things were done. After I finished the game back in March 2022, I'd occasionally speak with Ron a little bit and he was obviously concerned, like, 'Oh gosh, I hope everybody likes it,' and my feeling was like, 'There is no way you can't love this!' Clearly, there are some people who don't [laughs]. But when you are so locked into what it needs to be or what you feel it should be, you don't

271. *https://grumpygamer.com/when_i_made_another_monkeyisland*

realize how much you're shooting yourself in the foot with that. Artists need to have some space. They've got to have some space to create. There's a sense now in the gaming community, among a large chunk of the fanbase, that they should be very involved in the creative process and very involved in shaping what the game is and how it should be done. I think to myself: for a community that stridently and rightly fights for their media to be considered a true art form, they have a strong tendency to actually treat it like a dumb community [asset]. You have to decide. Are games art or not? If they are not, get in there, file your complaint, make a big ruckus, and make sure that the studio is making it exactly the way you think it should be made and vote with your dollars. If games are art, you've got to give the artists some room to do their thing."

Does Guybrush more or less share the same perspective as Ron, Dave, and the artistic team? Or does he more closely resemble those fans—including me—who carry on with their obsession, the idea of a secret, that's really just a 30-year-old joke from the developers? In the end, what's the point? "I can't speak for Ron and Dave in their personal lives, but you know, I wonder, in their heads, to what extent this is them letting go," Dominic tells me. "Like Guybrush. They need to let go. Guybrush is still him, but he reaches that level of peace with it. And I think that it holds for Ron and Dave hopefully." Dominic adds with a smile: "It's an indication of where they feel they've landed in their careers, in their lives. They've figured out who they are and have been able to let go of those things that drive us all."

Return to innovation

It would be wrong of me to sing the praises of *Monkey Island* over the course of over 200 pages, reflecting on the many innovations made by the saga from the standpoints of both storytelling and game design, without pointing out the discreet and yet undeniable audacity of *Return to Monkey Island*. "Thinking about the UI: I hate the current status quo,"[272] Ron Gilbert stated in 2020 in his reflections on the point & click sub-genre.

To say that people were counting on him and his new game to bring about a return to form for adventure games is an understatement. It's an indisputable fact: today's players appear to be more impatient than they were in the '90s. There are a thousand possible explanations for this, so it can't simply be boiled down to "things were better back in the day." For over 20 years now, the game design of adventure games has ostensibly suffered from this great paradox:

272. UI = user interface. A deep reflection from Ron Gilbert on his blog, dated November 17, 2020: *https://grumpygamer.com/dev_diary*

how can designers create good puzzles that are sufficiently difficult to pose a challenge while not being so frustrating that the player goes looking for the solution on the internet? With the decision to incorporate an adaptive help system into the game, Ron Gilbert was able to observe two important things during playtesting. First, players felt more at ease knowing that the game itself would progressively adapt to their concerns. From there, Gilbert discovered 30 years later that solving far-fetched puzzles does not necessarily bring the player satisfaction. That's not what they're looking for. "It was interesting to watch them play because they would hit a problem and they would immediately go to the hint,"[273] explains Ron. "It was just like five, maybe 10 seconds of thinking about it [before] the hint button. [...] They loved the game. There was nothing about going to that hint button that distracted, in any way, from their enjoyment of the game." And we can thank Dave Grossman for the precise calibration of the level of assistance provided by the ingenious hint system. Helping without making the player feel like they're sacrificing the pleasure of playing the game; immersing the player in the universe, whether they're a veteran or a novice, a child or an adult: those were the challenges faced by the creators. "I gained some useful experience working on games for kids over the previous decades because you have to be working on two levels. You've got to be working for the kids and for the adults who are playing with the kids. You have to give it to the kids without boring the adults. It's a very similar challenge to do something for an experienced audience and an inexperienced one," Grossman explains to the website *thegamer.com*. So, for *Return to Monkey Island*, the development team made the decision to adapt the gameplay by offering personalized help to the player according to the situation and their choices, all while maintaining the customary humor and the right ambiance. The type of assistance provided is known as a "diegetic hint system." While the result may not seem spectacular, it was nonetheless the end product of a very long and laborious development process carried out by the programmers. "The UI code is the most complex part of the system," Ron Gilbert stated on Twitter.

The other innovation likely to become a standard is what we can call "context-sensitive interactions." This feature is a response to one of the problems that had remained in an adventure game design that really hadn't changed much since *Maniac Mansion*. To know the real impact of a dialogue choice or an action, the player needed to execute that choice or action. Now, thanks to context-sensitive interactions, the player can simply hover the cursor of the mouse (or controller) over a character or an item to get a little text

273. *https://www.thegamer.com/ron-gilbert-and-dave-grossman-talk-monkey-island-working-with-disney-and-internet-toxicity*

preview of the potential result. Of course, the development team used that as an opportunity to insert some bits of humor, including jokes that merrily break the fourth wall. "We started the UI from *Delores* and, like I said, *Delores* was in some ways, kind of an R&D platform," Ron tells Laura Cress. "I had simplified the UI down for *Delores* [...] to have the verbs be a little more contextual. When you mouse over something in *Delores*, the only verbs that are there are the verbs that actually work. [...] So, that was the starting point. When we first started working on *Return to Monkey Island*, [...] the interface was exactly like it was in *Delores*. As we started playing around with that a little bit more, we kind of realized we don't have to say, 'Open the chest,' we could actually have a real sentence."

It's a simple yet effective idea that completely transforms the immersion you get from a classic adventure game without distorting its origins or its DNA. By putting forward this new system, Ron Gilbert and Dave Grossman were able to break another barrier. The interface would no longer take the form of a simple, mechanical system allowing the player to interact with the game's universe; instead, it would become a literal translation of Guybrush's thoughts. Instead of executing a classic command like "use this animal on this hacksaw," the player asks Guybrush what he thinks: "Hmm, that seems a little cruel to me. I don't want PETA to come down on me." Among the many design improvements, loading a saved game doesn't take you directly to the place where you left off, and instead takes you first to Guybrush and his son, sitting on a bench, ready to recontextualize the moment and the action left in suspense. *Return to Monkey Island* is overflowing with small details like that, elements that appear trivial but which make the player's experience so much more enjoyable, no matter their skill level.

What is Monkey Island?

Returning to Paris in late August 2022. We stroll along the tree-lined paths of the Tuileries Garden under a scorching sun. As we approach the end of our time together, Craig Derrick asks me an inevitable question: "In your opinion, what is it that makes *Monkey Island* so important to people? Why this game? What is it about *Monkey Island*?" This is a question that, of course, gets asked all the time. And it's one that I have hoped to answer in this book, or, failing that, at least provide some thoughts that might bring us closer to the truth. It's a question that inevitably hovers over all great works. And it was probably one of the first questions that Ron Gilbert and Dave Grossman asked themselves when they began discussing their likely sequel. Why were people asking Ron Gilbert to make a new *Monkey Island*? Gilbert, the creator of over 40 titles. Why not *Maniac Mansion*? Why not *Freddi Fish, Pajama Sam, Spy*

Fox, *DeathSpank*, or *The Cave*? "The game means a lot to a lot of people," says Ron.[274] "It was the game they grew up on; it was the first game they played as a kid. It was the game they shared with their siblings or shared with their father. You can't really just ignore that people are so passionate over it that they argue with us about the font that we chose. On some level, you do have to respect that."

I think that after having spent so much time asking myself this very same question, the best answer I've heard, the most honest answer I can think of, came from the mouth of Dominic Armato himself: "This story, these characters I mean... it has a way of subtly getting under your skin in a way a lot of stories don't. You know, part of it I feel is almost that it doesn't try so hard. It feels very genuine. As silly as it seems, because I'm saying this about an anachronistic game about pirates and rubber chickens with pullies in the middle and all that. But the tone and the characters, at that time, when [they] came out, all the LucasArts games of the era [were] unique. I wasn't an adventure game player; I was a LucasArts adventure game player. I liked the humor. I liked the warmth. All those games contained the first video game characters I connected with. And I think that may be the largest part of it. When you put it in the context of the time, maybe there was some stuff out there I wasn't playing, but what other video game characters were fleshed out enough that you were really connecting with? I don't think there was much. It's real, relatable and... it's so freaking charming. You know, it just sneaks up and it gets under your skin... and you fall in love with those characters. You identify with them." Dominic gives a big smile, as if daydreaming, and continues: "This is one of the things that Ron always harps on, and it's 100% true: nothing's ever going to replace a good story. No matter what your media is. It's a good story. It's enjoyable characters; it's people you want to spend time with. I mean, you have to when you're playing an adventure game. If you don't enjoy spending time with these people, you're not gonna get too far!"

Could that be the answer? So simple and so obvious. Could it be that we love *Monkey Island* so much because we enjoy spending time with Guybrush, Elaine, Stan, and Murray? Because listening to them tell us stories, whether they be credible or incredible, stupid or epic, is always a pleasure? That could be the key to a good game, and particularly to a GREAT adventure game. First and foremost, it's all about the characters. Can it be that Charles Cecil's *Broken Sword* remains vivid in our memories thanks to George Stobbart and Nico, rather than for its hackneyed conspiracy-driven plot lines? Can it be that *Grim Fandango* achieved cult status thanks to the charisma of Manny Calavera and the unforgettable Mercedes? Is *The Blackwell Legacy* such a memorable game

---

274. *https://www.thegamer.com/ron-gilbert-and-dave-grossman-talk-monkey-island-working-with-disney-and-internet-toxicity/*

because of Rosangela? I'd say probably. "I think that it is something that the game industry took a while to figure out," continues Dominic. "The LucasArts adventure team in the '90s, they were ahead of the curve on that. They understood the importance of story and characters. They understood that it's gonna mean more to people than pushing pixels in the long run. Of course, people get that now. I remember a discussion with Jake Rodkin,[275] because my kid at one point in time was kind of having his moment of, 'Oh, I want to be a game developer!' And I just mentioned that to Jake. He said: 'Tell him not to be a coder; we get all the coders we need. We need writers. We need artists. We need people who have studied storytelling and literature!' If you want to be in this industry, you need people who can be creative!"

The reason why *Monkey Island* has such staying power is because its developers, a bunch of hippies in *Star Wars* T-shirts, really understood before everyone else that great characters would stay with people, and they focused on that long before they worried about if the game itself was original, performed well, or was what people were looking for at the time.

Just like its gameplay, its comfortable design, and its visual style, *Return to Monkey Island* gives us yet another invitation: to reunite with the series' characters, to reconnect with our old charming, funny, and inoffensive friends and acquaintances. Except for the seagull, of course. By the way, Seagull, if you're reading this, just know that we miss you. All good games have seagulls, wouldn't you say so, *Loom*?

There's another secret of *Monkey Island*! Taking advantage of a slightly old-fashioned game design, and a genre that calls for players to take their time, by taking a seat on a bench, chatting, laughing, and getting emotional for no reason at all. How many modern games can claim to still offer us that kind of experience?

And now, ladies and gentlemen... Chapter 22! (Employees Only)

"It's just that I'm worried that the Secret can't possibly measure up to the effort and anticipation."

Elaine - *Return to Monkey Island*

"There is something about the ending of *Return to Monkey Island* that I'm not sure that a lot of people understand," Ron Gilbert tells Laura Cress. "The

275. Jake co-directed the fantastic games *Tales of Monkey Island* and *Firewatch* (among others).

original game was called *The Secret of Monkey Island* and we never really addressed what that secret was in any other games. When we started this game, we always said we really need to tell people what the secret of Monkey Island is. You don't want to just kick that football down the field another time. [...] As I conceived of the secret in 1988, when I first started working on this game and it got the title *The Secret of Monkey Island*, this was the actual secret of the game. It was that Guybrush was just in a giant amusement park."

There you go: that's the famous secret. Ron Gilbert serves it up to us and explains: "That whole concept was kind of abandoned early on in the development as the original game started to come to fruition." No grand finale, no ultimate climax or epic confrontation at the top of a ship's mast in the middle of a raging storm. Just this confirmation: indeed, the whole thing actually takes place in an amusement park. Exactly as Ron has always said. Let me remind you from the beginning of this book: "You see, one of my favorite rides in Disneyland is 'Pirates of the Caribbean.' You get on a little boat and it takes you through a pirate adventure, climaxing in a cannon fight between two big pirate ships. Your boat keeps you moving through the adventure, but I've always wished I could get off and wander around, learn more about the characters, and find a way onto those pirate ships."[276] But haven't we always known that deep down? And in the end decided that it wasn't what matters most?

Return to Monkey Island ends after Guybrush takes on the ultimate challenge, a puzzle in the form of a wheel (that looks eerily like the Dial-O-Pirate—a tribute to the original game's anti-piracy system), which opens the door that's supposed to lead to the secret. We discover that it in fact leads to an amusement park. Interestingly, you, the player, have the option to completely deny the truth and retrace your steps to remain in the illusion.

According to your actions, you'll experience any one of several different variations of the epilogue. But the true secret remains the same, and the bitter aftertaste it leaves you with is both a clever bit of writing and a nod to real life, as well as another "trick" from Ron Gilbert to not just give fans what they want. Yet another indication proving that obsession only leads to frustration—right Guybrush? Still, what remains interesting for us frustrated obsessive fans of *Monkey Island* is the revelation that all that we know about the previous games was delivered to us through the filter of Guybrush, with all of the fudging and bending of the truth that comes with that. As Elaine tells Guybrush at the very end: "Every time you tell that story, the ending gets stranger and stranger."

276. *The Adventurer* vol. 1.

Starting the game over would mean asking Guybrush to recount his adventures once again, and it would probably lead us to a different epilogue. And that's less about offering the player a new ending and more about illustrating the bigger point. The ending of *Return to Monkey Island* and its ultimate secret are not just pretty words, like those offered by Robert Louis Stevenson[277] (him again!) in his 1879 book *Travels with a Donkey in the Cévennes*, "For my part, I travel not to go anywhere, but to go. I travel for travel's sake." To be clear, the ending of *Return to Monkey Island* is not a true ending at all; it's an invitation to dive back into a new adventure.

Meanwhile, the amusement park is simply the answer to the question: "What is the true secret of *Monkey Island*?" The proof of this can be found on the commemorative plaque next to the amusement park's exit: "Historic Landmark: The Original Secret, a pirate adventure park. Established 1989 by R. Gilbert." Whether we're satisfied or not, our favorite Grumpy Gamer has given us the most direct answer possible to our question. What's interesting is that the answer may potentially only be of interest to the biggest fans among us–"employees only"; everyone else will likely be satisfied with a new ridiculous twist from a theme park that clearly appears to be based on the adventures of Guybrush Threepwood. For that latter group, when Guybrush opens Stan's little treasure chest and discovers a T-shirt that reads "I found the Secret of Monkey Island and all it was was this stupid T-shirt," they get to enjoy a funny joke. But for us die-hard fans, it's a disappointment that we've feared for so long–and that's so obvious–that most of the game's characters (and therefore the developers) gently warn us about.

"Boybrush: Dad! That was a silly ending! And it didn't even make any sense! You're terrible at endings!
– Guybrush: I thought you liked silly endings?..."

Return to Monkey Island is a metaphor for what it's like to be an adult and to want to take a stroll down our childhood memory lane. It's up to us to choose what type of adult we want to be... The kind who chooses to remain on the island and deny the truth, or the kind who chooses to just have fun with it...

"Guybrush, like us, is older now, and he's had a long and reasonably successful career. But he is mostly associated with something that happened a long time ago, and that feels unfinished to him. The game is a goofy pirate

---

277. I'll take this opportunity to remind you that Robert Louis Stevenson is still the greatest writer in the universe as he wrote the greatest novel: *Treasure Island* (1883).

adventure, the same as always, but also it's a story about trying to recapture the past, with all its alleged youthful strength and glory. Guybrush will not succeed and will fail at this. He will sort of get what he wants, but it won't be what he expected. I predict the same for us."[278]

Ron Gilbert and Dave Grossman

So long, old friends

On the social network Mastodon, Ron Gilbert shared some of his feelings after completion of the project: "I am so burnt out. As *Return to Monkey Island* was drawing to a close, I was filled with ideas for a seemingly endless list of projects I want to do next. As the game and press ended, I was even more invigorated. Then, I went on vacation for a week and realized how burnt out I was. It wasn't until I fully stopped moving that it all came crashing down. *Return to Monkey Island* was the most intense two years of my career. The pressure of making a sequel to a game loved by so many people and the stress of keeping it a complete secret was fun at first, but it's taken its toll on me. I rarely burn out. I like making games, and the fact that I can't do it right now only compounds the problem. I'm finding it hard to do the things I enjoy: playing games, reading, watching movies, etc. About the most I can do is stare into the distance like Guybrush at the end of *Return*. I'm slowly coming to the understanding that this is OK. It's what I need right now."

Then, a few weeks later, Ron returned to his old habits. He began coding again, joked around, devised tricks, and caused trouble with his secrets. For his part, Dominic Armato tells me: "It's... It's always hard for me because the truth is that, professionally speaking, there's nothing I'm prouder of in my life. Doing this character is the most amazing thing I'm most proud of and it's hard to put that away. When we go through one of these cycles and it comes and it builds again and people get excited, it is just the most wonderful feeling in the world. To be able to do it again, to have the creative freedom to do it again, and to get the energy, the love of people coming together and getting excited about it. But now, it's hard. If I had my way, we'd do this all the time. I love it so much." What do you think, fellow players, adventurers, pirates, and grown-up kids? Is that what we want too? I think I might have an answer to that...

Paris. August 2022. When I ask him the question, "Is it over for *Monkey Island*?," Craig Derrick smiles: "All I can say is that it won't depend on whether

---

278. An excerpt from the letter from the developers that the player unlocks when they finish *Return to Monkey Island*.

or not the game is a big success. It will depend solely on what people want, whether it's a video game or, who knows, some other form..."

Return to Monkey Island came out on September 19, 2022. It received generally positive reviews from video game media. And, as expected, its ending was divisive among fans. Half of them loved it and the other half hated it. Good ol' Ron: you'll always be a big kid!

The End?

Yup. That's literally the second-best ending of this book I've ever read.

THE MYSTERIES OF

MONKEY ISLAND

Appendices

Appendix 1: Mix-o-insults™

As I'm sure you know, a duel isn't just about the physical abilities of two fearsome pirates. No! In the pirate world, a proper duel is all about stinging insults and great comebacks. If you want to win, there's no better way than to take down your adversary with a phrase that cuts like the sharpened blade of a cutlass. Thankfully for you, matey, I've prepared for you the Mix-o-insults™!

I've chosen 15 of the cleverest insults; your job is to find the right response, the only unstoppable comeback. The one that might take you further down the dark and dangerous paths of Mêlée Island. Each correct response earns you one point. So, answer your opponent's zingers, add up your points, and see where you stand on the official self-evaluation rubric from the International Federation of *Monkey Island* Insult Fighting™ (the esteemed IFMIIF™).

1 - You fight like a dairy Farmer!
A.   I had my cat laminated.
B.   Support your local PTA.
C.   How appropriate. You fight like a cow!

2 - I've spoken with apes more polite than you!
A.   Oh, that is so cliché.
B.   I'm glad to hear you attended your family reunion!
C.   Then be a good dog.

3 - People fall at my feet when they see me coming!
A.   When I'm done with YOU, you'll be a boneless filet.
B.   Even BEFORE they smell your breath?
C.   Too bad no one's ever heard of YOU at all.

4 - If your brother's like you, better to marry a pig.
A.   You make me think somebody already did.
B.   Your hemorrhoids are flaring up again, eh?
C.   You're stupid.

5 - My last fight ended with my hands covered with blood.
A.   Then be a good dog. Sit! Stay!
B.   Then perhaps you should switch to decaffeinated.
C.   Your hemorrhoids are flaring up again, eh?

6 - My attacks have left entire islands depopulated!

A.   With your breath, I'm sure they all suffocated.

B.   Why? Did you want to borrow one?

C.   Even BEFORE they smell your breath?

7 - Would you like to be buried, or cremated?

A.   Never before have I seen someone so sissified!

B.   With you around, I'd prefer to be fumigated.

C.   Could I get my parking ticket validated?

8 - I have never seen such clumsy swordplay!

A.   Of all crafts, my favorite is papier-mâché.

B.   You would have, but you were always running away.

C.   I'll meet you in the foyer.

9 - My tongue is sharper than any sword.

A.   First, you'd better stop waving it like a feather-duster.

B.   I would be in real trouble if you ever used them.

C.   I like my steak chicken-fried.

10 - I can't rest 'til you've been exterminated!

A.   My fishing hook is always live-baited.

B.   I fear our government's funds are being misappropriated.

C.   Then perhaps you should switch to decaffeinated.

11 - Killing you would be justifiable homicide!

A.   Hydraulic suspension guarantees a nice smooth ride.

B.   I sent a letter to the King of Portugal, who never replied.

C.   Then killing you must be justifiable fungicide.

12 - This is the END for you, you gutter crawling cur!

A.   How appropriate. You fight like a cow!

B.   And I've got a little TIP for you, get the POINT?

C.   No way! You'll never ketchup to my level!

13 - Have you stopped wearing diapers yet?

A.   You're ugly

B.   You run THAT fast?

C.   Why? Did you want to borrow one?

14 - I will milk every drop of blood from your body!
A.   How appropriate, you fight like a cow!
B.   You make me think somebody already did.
C.   Even BEFORE they smell your breath?

15 - Your sword is as sharp as a banana!
A.   I'll be sure to break you fast!
B.   Yeah! Like a doofus! Who's an amazing fighter!
C.   I'll still pear (pare) you down to size.

Answers:
1-C, 2-B, 3-B, 4-A, 5-C, 6-A, 7-B, 8-B, 9-A, 10-C, 11-C, 12-B, 13-C, 14-A, 15-C

* * *

The official self-evaluation rubric from the International Federation of *Monkey Island* Insult Fighting™

If you earned 0 to 3 points: You're at "Dairy Farmer" level
You really need to rethink your career choice. You can't just show up and say, "I want to be a pirate!" and immediately join the Brethren of the Coast. You stand almost no chance of survival on a pirate-infested island. We suggest that you change careers and become a politician or an accountant, a profession in which posting funny cat videos on social media is seen as the pinnacle of humor.

If you earned 4 to 7 points: You're at "Fan of Sierra™ Games" level
It's just us here, you can admit it. You bought this book totally at random or just out of curiosity, but the truth is you've spent hundreds of hours playing *King's Quest* and you're one of those weird people who like games made by Sierra. Your kind of video game universe is more multicolored ponies and pixelated daisies rather than the harsh world of pirates and scoundrels. Don't beat yourself up about it, we all have our own issues.

If you earned 8 to 12 points: You're at "Legitimate Pirate" level
A good effort. You're not a bad student. Sometimes funny, sometimes miss the mark. Still, with a bit of hard work you might learn to be decently quick-witted. Spend some time practicing with family, or with your colleagues or teachers. I'm sure they'll be able to appreciate a well-aimed insult.

If you earned 13 to 15 points: You're at "Sword Master" level

Ahoy! You've earned the eternal respect of the very professional International Federation of *Monkey Island* Insult Fighting™. I can only imagine the many hours you must have spent in front of a mirror insulting your own reflection. Your wit is your most dangerous weapon and you stand a real chance against the Sword Master of Mêlée Island.

Appendix 2: Mojo-credits™

Ron Gilbert

Game director for *The Secret of Monkey Island* **and** *Monkey Island 2: LeChuck's Revenge*

Born in 1964 in La Grande, Oregon. In the early 1980s, Ron Gilbert quickly learned his way around the machine that would become his favorite computer, the Commodore 64. Intrigued by the potential of the BASIC programming language, and frustrated by being unable to partake in the joys of video games from the comfort of his home, he decided to personally copy and redevelop the games he found at local arcades. He started his career at Human Engineered Software as a programmer. While there, he created his first tools for graphics development before the company went out of business. He then landed at Lucasfilm just three years after its founding, in 1985. He provided his skills to the adaptation of *Koronis Rift* and *PHM Pegasus* for the C64, under the direction of Noah Falstein. During the same period, he began imagining a new form of video game storytelling, embodied in a still poorly conceived project: *I Was a Teenage Lobot*. With the help of Gary Winnick, the game was gradually fleshed out and became *Maniac Mansion*, which was released in 1987. That game ran on a brand-new game engine of their own invention: the SCUMM engine.

It was followed by two of the studio's most renowned titles, *The Secret of Monkey Island* (1990) and *Monkey Island 2: LeChuck's Revenge* (1991), after which Ron decided to found his own company: Humongous Entertainment. Gilbert has always preferred the atmosphere of working in a small team with a certain level of independence. From 1992 to 1997, he and his company created games for young children, which were particularly popular in North America. They included *Freddi Fish*, *Fatty Bear*, *Pajama Sam*, and *Spy Fox*. In 1997, Chris Taylor, a young designer, made a proposal to Ron for a real-time strategy game project: *Total Annihilation*. After that, working with Dave Grossman, he decided to focus on a new evolution in the design of adventure games with a game given the working title *Good & Evil*. However, the company began to struggle and its financing collapsed. In 2001, Ron Gilbert started again from square one and founded Hulabee Entertainment to continue creating more modest adventure games for kids: *Moop & Dreadly*, *Ollo in the Sunny Valley Fair*, and more. After serving as a consultant for *Penny Arcade Adventures*, Ron became the creative director of Hothead Games in 2008, where he developed *DeathSpank* (2010), followed by the adventure game *The Cave* (2013) for Double Fine, a project on which he reunited with his old colleague Tim Schafer. In 2014, he launched a Kickstarter campaign with Gary Winnick to fund the development of his triumphant return to the point & click sub-genre, releasing *Thimbleweed Park* in 2017. A true lover of programming, Ron Gilbert continues to code for over five hours a day, both on weekdays and even on weekends.

Tim Schafer

Programmer for *The Secret of Monkey Island* and scenario writer for *Monkey Island 2: LeChuck's Revenge*

Born in 1967 in Sonoma, California. After Ron Gilbert, he is probably the second most iconic figure tied to LucasArts adventure games. Immediately after college, he answered an ad for a job at Lucasfilm Games, highlighting his writing chops and his humor. After joining the company's ranks as a "Scummlet," an entry-level job in which new employees learned to use the SCUMM engine, he worked with Ron Gilbert on writing scripts and dialogue for *The Secret of Monkey Island* (1990). It was with *Monkey Island 2: LeChuck's Revenge* (1991) that Tim took on a more prominent role at the studio. He and his colleague Dave Grossman were put in charge of writing all of the game's dialogue. Again with Dave Grossman, he took over from Ron Gilbert and designed *Day of the Tentacle* (1993), the sequel to *Maniac Mansion*. The game's critical success earned Schafer a promotion, allowing him to direct his first big personal project, *Full Throttle* (1995). Three years later, he gave the genre a timeless classic, *Grim Fandango* (1998). In 2000, he decided to leave the nest and founded the studio Double Fine Productions. There, he created the cult platform game *Psychonauts* (2005), then, having always been a fan of rock 'n' roll, he got actor and musician Jack Black to fill the lead role in *Brutal Legend* (2009). This was followed with more modest productions like *Costume Quest* (2010) and *Stacking* (2011), as well as *The Cave* (2013), which he asked his old mentor, Ron Gilbert, to direct. In 2012, he made a splash by successfully completing one of the first big crowdfunding campaigns in video game history for *Broken Age* (2014). Following that, he made a deal with Disney allowing him to produce HD ports of his old glories *Day of the Tentacle* and *Full Throttle*. In 2017, he received the highest honor as a developer with a Lifetime Achievement Award from the Game Developers Choice Awards, joining the likes of Will Wright (*The Sims*), Shigeru Miyamoto (*Mario*, *Zelda*),

Hideo Kojima (*Metal Gear*), and Amy Hennig (*Uncharted*). In 2021, he released *Psychonauts 2*, which he wrote and co-directed.

Dave Grossman

Programmer for *The Secret of Monkey Island*, scenario writer for *Monkey Island 2: LeChuck's Revenge*, and game director for *Tales of Monkey Island*

Born in 1967. After first falling in love with video games while playing titles like *Colossal Cave Adventure* on his family's computer, Dave joined Lucasfilm Games in 1989 as a "Scummlet." He and Tim Schafer formed a duo that developed the dialogue for *The Secret of Monkey Island* (1990) and *Monkey Island 2: LeChuck's Revenge* (1991). After spending a few months working on the production of an early version of *The Dig* (which wouldn't be released until 1995), he returned to working with Schafer to create *Day of The Tentacle* (1993), the sequel to *Maniac Mansion*. After that great success, Dave developed doubts about LucasArts' new management and decided to leave the company. After a long bicycle journey from San Francisco to Canada, he reunited with Ron Gilbert in 1996 and helped write the scenario for *Total Annihilation* (1997). At the same time, he worked on writing a handful of children's books and collections of poems. He eventually returned to the world of video games by joining Telltale Games, where he directed *Sam and Max Save the World* (2007), *Wallace & Gromit* (2009), then *Tales of Monkey Island* (2009). He helped write *The Walking Dead* (2012) and *The Wolf Among Us* (2013), two of the studio's biggest hits. He left the position of head writer and senior editor at Telltale to join Reactive Studios in 2014. There, he has worked on several projects to adapt video games for mobile devices, in addition to the development of a new concept for audio-based games.

Larry Ahern

Animator for *Monkey Island 2: LeChuck's Revenge* and game director for *The Curse of Monkey Island*

Larry was a young freelance artist when he joined Lucasfilm Games in November 1990. Up to that point, he had used his artistic talents to design T-shirts, mugs, and other souvenir-like items. He was placed in one of the studio's teams of trainees using in-house artistic tools, working alongside Anson Jew, Mike McLaughlin, and Peter Chan. The three of them learned to use Deluxe Paint and Deluxe Paint Animator, the two most popular tools at the time for creating graphics. Larry has a very cartoonish style, and when the company had to decide to assign him to work on production of *Monkey Island 2* or the very serious *The Dig*, they naturally put him on the team for... *The Dig*. The project, which was supervised by Dave Grossman at the time, began to stall and so the team was reassigned to work with Ron Gilbert. For *Monkey Island 2*, Larry was able to get his feet wet by producing some of the character animations. He went on to become the head animator for *Day of the Tentacle* (1993) and then the art director for *Full Throttle* (1995). In 1997, along with Jonathan Ackley, he directed the third installment in the adventures of Guybrush Threepwood. After that, he worked on the sequel to *Full Throttle*, but the project's cancelation pushed him toward the exit. He jumped ship to Microsoft, where he worked on the game *Blood Wake* (2001), a naval combat game exclusively for the brand-new Xbox. After doing some of the art for *Flight Simulator X* (2006), he reunited with a LucasArts alumnus, Mike Levine, to found the studio Crackpot Entertainment, which released its first title in 2008, *Insecticide*, a platform game for the PC and Nintendo 3DS. While it was originally designed to be a story in two parts, unfortunately, the second episode was never produced. Larry Ahern then reunited with his old friend Jonathan Ackley when he joined the Disney team responsible for developing new rides for the Disney theme parks. Together, they designed the live-action role-playing game *Sorcerers of the Magic Kingdom* (2012). Larry continues to work for Walt Disney Imagineering to this day.

Jonathan Ackley

Game director for *The Curse of Monkey Island*

Jonathan joined the ranks of LucasArts in 1992 as a "Scummlet." He took part in the development of *Day of the Tentacle* (1993) and became friends with Larry Ahern. Their shared passion for the saga of Guybrush Threepwood led them to propose a script that would become *The Curse of Monkey Island* (1997). At the same time, Jonathan participated as a freelancer in various projects at the studio Rocket Science Games, including the notable and off-the-wall *Cadillacs & Dinosaurs: The Second Cataclysm*, a rail shooter for the Sega CD released in 1994, and he even participated as a voice actor in the game *Loadstar: The Legend of Tully Bodine* (1994). In 2000, he left LucasArts and joined Walt Disney Imagineering to develop new rides for the Disney theme parks. In 2012, he co-designed with Larry Ahern *Sorcerers of the Magic Kingdom*.

Sean Clark

Game director for *Escape from Monkey Island*

In 1990, Sean Clark joined the ranks of LucasArts as one of the new programmers using the SCUMM engine. He cut his teeth on the improved versions of *Loom* and *The Secret of Monkey Island* for the Japanese computer FM Towns. He continued providing his talents as a developer on *Indiana Jones and the Fate of Atlantis* (1992) and *Day of the Tentacle*. In 1993, he and his colleague Michael Stemmle were assigned to direct *Sam and Max Hit the Road*, the cult title inspired by Steve Purcell's comic-book universe. With his new directorial status, he took over development of the phantom project known as *The Dig*, which was finally released in 1995. After dabbling in several of the studio's aborted projects, he directed LucasArts' final adventure game, *Escape from Monkey Island* (2000), with Michael Stemmle. Since his departure from LucasArts in 2002, Sean Clark has worked on a handful of lesser-known mobile games from studios like Electronic Arts and Big Fish Games.

Michael Stemmle

Game director for *Escape from Monkey Island* and *Tales of Monkey Island*

As a young man, Michael spent many years at LucasArts. In 1990, he became a regular tester, in spite of not having any formal training, doing testing on the puzzles of *The Secret of Monkey Island* before doing small touch-ups on the graphics for the game's Amiga adaptation. He was even assigned to prepare the game's demo. As an accomplished multitasker, he was able to work on Deluxe Paint while also helping program games using the SCUMM engine, particularly for *Indiana Jones and the Fate of Atlantis*. With Sean Clark, he directed the fabulous *Sam and Max Hit the Road* (1993), then went solo to direct *Star Wars: Rebel Assault 2* (1995) and *Afterlife* (1996). In 2000, he directed *Escape from Monkey Island* alongside Sean Clark. After his departure from LucasArts in 2003, he rejoined his former colleagues at Telltale, where he directed the series *Strong Bad's Cool Game for Attractive People* (2008), then, most notably, *Tales of Monkey Island* (2009) alongside Dave Grossman. He then worked on *Sam & Max season 2* (2010), *Back to the Future* (2011), and even *Tales from the Borderlands* (2014) before leaving the company. Today, he is a freelancer, providing his game design expertise to various studios.

Steve Purcell

Artist for *The Secret of Monkey Island, Monkey Island 2: LeChuck's Revenge*, **and** *The Curse of Monkey Island*

Steve, a California native, quickly rose to notoriety when, in 1980, he published a comic strip in the highly respected monthly publication of the California College of Arts and Crafts in San Francisco. Thus were born Sam and Max, Freelance Police. From 1982 to 1987, Steve Purcell provided his services as a talented illustrator to Marvel Comics, Chaosium, and for Steve Moncuse's comics series *Fish Police*. In 1988, Steve was hired by Lucasfilm Games as a temp for a project that was ultimately scrapped. He was then rehired a few weeks later to create the animations for the David Fox game *Zak McKracken and the Alien Mindbenders* (1988). He created the game box illustrations for *Maniac Mansion, The Secret of Monkey Island* (1990), and *Monkey Island 2: LeChuck's Revenge* (1991), in addition to serving as the art director for the latter two games. While working for Lucasfilm, he continued creating outside illustrations and comics, releasing several installments in the *Sam & Max* series and creating the saga *Defenders of Dynatron City* (1992) for Marvel.

With positive reader feedback on the adventures of *Sam & Max* published in *The Adventurer*, the studio's magazine, LucasArts decided to launch production of *Sam and Max Hit the Road* (1993), with Purcell supervising the game's art. After participating in various projects, including the conceptual illustrations for the future *Curse of Monkey Island* (1997), Steve left the company. He joined the Canadian studio Nelvana and produced the animated series *The Adventures of Sam and Max: Freelance Police* (1997), which was broadcast on Fox Kids in the U.S. and YTV in Canada. Steve then returned to San Francisco, where he joined ILM and created a number of concepts for a project based on *Frankenstein* (the movie was never made, but the concept art was partially repurposed for Stephen Sommers' *Van Helsing*, though Purcell was not credited). After that, he worked on an animated movie adaptation of the *Monkey Island* series, but once again, the project was canceled.

In 2002, Steve Purcell joined Pixar, the famous studio responsible for *Toy Story* (and largely made up of former employees of Lucasfilm from the company's early days). He helped out on *Cars* (2006) (notably lending his voice to certain side characters) and Brad Bird's *Ratatouille* (2007). His took on his first big project with *Brave* (2012), which he co-directed with Brenda Chapman and Mark Andrews. In 2014, he directed the animated short *Toy Story: That Time Forgot*. He still works for Pixar to this day, continuing to develop feature-length animated films.

Michael Z. Land

Composer for *The Secret of Monkey Island*, *Monkey Island 2: LeChuck's Revenge*, *The Curse of Monkey Island*, *Escape from Monkey Island*, *Tales of Monkey Island*, *and Return to Monkey Island*

A Massachusetts native, Michael Z. Land studied musical theory at Harvard from 1979 to 1984. He became an educator, then an engineer at Lexicon, where he developed MIDI musical interfaces. In 1990, he hastily joined Lucasfilm Games and Ron Gilbert's team, creating the full score for *The Secret of Monkey Island* in a matter of weeks. The next year, with his colleague Peter McConnell, he created the revolutionary iMUSE interactive music system, which was immediately put to use in *Monkey Island 2: LeChuck's Revenge* (1991). In the following years, he created some of the studio's greatest soundtracks, including for *Indiana Jones and the Fate of Atlantis* (1992), *Star Wars X-Wing* (1992), *The Dig* (1995), *The Curse of Monkey Island* (1997), and *Escape from Monkey Island* (2000).

On top of his composing work, he has continued to teach and study music theory, focusing on classical instruments like the cello.

Appendix 3: LucasArts™ classics

Throughout this book, I have regularly referred to a number of cult adventure games created by Lucasfilm/LucasArts. In order to avoid bogging down the story of *Monkey Island* with information on games not directly related to its universe, I chose to not cover these games in the main text. However, I knew that astute point & click fans such as yourselves would not forgive me if I neglected to talk about them in greater detail. So, here they are in this appendix.

Loom™

Brian Moriarty was a young developer when he cut his teeth in the video game industry while working for the newsletter *ANALOG Computing* (an acronym for "Atari Newsletter and Lots of Games"). In the 1980s, computer industry publications regularly offered budding coders pages of complete computer source code that they could copy into an interpreter (BASIC, an assembler, etc.) on their own computer and customize however they pleased. It was a more or less educational way of sharing code in the pre-internet era. In his role at the newsletter, Moriarty published the complete code for two games: *ANALOG: Adventure in the 5th Dimension* (1983) and *Crash Dive!* (1984). He thus got the attention of a Massachusetts-based company named Infocom that specialized in producing high-quality text-based games, including the famous *Zork* and *The Hitchhiker's Guide to the Galaxy*. While at Infocom, Brian Moriarty wrote probably one of the greatest masterpieces of the genre, the incredibly austere yet rich *Trinity*. Listed a number of times as one of the world's best major interactive fiction games after arriving in the mid-1980s, in the early days of video games, Moriarty's game presents an alternative reality in which the player is confronted with the raw horrors of death and a dark, depressing, dreamlike setting. A poetic gem, *Trinity* makes the player a witness to a number of the most destructive scenes in the history of nuclear weapons. From Nagasaki to tests in Nevada, Siberia, and outer space, the player becomes a constantly fleeing witness to the destructive power of humanity against an outraged natural world. With excellent writing, delivering a delicious blend of *Alice in Wonderland* and dark poetry, *Trinity* is a triumph of aesthetic pessimism as rarely seen in video games. Although it has regularly received accolades over the years, the title remains a mostly forgotten masterpiece and may be out of reach for players whose English isn't as strong. The game was released on May 9, 1986, for the Amiga, Atari ST, and PC.

Noah Falstein soon took notice and Moriarty received an offer to join Lucasfilm to start work on a new game using the SCUMM engine, which Ron Gilbert and Aric Wilmunder had been working tirelessly to develop. Brian arrived in the summer of 1988 as the entire company was pounding away at *Maniac Mansion*. Moriarty could hardly believe this incredible opportunity that had fallen into his lap. He realized that the development team was working with far greater freedom of resources compared to the constraints he'd worked under at Infocom, and the in-house game engine promised to provide the technical capabilities necessary to realize his poetic dreams on the computer screen. However, Brian didn't quite fit into the studio's atmosphere: "I chuckled along with everyone else at the humor in previous Lucasfilm adventures (including *Monkey Island*, which was under development at the same time as *Loom*). But from its conception, the aesthetic of *Loom* seemed to call for a more earnest treatment. I didn't want it to come across as solemn or portentous, but I felt that adopting the 'house style' of sardonic, self-referential humor might detract from the player's sense of immersion in Bobbin's world. The game does contain moments of sly humor, a few outrageous sight gags (such as the death of Bishop Mandible), and at least one inside joke ('I have a very bad feeling about this'[279])."

Thus *Loom* didn't take long to enter production, at the same time as a new secret project from Ron Gilbert. While most of Lucasfilm Games' two dozen employees in 1989 were working on the development of *Indiana Jones and the Last Crusade*, Moriarty played around with the SCUMM engine to better understand its technical capabilities. It was at that point that he came up with the story of Bobbin Threadbare, a member of the mysterious Guild of Weavers who must undertake a long journey through a fantasy world to find his kin, who have been transformed into swans... "The fundamental inspiration for the game was the title itself. '*Loom*' is a luscious word with many diverse meanings. It suggests weaving, but also 'looming' in the sense of towering over something, evoking mountains, power, and menace. It also shares the sound of words that bring to mind feelings of darkness and secrecy, such as gloom, womb and tomb. [...] Throw in a dose of Mythology 101, an undead bad guy and my trademark fondness for extra dimensions [note: a reference to *Trinity*], and you get what eventually became *Loom*."[280] The radical change

279. Practically a compulsory line in any *Star Wars* or *Indiana Jones* movie – Interview: *http://www.arcadeattack.co.uk/brian-moriarty/*
280. *https://web.archive.org/web/20111210185701/http://www.adventureclassicgaming.com/index.php/site/interviews/212/*

in ambiance pleased Steve Arnold and the rest of the team. They were all fans of *Trinity*, and it seemed like the studio might have come up with a poetic game capable of rivaling Infocom's masterpiece. "Once the basic concept was settled, I discussed it with Gary Winnick, the lead animator, and Mark Ferrari, the background artist. We found ourselves gravitating towards Walt Disney's *Sleeping Beauty* as a model for the look and feel of the game. [...] Mark did an amazing job adapting this look to the 16-color EGA palette. The other major influence was Tchaikovsky's ballet *Swan Lake*. It's one of my favorite pieces of music. The majestic sweep and melancholy atmosphere seemed perfect for a wistful story like *Loom*. All of the music for the game was transcribed note by note from Tchaikovsky's score. I also borrowed the swans, the owls, and a few other elements from the scenario of the ballet."[281]

While Moriarty's previous creations leaned into a level of difficulty that would be seen as punishing for today's players, for *Loom*, he decided to scrupulously follow the commandments of Ron Gilbert. He selected the very best parts from the early versions of his scenario, keeping only the story's essence and the main plot and prioritizing storytelling efficiency over situations more directly related to gameplay. He made it a point of honor to construct puzzles that fit into the deeper logic of the story. He pushed this systematic streamlining to the point that the game's text-based interface disappeared completely: no more verbs or inventory. All it took was a double-click to interact with an object or character, and unlike *Indiana Jones and the Last Crusade*, the dialogue was linear, without the response trees that would appear in the studio's subsequent releases. Instead, Moriarty and Winnick came up with an original system in which Bobbin would use a musical instrument to influence his surroundings. Thus, the player composes a series of notes to create magic spells with different effects according to the rhythm and melody.

In January 1990, the game was ready. In the very first version, an audio cassette tape was included in each game box, allowing the player to listen to a narrated prologue before starting the game (unfortunately, floppy disks at the time didn't have enough room to include digitalized voices). After several ports for the FM Towns, Amiga, Atari ST, and Macintosh, *Loom* received a 256-color VGA version on CD-ROM in which the voices were directly integrated, along with reorchestrated music. Science fiction writer Orson Scott Card[282] was incredibly impressed with the game, which he discovered on a visit to Skywalker Ranch. He ended up lending his voice and writing some pieces of dialogue for the CD-ROM version.

Once again, Moriarty received praise from critics. *Loom* holds a special place in the hearts of fans of classic point & click adventure games. It offers

---

281. *http://www.adventureclassicgaming.com/index.php/site/interviews/212/*
282. *Ender's Game, The Tales of Alvin Maker.*

a refreshingly poetic change of pace, in spite of its dark and slightly demoralizing universe. For yours truly, just hearing the opening notes of Tchaikovsky's famous ballet triggers a wave of nostalgia. The game never found its audience and was viewed as a relative commercial failure compared to the studio's other productions. Still, *Loom* was the first game to apply Ron Gilbert's precepts and gave a dazzling demonstration of their effectiveness and modernism, just a handful of months before Gilbert's mysterious project, *The Secret of Monkey Island*.

Indiana Jones and the Fate of Atlantis™

After the success of *Indiana Jones and the Last Crusade*, it's no surprise that LucasArts made it a priority to give the game a sequel, benefiting from the latest adjustments to the SCUMM engine. Since David Fox was already busy on another secret project entitled *The Dig*, development was entrusted to Hal Barwood in 1990. Barwood was already an industry veteran within LucasArts' young team. In 1970, he worked with George Lucas as a special effects designer for his *THX 1138*, then with Steven Spielberg to write the scripts for *Sugarland Express* and for the fantastic *Close Encounters of the Third Kind*. In 1980, in the middle of writing the next Matthew Robbins film, *Dragonslayer*, Barwood discovered a new passion for video games, sensing that they offered an exceptional new form of storytelling. He then directed his one and only feature-length horror film, *Warning Sign*, which failed to achieve much success. In 1990, his great relationship with George Lucas, his impressive résumé, and his desire to write for video games led him directly to the director's chair for the new *Indiana Jones* adventure game from Lucasfilm Games.

Barwood almost immediately rejected the first draft of the game scenario, which was based on an unproduced script entitled *Indiana Jones and the Monkey King*, which had been written by Chris Columbus[283] four years earlier for Steven Spielberg. Barwood managed to convince the studio's bigwigs to let him write an original scenario for the franchise. To do so, he enlisted the expertise of Noah Falstein, who had previously worked on *Indy 3*. After pondering a story set in England and centering on the myth of Excalibur, Barwood and Falstein ultimately agreed on Atlantis as the location for a new quest for our favorite whip-cracking explorer. Production advanced at a strong pace in parallel to the

---

283. Chris Columbus went on to direct *Harry Potter and the Sorcerer's Stone* and its sequel *Harry Potter and the Chamber of Secrets*. In 1986, at the request of Steven Spielberg, who particularly enjoyed Columbus' work as a writer on *Young Sherlock Holmes* (1985, Barry Levinson), he wrote an original script for the highly anticipated third episode in the adventures of Indiana Jones. However, Lucas and Spielberg preferred the script written by Jeffrey Boam, entitled *Indiana Jones and the Last Crusade*.

development of *Monkey Island 2: LeChuck's Revenge*, the studio's next major title. As such, *Indiana Jones and the Fate of Atlantis* reaped the benefits of technical improvements made to the SCUMM engine by Ron Gilbert, including for the generation of high-resolution backgrounds, native management of 256 colors, and, most importantly, dubbing (though of dubious quality) for each of the characters, as the title would be immediately released on CD-ROM.

Interestingly, the animations of the main characters were "rotoscoped".[284] Thus, Steve Purcell, with his trusty hat, and his future wife, Colette Michaud, stood in for Indy and Sophia, respectively. In the art department, William Eaken, Mark Ferrari (who was already working on *The Secret of Monkey Island*), James Dollar, and Avril Harrison delivered one of the most inspired and faithful interpretations of the *Indiana Jones* universe. Not only was the script excellent, but the design of the puzzles was remarkable, the humor ubiquitous, and the pacing was perfectly matched to the game's cinematic inspiration. *Indiana Jones and the Fate of Atlantis* is the true fourth installment in the saga, in addition to being one of the best point & click games ever created.

In 1939, at the dawn of World War II, Indy teams up with Sophia Hapgood, a psychic and archaeology lecturer specializing in Atlantis, to search for a mythical text by Plato, the Hermocrates, which will supposedly guide them to the lost continent. A race against the Third Reich leads our duo across the Mediterranean, then under the sea to the legendary city. Of course, the quest ends in total destruction, like any other archaeological find discovered by an adventurer worth his salt.

Released in June 1992, the title was an immediate hit. The game was a smashing success, both critically and commercially. It was the most successful adventure game ever created by LucasArts, with sales easily exceeding one million units. A sequel was soon in the works, led by Hal Barwood, Joe Pinney, and Aric Wilmunder. A few months later, the scenario for *Indiana Jones and the Iron Phoenix* was unveiled at the European Computer Trade Show, but the game's subject matter immediately received a cold response from German distributors. In the game, Indy was supposed to fight a cult led by Nazis who had taken refuge in Bolivia and hoped to resurrect Adolf Hitler. The topic was politically sensitive for a freshly reunified Germany, and LucasArts couldn't give up the lucrative Teutonic market, where adventure games were particularly popular. In the end, the scenario written by Hal Barwood was adapted into a comic book series.[285]

---

284. Rotoscoping is an animation technique in which a real actor is filmed, then the animator draws their image frame by frame from the film.
285. Published by Dark Horse Comics and written by Lee Marrs.

Day of the Tentacle™

Having barely recovered from the release of *Monkey Island 2*, Ron Gilbert and his two collaborators quickly convinced the management of LucasArts to create a sequel to their critically acclaimed *Maniac Mansion*. The small team began an intense period of brainstorming in hopes of once again pushing the limits of the adventure game genre. Weeks before his departure from the company, Ron proposed that they use time travel as the foundation of their game design. It was an absolute stroke of genius! Moreover, it turned out to be Ron's main and most decisive contribution to the game as he left the project in January 1992. Naturally, Dave Grossman and Tim Schafer took over management of the project. They had risen quickly through the ranks since they started at Lucasfilm in August 1989 as mere "Scummlets." They had definitively proven their humor, talent, and creativity. After a month of back and forth and intense writing, they delivered a complete design document to the studio's management in February 1992, entitled *Maniac Mansion II: Day of the Tentacle*.

The document briefly summarized the story of the game: "Tentacles eat toxic waste, get smart, take over the world. Dr. Fred tries to save the day, puts kids in experimental time machine. Things go awry, time machine crippled. One kid sent two hundred years into the past, one two hundred years into the future, one left in the present. Kids must fix time machine, get back together, use time machine to prevent world domination by tentacles." It's probably the stupidest synopsis ever written, but the most brilliantly designed adventure game to this day.

From *Maniac Mansion*, Grossman and Schafer only kept a handful of carefully chosen characters. The mauve tentacle, of course, which became the main antagonist, but also Dr. Fred and Bernard, the ultimate nerd. Schafer proposed the character Hoagie, based on a fan of the metal group Megadeth who he had met, and Grossman took inspiration from his ex-girlfriend for the character Laverne. On the artistic side of the project, while the music was again composed by the trio of Clint Bajakian, Peter McConnel, and Michael Z. Land, the graphics were entirely delegated to Peter Chan (for the backgrounds) and Larry Ahern, for the design of the characters. Moreover, *Day of the Tentacle* received its greatest praise for the peculiar style of its graphics. The character sprites were bigger than usual and, most notably, their facial animations were particularly well-crafted. It was another innovation moving video games closer to cartoons, as was Larry Ahern's goal, and the result was very successful. The game cleverly blended humor with the typical sarcasm found in LucasArts' productions, while adding in a dose of more visual and blatant situational comedy, which would become a standard for the studio, but also for adventure games from competitors.

Finally, *Day of the Tentacle* became the studio's first title to receive full dubbing of the characters from the moment of its release. The title was released on CD-ROM from day one, although a version of the game without the voices was also released for players of more modest means who weren't yet lucky enough to own a precious CD-ROM drive. The result made a splash as *Day of the Tentacle* undeniably blew audiences away when it was released in June 1993. Video game media described it as a marvel with extraordinary graphics, delivering a charming homage to Tex Avery's *Looney Tunes*. Still, the curse of LucasArts' original titles struck yet again. At the time of its release, the game sold just over 80,000 copies. The results brought disappointment, but that faded away with time as the game developed a cult following. It eventually received a "remastered" version produced by Double Fine Studios[286] in January 2015, and the game hasn't aged one bit...

Sam and Max Hit the Road™

While Dave Grossman and Tim Schafer were working away at *Day of the Tentacle*, the LucasArts "B team," the very same one that had developed *Indiana Jones and the Fate of Atlantis*, was looking for their next project. Sean Clark and Michael Stemmle, who had been assistant designers on *Fate of Atlantis*, took the reins of the new project, which they wanted to be set in a totally new universe. Steve Purcell, in addition to his work as an artist for the studio's various games, regularly produced for *The Adventurer*, the LucasArts magazine, a page dedicated to his comedic duo of antiheroes, Sam and Max, parodying the firm's games. It quickly became clear that Purcell's comic book universe deserved its own game. Michael Stemmle recalls: "When I began working at Lucasfilm Games, I was dimly aware of *Sam & Max*, but had never bought a comic. Once I started, however, I was quickly immersed in the characters, since the company had adopted them as the unofficial company mascots. Heck, the training environment for the SCUMM system was a primitive version of the *Sam & Max* office. By the time I was assigned to *Hit the Road*, I was a huge fan... almost by osmosis."[287] Steve Purcell and his future wife, Colette Michaud, became integral parts of the new project, which was mainly adapted from the comic *On the Road*, released in 1989. In the comic, the two pals go on a road trip across the United States. The ideal pretext for visiting many different imaginary environments from the brilliant mind of Steve Purcell. "The *Hit the Road* story borrowed a number of elements that cropped up in the comics, like

---

286. Double Fine Studios, founded by Tim Schafer in 2000, which went on to produce a number of marvels, including *Psychonauts*, *Broken Age*, and *The Cave*.
287. *https://mixnmojo.com/features/sitefeatures/LucasArts-Secret-History-Sam-and-Max-Hit-the-Road/4*

the Cone of Tragedy, the Giraffe-Necked Girl, and so forth." As with *Day of the Tentacle*, which came out a few months before it, *Sam and Max Hit the Road* was fully dubbed, with Steve Purcell supervising that whole process. And the voices were a huge hit, accompanied by the jazzy score composed by Michael Z. Land and his team.

Visually, *Sam & Max* was a real feat for its time. The graphics were refined, and better management of the PC's internal memory allowed the team to work wonders with the SCUMM engine, particularly when it came to the character animations. Above all, the game's greatest innovation was that, for the first time in an adventure game, the developers completely did away with the verbs. As such, *Sam & Max* marked an important milestone in the history of point & click adventures. The interface was still controlled entirely with the mouse, but with just a contextual cursor that could be switched by right clicking to select a desired action (look, take, act, etc.). It was a bold and decisive choice for the time and the conventions of the genre, but one that was justified in that it gave more room for the game's backgrounds and, in particular, to add some spice to the dialogue. As Steve Purcell put it, "Nothing would kill a joke worse than reading it before you hear it."[288] In any case, this choice went on to become best practice, both at LucasArts and at competing studios. Once again, LucasArts was the main driver of advancements in game design for point & click titles.

To offer a change of pace from the intense phases of searching imposed by a difficulty level that was much too high (though to the liking of many players), Clark and Stemmle also decided for the first time to incorporate into the game some wild arcade game phases that contrasted radically with the classic gameplay of adventure games. It was a laudable effort, but the results were very questionable from a gameplay perspective. Moreover, some of the mini-games became particularly notorious for their gratuitous cruelty, like one involving smashing innocent rats with a mallet.

Once again, the new LucasArts game received rave reviews from critics when it was released in November 1993, just months after *Day of the Tentacle*. Hilarious, sarcastic, mean, splendid... The game was showered with adjectives, and rightfully so. *Sam and Max Hit the Road* is, without a doubt, the funniest, richest, and most acerbic of the studio's games, with its only downsides being its difficulty, the arcade mini-games with mediocre gameplay, and certain puzzles that make you want to pull your hair out.

Notably, a sequel was planned some years later, in 2001, by the studio Infinite Machine, founded by alumni of LucasArts. *Sam and Max Plunge Through Space* was supposed to launch our two antiheroes into space, exclusively on the Xbox. However, even though the scenario had been written and a functional

---

288. *Retro Gamer Magazine*, No. 22 (March 2006).

demo had been made, the project was abandoned. Immediately thereafter, *Sam and Max: Freelance Police* was planned as a direct sequel by LucasArts in 2002, but when the studio turned in a radically different direction in the early 2000s, the project was again killed in its infancy. Finally, in 2006, *Sam & Max: Season One - Save the World* was developed by Telltale Games under the direction of... Dave Grossman.

Full Throttle™

After a few weeks of well-earned rest following the release of *Day of the Tentacle*, Dave Grossman announced that he too would be leaving the company to join Ron Gilbert at Cavedog Entertainment, where he would be in charge of the scenario for *Total Annihilation*. However, as we've seen, Grossman could never keep away from the *Monkey Island* series. Even though it had lost two of its greatest game designers, LucasArts didn't abandon the adventure game segment. The company kept churning out *Star Wars* titles at a rapid pace, which easily kept money flowing in. Meanwhile, LucasArts still wanted to keep producing original licenses as a way of affirming the studio's identity.

With that ambition, Tim Schafer, this time serving as the sole captain of the ship, proposed several ideas to the company's management: a game based on the adventures of a biker gang, another on the Mexican Day of the Dead celebration, and finally, a spy game. Although they had some doubts about the unusual subject and seriousness of the first idea, the LucasArts big shots felt that it was probably the least objectionable of the three. A few weeks later, Schafer slid the script for *Full Throttle* onto his manager's desk. "There are different movies that made me want to make these different games [the three ideas mentioned above]. *Yojimbo*[289] and *The Road Warrior*[290] made me want to make *Full Throttle*. *Grim Fandango* is obviously *Casablanca*[291] and *The Thin Man*.[292] I had this idea for a spy game that was *Three Days of the Condor*[293] and Hong Kong wire-fu Jet Li movies,"[294] explains Tim Schafer. The scenario made the studio's management nervous: its universe was dark and apocalyptic,

289. A fantastic samurai film by Akira Kurosawa, *Yojimbo* (meaning "bodyguard," 1961) was adapted by Sergio Leone into a Western entitled *A Fistful of Dollars*, starring Clint Eastwood.
290. *Mad Max 2*, as it was entitled in its native Australia, directed by George Miller (1982). Enough said.
291. *Casablanca* is a 1947 masterpiece of film noir, starring Humphrey Bogart and Ingrid Bergman and directed by Michael Curtiz.
292. Another black-and-white classic, directed by W.S. Van Dyke and released in 1934.
293. *Three Days of the Condor*, directed by Sydney Pollack (1975), starring Robert Redford and Faye Dunaway.
294. *https://www.rollingstone.com/culture/culture-features/full-throttles-tim-schafer-on-mark-hamill-and-being-asked-not-to-touch-george-lucas-122561/*

contrasting perhaps a bit too starkly with LucasArts' previous adventure game successes. However, Schafer reassured them: "One of the funny things about pitching *Full Throttle* was that it didn't sound like a comedy at all. And I wouldn't say it was a comedy. At a high concept, it's a biker on the run for a crime that he didn't commit. There's nothing funny about that. But then when he tries to pick up a piece of meat, or something that he doesn't want to put his lips on, that can be funny. That's an interesting thing to pitch to people: 'It's going to be serious from 10,000 feet in the air, but it's going to be funny on the ground.'"

The main positive qualities of *Full Throttle* can be boiled down to three things: personality, scene-setting, and rock 'n' roll. Its *Mad Max*-style universe and its impeccably written characters, all hardened and a bit crazy, prove Tim Schafer's immense talent as a storyteller. Schafer wrote the game's entire script on his own, with just a little assistance from Larry Ahern, who worked more on the gameplay and puzzle aspects. The biggest leap forward compared to the studio's previous productions was that the game was directed in an almost cinematic style. The SCUMM engine was stretched to its limits to give life to the dynamic camera shots, which more than ever before added an extra dimension to the player's immersion in the game's ghost-town atmosphere. And while the setting may have that apocalyptic, ghost-town feel, it still delivers an absolutely wild sense of rage and dynamism. From its opening scene, with a car flying down the highway, to its final, tragicomic shot, *Full Throttle* is a veritable rock opera. Peter McConnell, this time solely responsible for producing the game's soundtrack, looked for a musical group capable of embodying the hero, Ben Throttle, and his gang. McConnell recalls: "We were like, 'How are we ever going to have music that rocks as hard as what we're trying to get across here, with this biker?' I liked *Superunknown*,[295] the Soundgarden album that had a song called 'Kickstand' on it. We thought, 'This is a sign from the rock 'n' roll gods that we need to get this song.' We made a trip down to L.A., rented a convertible and drove to A&M Records and pitched them on it. It was going really well, until they realized we weren't going to give them any money." With Soundgarden out, McConnell happened to hear a few songs from a San Francisco-based group called The Gone Jackals on an obscure college radio station. It felt almost too good to be true. After a bit of back and forth, The Gone Jackals agreed to provide the music for the game's entire soundtrack, which actually became what the band is best known for. It was a success on all fronts.

With a budget of over $1.5 million, the game was the studio's most expensive ever at that point. It finally hit the shelves in April 1995. While *Full Throttle* is undeniably one of LucasArts' great classics and has left an impressive legacy,

---

295. The famous album from the grunge rock band Soundgarden, whose hit *"Black Hole Sun"* was an international sensation.

it's not without its faults. Its arcade-game interludes are totally unplayable. The game is also very simple–perhaps too simple for its era–and ends very quickly. Still, the game's incredible personality, its improved playability, its dazzling game design, and its excellent dubbing (including the notable participation of Mark Hamill[296] himself!) make it a true masterpiece. Moreover, its "remastered" version, produced by Double Fine Productions in 2017 for the PC, PS4, and PS Vita, is a real delight and hasn't aged a bit.

Grim Fandango™

After finishing his work on *Monkey Island 2*, Tim Schafer was brimming with ideas for projects, particularly one based on the Day of the Dead (*Día de los Muertos*), the Mexican holiday celebrating loved ones who have passed away. This was before he finally decided to launch production of *Full Throttle*. So, in 1995, after the release of the latter, Schafer revisited the idea of a Day of the Dead-inspired game. Sensing that adventure games were declining in popularity, LucasArts asked him to launch a more ambitious project based on a new license. Thus, Tim pitched his idea to them, adding a touch of inspiration from his favorite films noir, like *Casablanca* and *The Maltese Falcon*. While writing of the game was finished quickly, the production phase proved to be a nightmare. Eventually, the team decided to abandon the old SCUMM engine. *Deeds of the Dead*, as the project was dubbed, would be the studio's first adventure game since *Labyrinth* to be developed without Ron Gilbert's engine.

Tim Schafer, in an interview given to the famous website *MixnMojo*, recounts what that transitional era was like: "Everybody was pushing for 3D at the time. We were the old 2D hold-outs in the graphic adventure department. We always thought it looked better. Although on *Throttle* we did make 3D models of the bikes and the trucks and a lot of the things used in the action sequences. Then we rendered them out and painted over them. But I thought 3D looked so bad back then. Until I saw *BioForge*[297] and I loved how dramatically the camera angles changed as you walked around. That was one thing we couldn't do with 2D: have quick camera angle changes. So, that kind of seduced me into the world of 3D."[298]

The commercial success of *Full Throttle* meant that the studio's management gave the game designer a certain level of freedom to do what he wanted. The only real criticism came from Hal Barwood, who didn't care for the name *Deeds*

---

296. The real-life Luke Skywalker, who is also a talented voice actor, notably lending his voice to the unforgettable Joker in *Batman: The Animated Series*.
297. Developed by Origin Systems in 1995. *BioForge* is an avant-garde, science fiction, 3D, third-person adventure game.
298. *https://mixnmojo.com/features/sitefeatures/LucasArts-Secret-History-Grim-Fandango/7*

of the Dead. After a few weeks, it was changed to *Grim Fandango*. While the studio was best known for 2D games, LucasArts was already accustomed to 3D productions by that point. As such, the team decided to use the "Sith engine," which was already in use for one of the company's other productions, *Star Wars Jedi Knight: Dark Forces II*.[299] One of the team's programmers, Bret Mogilefsky, was already comfortable with the Lua scripting language and proposed that they use it to simplify the designers' work. "In the beginning, we just said we were going to take the *Jedi Knight* engine and add a scripting language to it," Tim Schafer recalls. "I remember Ray Gresko saying, 'That sounds easy. That would take about three brain cells to do that.' Turned out to be a little more complicated in the end, but these things usually are. I think it took at least nine brain cells, if I remember correctly. Which meant we had to hire four programmers! (haha, programmer burn.)" The new game engine, dubbed GrimE, would allow the characters to move around in 3D on "high-resolution" pre-rendered backgrounds. Best of all, it retained the flexibility and accessibility of the SCUMM engine. This small revolution allowed designers to use their creation tools just about as easily as they could with the studio's historic game engine.

Development of *Grim Fandango* took three long years, a record at the time, with a large budget of over $3 million. "We had every shot storyboarded and the puzzles all planned, so there wasn't much room to wander away from the vision of the game. But the implementation was nasty, and we mostly just all worked too hard and burned ourselves out. After the project, I had to go home and not come into the office for three months." The game was finally released for the PC on October 30, 1998. It met with success, selling almost 500,000 copies, turning a profit in spite of the long production and the game's exceptionally large budget.

It proved to be one of the greatest adventure games of all time. The game presents the adventures of Manny Calavera, a travel agent assigned to help struggling souls make their way through the Land of the Dead, as he searches for the beautiful Mercedes "Meche" Colomar. It's a romantic ode to the film noir genre. The scenario, which is surprisingly deep, cleverly blends seriousness, sarcastic humor, and dramatic tension. To top it all off, the soundtrack by Peter McConnell is absolutely fantastic, combining jazz, the music of Hollywood films, and Mexican folk tunes. *Grim Fandango* is often named one of the best—if not *the* best—adventure games of all time. Above all, it allowed LucasArts to once again blow its competitors out of the water. The studio would remain the undeniable and uncontested champion of adventure games.

---

299. The sequel to the excellent FPS *Star Wars: Dark Forces*. The sequel was released in 1997, directed by Justin Chin, with game design by Peter Chan.

The Dig™

It's almost as if every studio has its own legendary, phantom-like project... and for LucasArts, that game is without a doubt *The Dig*, a title that eventually achieved cult status, but which was viewed as cursed because of its six long years of development with many different iterations. In fact, more has probably been written about the game's development than about the final product. And yet, the game's credits present a real dream team: Steven Spielberg as a scenario writer; ILM responsible for creating some of the cinematics; no less than five different game designers, namely Noah Falstein, Dave Grossman, Brian Moriarty, David Fox, and Sean Clark; and dialogue written by author Orson Scott Card. It was LucasArts' first "adult" science fiction project, based on serious scientific ideas. However, what was supposed to be a flagship for the studio, the *2001: A Space Odyssey* of video games, ended up digging itself into a colossal hole and turning into an ailing game out of sync with the times.

But I'm getting ahead of myself. In 1985, the director of *Indiana Jones* came up with a new story for the series *Amazing Stories*,[300] on which he was a producer. It was a cross between *Forbidden Planet*–a sci-fi retelling of William Shakespeare's *The Tempest* in which the ruins of an ancient extraterrestrial civilization appear–and *The Treasure of the Sierra Madre*, a movie in which three miners amass a fortune worth of gold, but end up trying to kill each other out of hatred and madness. Spielberg developed the story, but quickly realized that it would be too ambitious for television and much too expensive to make as a movie. The idea was filed away in a drawer, until Lucasfilm Games pulled it back out in 1989 with the possibility of turning it into a prestigious video game. Writing of the scenario was entrusted to Noah Falstein, with occasional help from Dave Grossman. After a few months of writing, as they were too busy finishing up the development of *Indiana Jones and the Fate of Atlantis*, the project was handed over to Brian Moriarty. He decided to throw away 80% of the work Falstein had completed. Moriarty created additional main characters, added an entire sub-plot about a Japanese businesswoman responsible for financing the space expedition, reworked the visuals one by one to convert the style to something more dreamlike, and developed an interface based on changing contextual icons similar to those in his previous game, *Loom*. Originally planned for a release in 1993, the game's development encountered significant delays due to back and forth between Moriarty, with his very complex, scientific vision, and LucasArts' management, who worried

300. *Amazing Stories* was a fantasy TV series created and produced by Steven Spielberg. It was broadcast on the American TV channel NBC for two seasons between 1985 and 1987. As an anthology series featuring fantasy stories, various episodes were directed by talented individuals like Clint Eastwood, Martin Scorsese, Robert Zemeckis, and Joe Dante.

that the game would be unsuitable for the mass market. *The Dig* became such a notorious project that the studio's employees avoided every meeting about it like the plague.

In late 1993, Brian Moriarty threw in the towel and immediately left the game studio to join the educational branch of Lucasfilm. The project then fell to Dave Grossman, who tried to rework Moriarty's script by reincorporating Falstein's original vision. The release was pushed back to September 1994, but it quickly became clear that the game would not be fully functional and ready in time. Grossman in turn abandoned both the cursed project and the company, and *The Dig* was finally entrusted to Sean Clark. He enlisted the help of Bill Tiller, a prodigious young graphic artist, and Michael Z. Land to bring Spielberg's vision to life. The game engine that they originally planned to use, StoryDroid,[301] was abandoned in favor of the trusty old SCUMM engine, of which the developers had a much better command. The team eliminated a few of the main characters that Moriarty had planned in order to save time on animation. They also cut down on many of the puzzles.

The Dig was finally released in November 1995 for the PC and Mac. While the voices and setting were fairly well received and sales were not bad (reportedly around 300,000 copies), the game was criticized for its outdated technology, its brutally difficult puzzles, and its literalness, which was quite unusual for LucasArts' productions. And we have to admit, the final product is typical of a cursed game. Disjointed, pointlessly complex, and poorly thought-out, with completely meaningless sub-plots, the effects of the tortuous development can be felt by anyone courageous enough to invest time and effort in the game. That said, the score by Michael Z. Land, with its ambient-electronic style, is absolutely sumptuous, and the oppressive atmosphere, a mix between apocalyptic and space-age lyricism, is the stuff of dreams. In spite of its faults, *The Dig* is a legendary game with wild, captivating ambitions, which on their own are enough to pique the curiosity of a sophisticated retrogamer.

301. There's not much information out there about the short-lived game engine StoryDroid, but it appears that it was developed in-house specially for *The Dig* and for a time was also supposed to be used for development of the game *Instruments of Chaos starring Young Indiana Jones*, released in 1994 for the Sega Genesis (a.k.a. Mega Drive).

Appendix 4: *Plank of Love*™

Song performed by Guybrush and Elaine Marley-Threepwood

Guybrush:
I was a lucky sailor,
As free as a tropical breeze,
But your love clapped me in irons,
And I can't reach the keys!
Now my heart is in your brig,
And I know it's not the only lodger,
But since you cast away my love,
I'm no longer a Jolly Roger.
All: *Plank of Love!*
Guybrush: *Don't make me take that one last step.*
All: *Plank of Love!*
Guybrush: *Why must you treat me like a schlep?*
I'd keep an even keel,
But it's a dirty deal!
There's no appeal!
And now I must walk this plank of love.
Darling, please be mine,
Only you can make me whole.
Your love is the lime
For the scurvy in my soul.
I used to dream of sunken treasure,
But now my only wish is
To be staying here with you tonight,
Instead of sleeping with the fishes.
All: *Plank of Love!*
Elaine: *I love you, though I know I shouldn'.*
All: *Plank of Love!*
Elaine: *I'll walk with you down that plank so wooden.*
My heart's been cursed,

By your love coerced,
In thoughts of you I am immersed!
And now I must walk this plank of love.
Guybrush: *You've got the booty I want the most,*
I'm not talking about your money.
My life's as dry as whole-wheat toast,
Without you, my Plunder-Bunny.
Elaine: *You know you've got my soul shanghaied!*
Not even all your corny jokes'll
Make me wish that I was not your bride
When you carry me across your fo'c'sle.
All: *Plank of Love!*
Guybrush: *Don't drown me in the ocean salts.*
All: *Plank of Love!*
Guybrush: *Don't think my song is only schmaltz.*
Elaine: *You're a pirate mighty.*
Guybrush: *You're my Aphrodite.*
Both: *Next to you, my heart feels flighty,*
And now I must walk this plank of love.
Guybrush: *But now our love's in danger,*
You're a statue made of gold.
It makes my heart sink like an anchor,
Keeping you in my cargo hold.
Elaine, I can't wait to see you
In a sparkling wedding gown,
But if I can't break that curse soon,
I'm gonna have to melt you down.
All: *Plank of Love!*
Guybrush: *I hope that curse breaks quick...*
All: *Plank of Love!*
Guybrush: *'Cause the balloon payment's due soon on this ship.*

Author's Acknowledgments

First, I would like to give special thanks to Nicolas Courcier and Mehdi El Kanafi, who placed their trust in me again, this time working solo. They always give their all, they're cool, and they're totally fearless. And, of course, I can't go any further without paying tribute to Bruno Provezza, without whom none of this would have been possible.

Next, thank you to everyone who supported me (and put up with me) without belittling me throughout this long year of writing, providing me with details, valuable information, and enlightening discussions. First and foremost, Pierre Salard, a walking, talking francophone encyclopedia of LucasArts. Also Charlotte Courtois, for her fascinating research. And Gilles Peyroux, for his support and willingness to talk.

Thank you to Sylvain Sarrailh and Steve Purcell for agreeing to illustrate the cover of this book. I have no doubt that many people will buy it just so they can admire your fantastic illustrations... and hopefully they'll get around to actually reading it one day!

Thank you to the community of *Monkey Island* fans who, for nearly 30 years, have kept conversations alive, produced fascinating articles, kept tabs on every bit of news, and harassed Disney to get them to hand the franchise over to Ron Gilbert. In particular, thank you to *scummbar.com*, *mixnmojo.com*, *worldofmi. com*, and *monkeyisland.fr*. The work you do is amazing!

Thank you to my parents, who bought me my Amiga 500 when I was 11 years old, not knowing that they were sending me off on a virtual adventure that continues to this day. Thank you to my friends, especially Clément Sablet, for their constant support. And thank you to all of my family members who feigned interest in what I was telling them, backed up with wild gestures and mimed sword fighting (and also those who put up with listening to over 5,000 hours of pirate reggae over the last few years). And, of course, big hugs to Antoine, my little Mighty Pirate™, Lise, Madyson, Tristan, and all the other kids who hopefully will one day be lucky enough to walk the roads of Mêlée Island.

Thank you for reading this book through to the end. You are the living proof that one can enjoy video games and still cultivate one's mind with fine literature.

No animals were harmed in the writing of this book.

Never pay more than $20 for a video game.

Any resemblance to real-life people or events is not at all coincidental.

Now maybe it's time to go do something more stimulating to the mind, like playing a video game, leaving comments on YouTube videos, or trolling people on social media.

Also available from Third Éditions

Berserk. With Darkness Ink
BioShock. From Rapture to Columbia
Dark Souls. Beyond the Grave - Volume 1
Dark Souls. Beyond the Grave - Volume 2
Devolver: Behind the Scenes. Business and Punk Attitude
Fallout. A Tale of Mutation
Halo. A Space Opera from Bungie
JoJo's Bizarre Adventure. Manga's Refined Oddball
Metal Gear Solid. Hideo Kojima's Magnum Opus
Resident Evil. Of Zombies and Men - Volume 1
Sekiro. The Second Life of Souls
The Heart of Dead Cells
The Impact of Akira. A Manga [R]evolution
The Legend of Dragon Quest
The Legend of Final Fantasy VI
The Legend of Final Fantasy VII
The Legend of Final Fantasy VIII
The Legend of Final Fantasy IX
The Legend of Final Fantasy X
The Legend of Kingdom Hearts - Volume 1: Creation
The Rise of the Witcher. A New RPG King
The Strange Works of Taro Yoko. From Drakengard to NieR: Automata
The Works of Fumito Ueda. A Different Perspective on Video Games
The Works of Hayao Miyazaki. The Japanese Animation Master
Zelda. The History of a Legendary Saga - Volume 1
Zelda. The History of a Legendary Saga - Volume 2: Breath of the Wild

Legal submission: October 2023